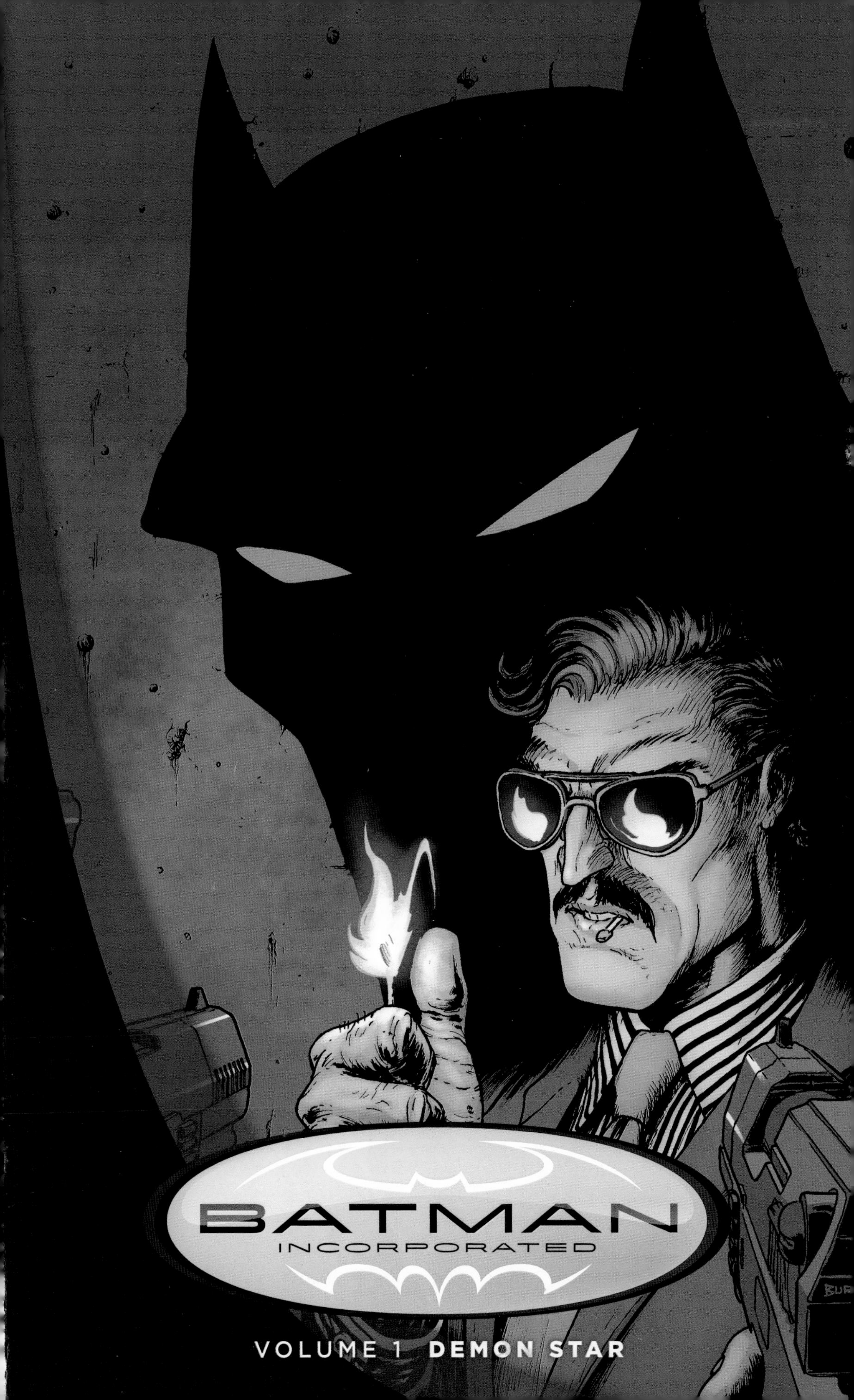
BATMAN
INCORPORATED
VOLUME 1 DEMON STAR

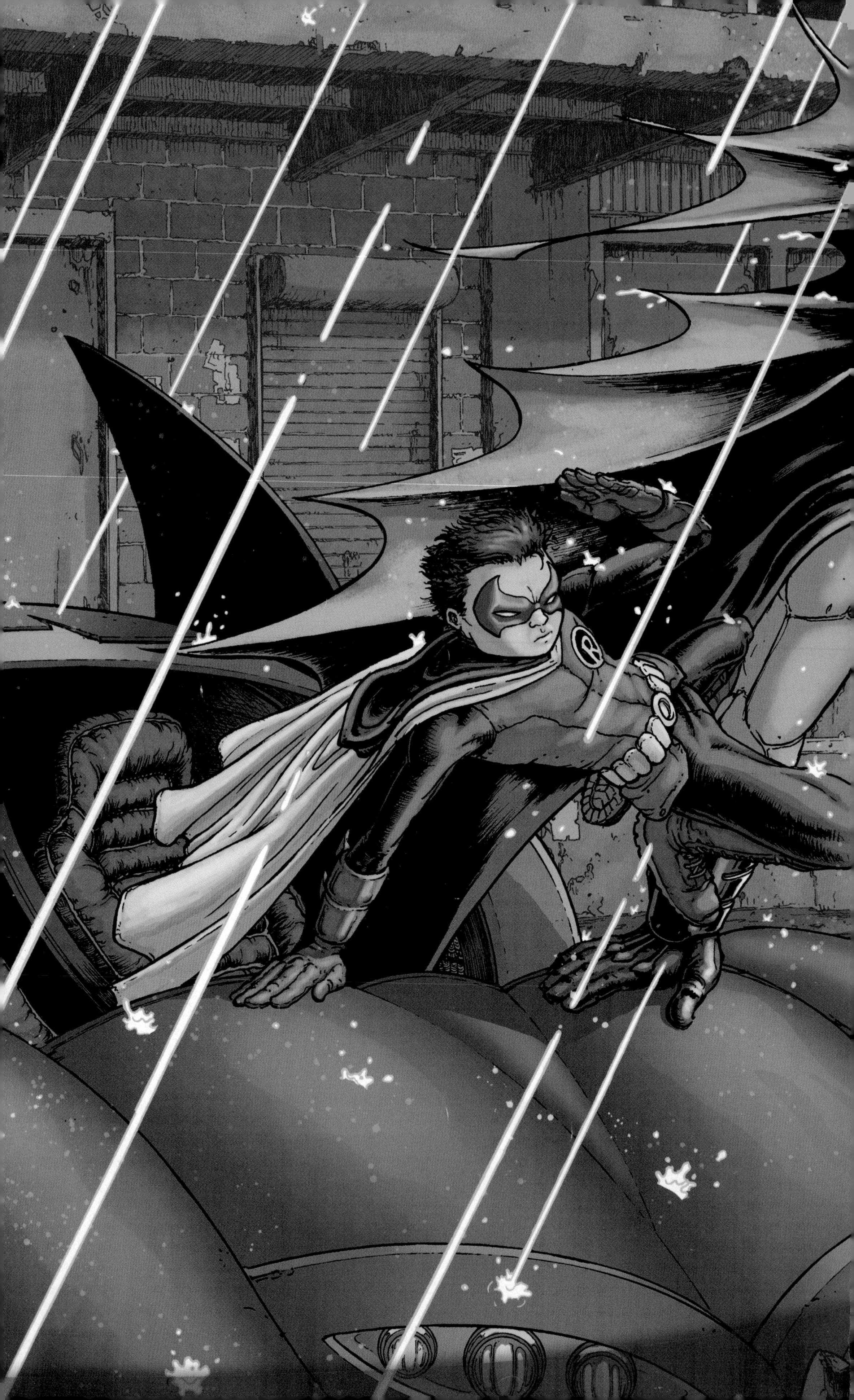

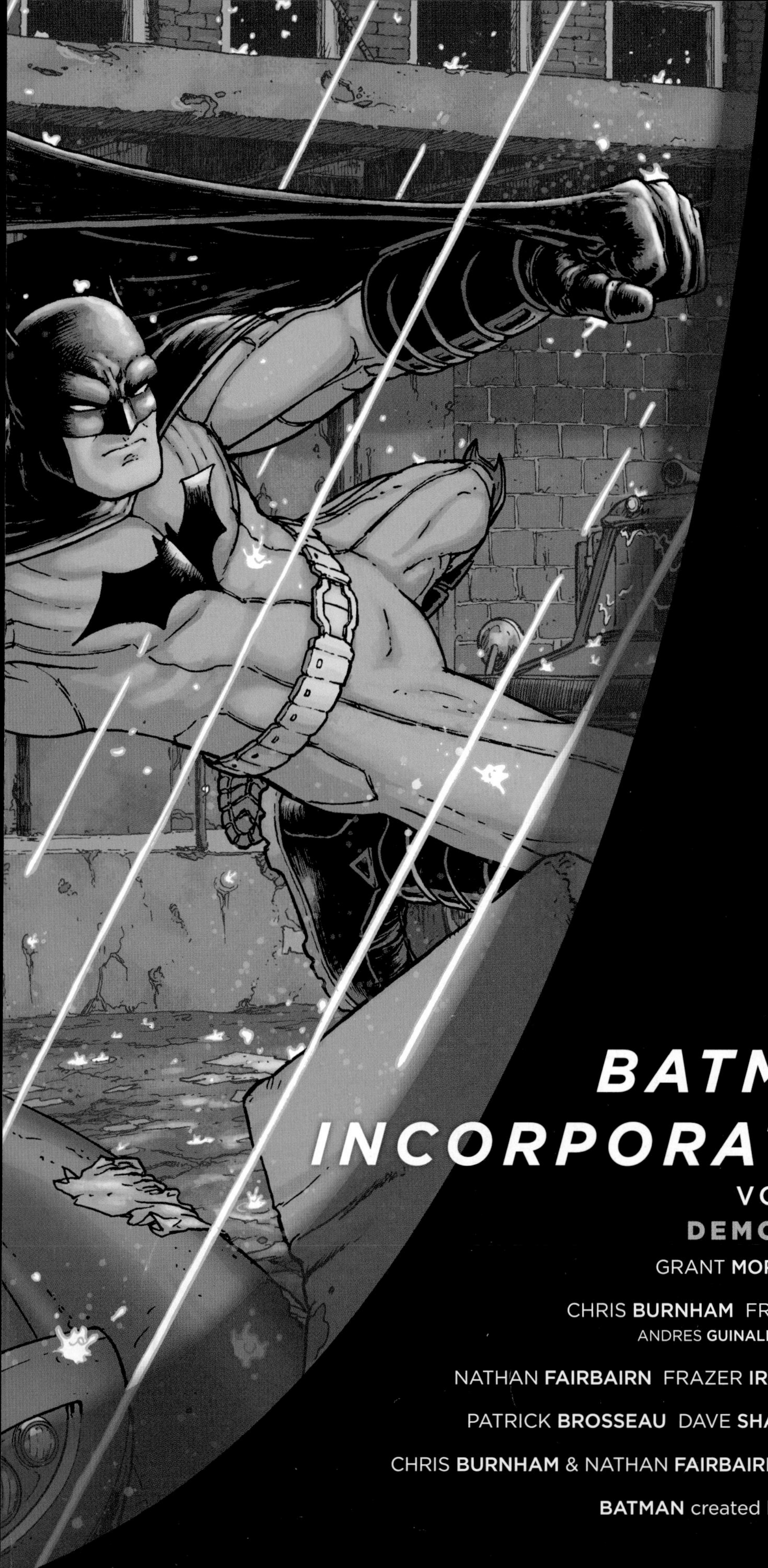

BATMAN INCORPORATED

VOLUME 1
DEMON STAR

GRANT **MORRISON** writer

CHRIS **BURNHAM** FRAZER **IRVING**
ANDRES **GUINALDO** & **BIT** artists

NATHAN **FAIRBAIRN** FRAZER **IRVING** colorists

PATRICK **BROSSEAU** DAVE **SHARPE** letterers

CHRIS **BURNHAM** & NATHAN **FAIRBAIRN** cover artists

BATMAN created by BOB **KANE**

MIKE MARTS Editor – Original Series BRIAN SMITH Associate Editor – Original Series
RICKEY PURDIN Assistant Editor – Original Series PETER HAMBOUSSI Editor
ROBBIN BROSTERMAN Design Director – Books ROBBIE BIEDERMAN Publication Design

BOB HARRAS VP – Editor-in-Chief

DIANE NELSON President DAN DIDIO and JIM LEE Co-Publishers
GEOFF JOHNS Chief Creative Officer
JOHN ROOD Executive VP – Sales, Marketing and Business Development
AMY GENKINS Senior VP – Business and Legal Affairs NAIRI GARDINER Senior VP – Finance
JEFF BOISON VP – Publishing Operations MARK CHIARELLO VP – Art Direction and Design
JOHN CUNNINGHAM VP – Marketing TERRI CUNNINGHAM VP – Talent Relations and Services
ALISON GILL Senior VP – Manufacturing and Operations HANK KANALZ Senior VP – Digital
JAY KOGAN VP – Business and Legal Affairs, Publishing JACK MAHAN VP – Business Affairs, Talent
NICK NAPOLITANO VP – Manufacturing Administration SUE POHJA VP – Book Sales
COURTNEY SIMMONS Senior VP – Publicity BOB WAYNE Senior VP – Sales

BATMAN INCORPORATED VOLUME 1: DEMON STAR

DC Comics, 1700 Broadway, New York, NY 10019
A Warner Bros. Entertainment Company
Printed by RR Donnelley, Salem, VA, USA. 4/5/13. First Printing.

HC ISBN: 978-1-4012-3888-9
SC ISBN: 978-1-4012-4263-3

Library of Congress Cataloging-in-Publication Data

Morrison, Grant, author.
Batman, Incorporated. Volume 1, Demon Star / Grant Morrison, Chris Burnham.
pages cm
"Originally published in single magazine form in Batman, Incorporated 0-6."
ISBN 978-1-4012-3888-9
1. Graphic novels. I. Burnham, Chris, 1977- illustrator. II. Title. III. Title: Demon Star.
PN6728.B36M675 2013
741.5'973—dc23
2012050769

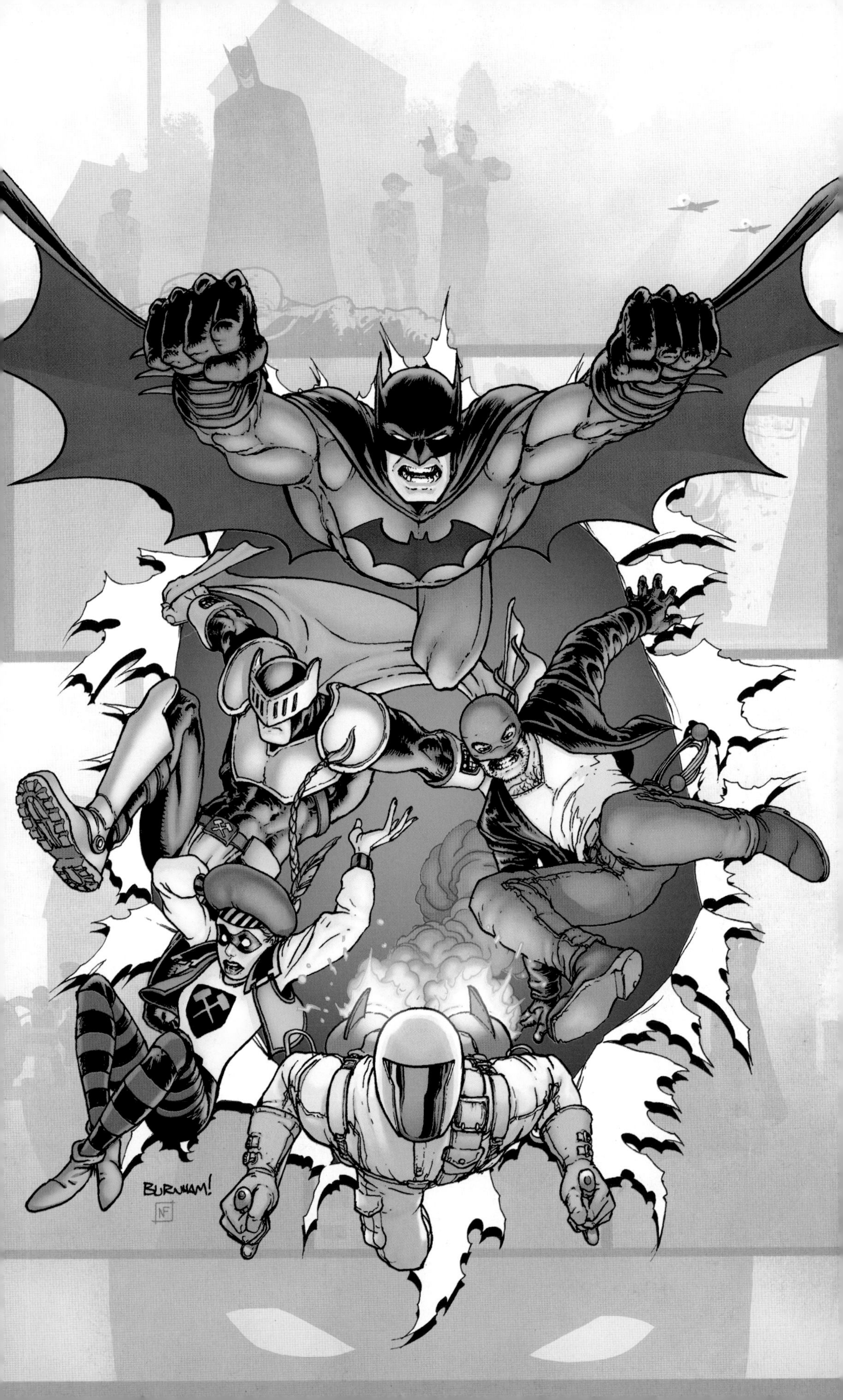
BURNHAM!
NF

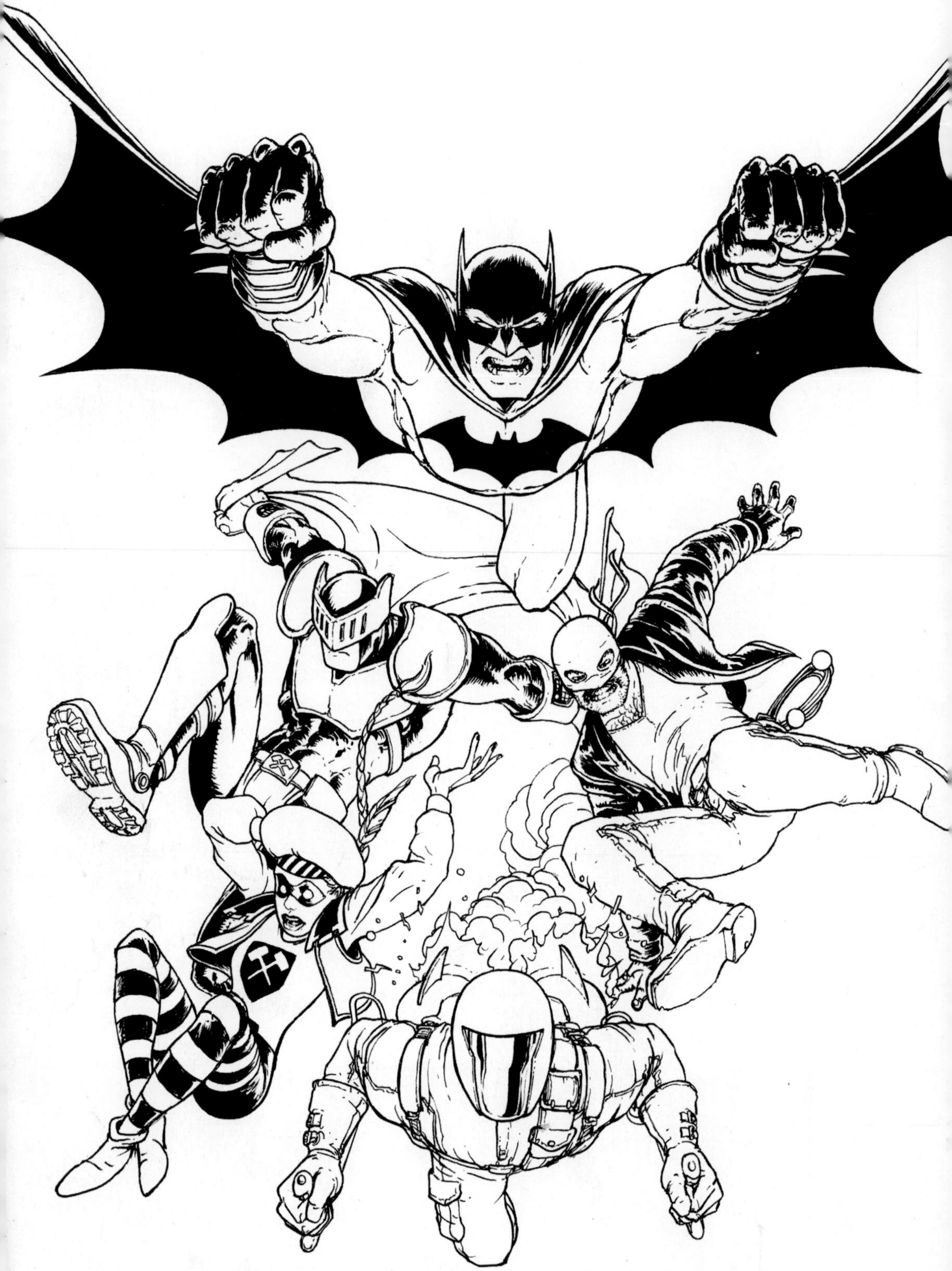

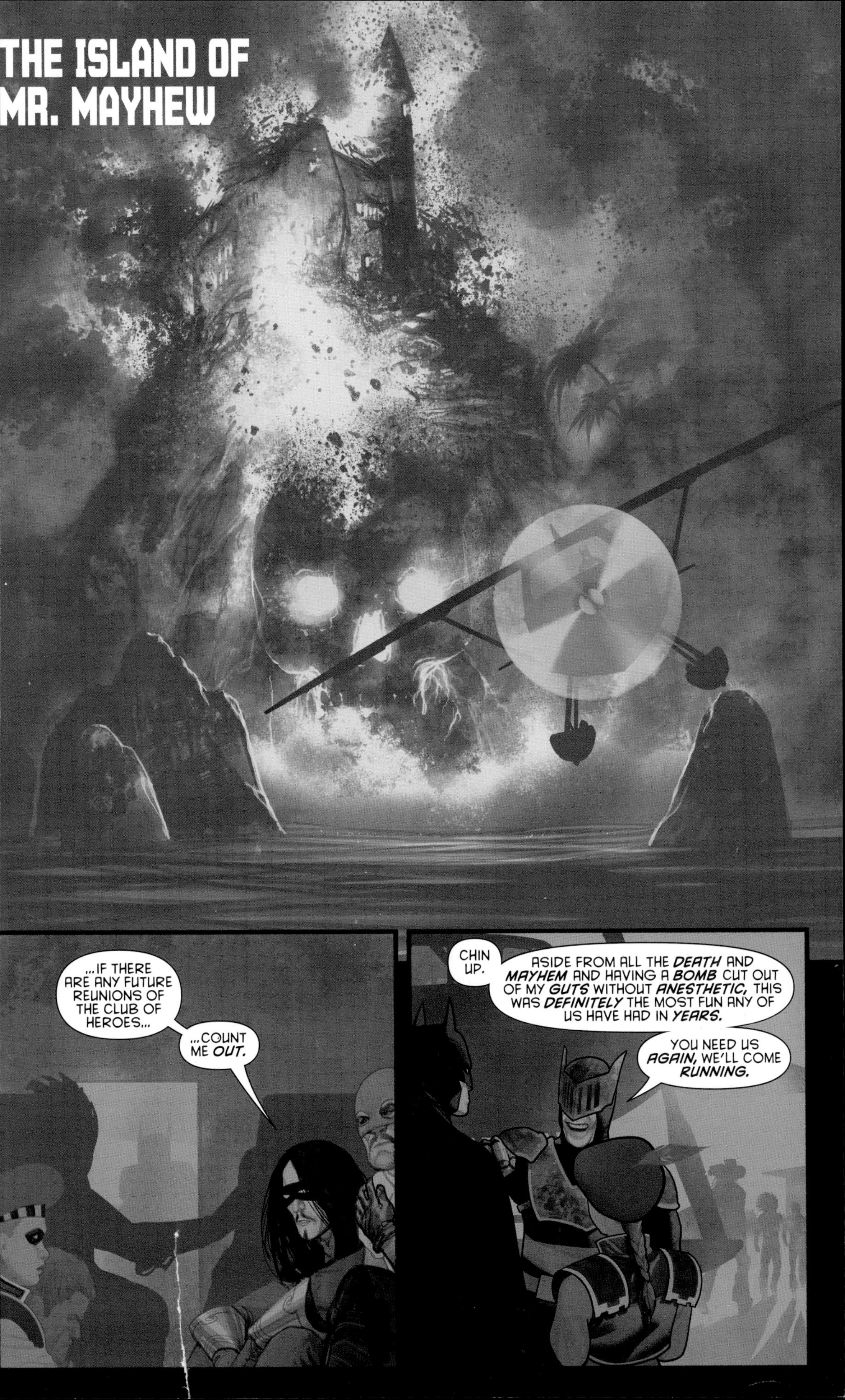
THE ISLAND OF MR. MAYHEW
...IF THERE ARE ANY FUTURE REUNIONS OF THE CLUB OF HEROES...
...COUNT ME OUT.
CHIN UP.
ASIDE FROM ALL THE DEATH AND MAYHEM AND HAVING A BOMB CUT OUT OF MY GUTS WITHOUT ANESTHETIC, THIS WAS DEFINITELY THE MOST FUN ANY OF US HAVE HAD IN YEARS.
YOU NEED US AGAIN, WE'LL COME RUNNING.

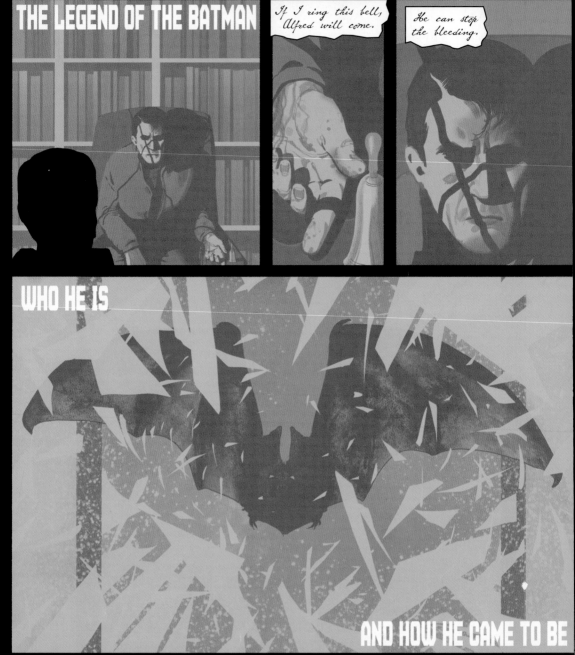

THE LEGEND OF THE BATMAN

If I ring this bell, Alfred will come.

He can stop the bleeding.

WHO HE IS

AND HOW HE CAME TO BE

THAT'S IT.

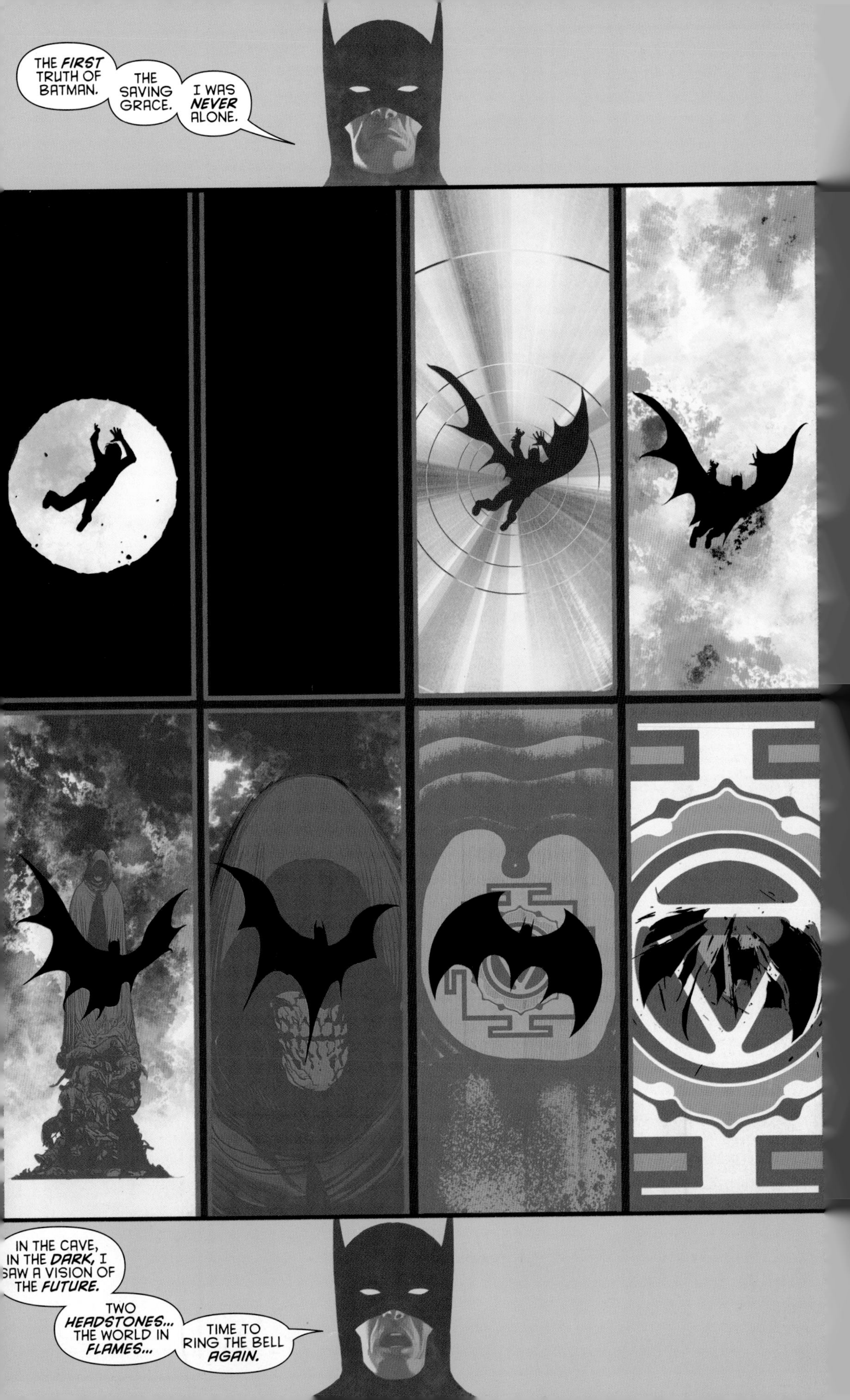
THE FIRST TRUTH OF BATMAN.
THE SAVING GRACE.
I WAS NEVER ALONE.
IN THE CAVE, IN THE DARK, I SAW A VISION OF THE FUTURE.
TWO HEADSTONES... THE WORLD IN FLAMES...
TIME TO RING THE BELL AGAIN.

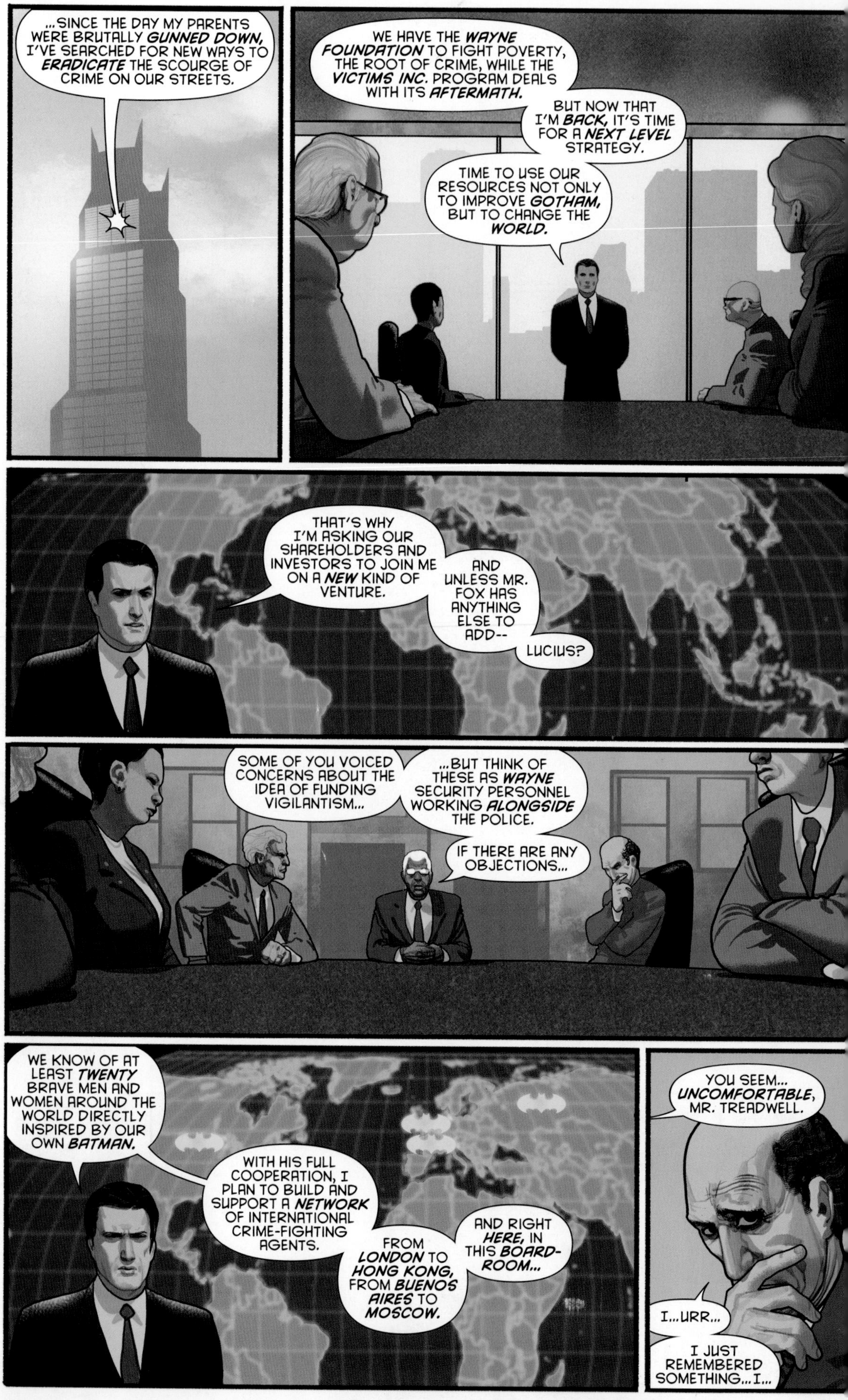
...SINCE THE DAY MY PARENTS WERE BRUTALLY GUNNED DOWN, I'VE SEARCHED FOR NEW WAYS TO ERADICATE THE SCOURGE OF CRIME ON OUR STREETS.
WE HAVE THE WAYNE FOUNDATION TO FIGHT POVERTY, THE ROOT OF CRIME, WHILE THE VICTIMS INC. PROGRAM DEALS WITH ITS AFTERMATH.
BUT NOW THAT I'M BACK, IT'S TIME FOR A NEXT LEVEL STRATEGY.
TIME TO USE OUR RESOURCES NOT ONLY TO IMPROVE GOTHAM, BUT TO CHANGE THE WORLD.
THAT'S WHY I'M ASKING OUR SHAREHOLDERS AND INVESTORS TO JOIN ME ON A NEW KIND OF VENTURE.
AND UNLESS MR. FOX HAS ANYTHING ELSE TO ADD--
LUCIUS?
SOME OF YOU VOICED CONCERNS ABOUT THE IDEA OF FUNDING VIGILANTISM...
...BUT THINK OF THESE AS WAYNE SECURITY PERSONNEL WORKING ALONGSIDE THE POLICE.
IF THERE ARE ANY OBJECTIONS...
WE KNOW OF AT LEAST TWENTY BRAVE MEN AND WOMEN AROUND THE WORLD DIRECTLY INSPIRED BY OUR OWN BATMAN.
WITH HIS FULL COOPERATION, I PLAN TO BUILD AND SUPPORT A NETWORK OF INTERNATIONAL CRIME-FIGHTING AGENTS.
FROM LONDON TO HONG KONG, FROM BUENOS AIRES TO MOSCOW.
AND RIGHT HERE, IN THIS BOARD-ROOM...
YOU SEEM... UNCOMFORTABLE, MR. TREADWELL.
I...URR...
I JUST REMEMBERED SOMETHING...I...

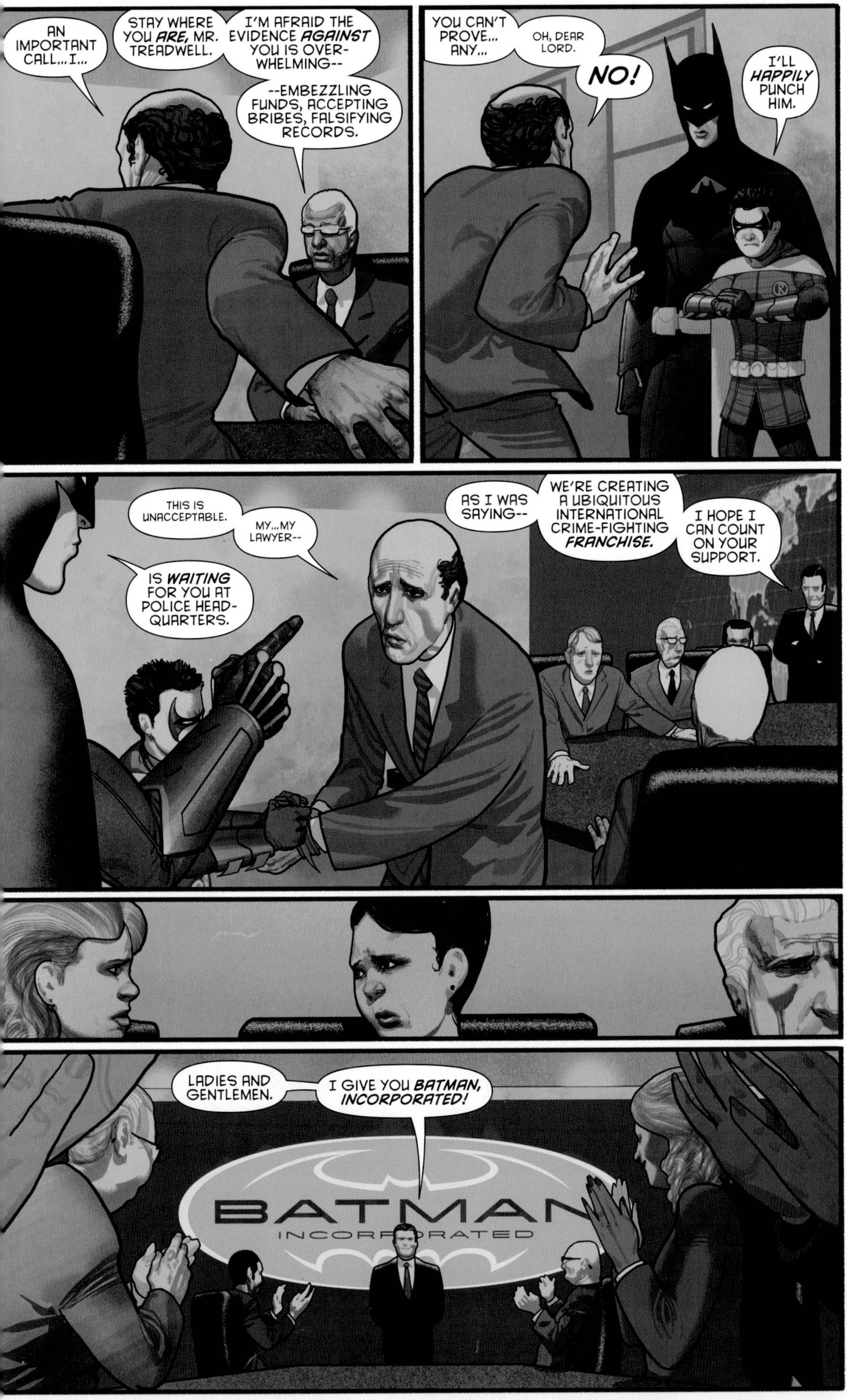
AN IMPORTANT CALL... I...
STAY WHERE YOU ARE, MR. TREADWELL.
I'M AFRAID THE EVIDENCE AGAINST YOU IS OVER-WHELMING--
--EMBEZZLING FUNDS, ACCEPTING BRIBES, FALSIFYING RECORDS.
YOU CAN'T PROVE... ANY...
OH, DEAR LORD.
NO!
I'LL HAPPILY PUNCH HIM.
THIS IS UNACCEPTABLE.
MY... MY LAWYER--
IS WAITING FOR YOU AT POLICE HEAD-QUARTERS.
AS I WAS SAYING--
WE'RE CREATING A UBIQUITOUS INTERNATIONAL CRIME-FIGHTING FRANCHISE.
I HOPE I CAN COUNT ON YOUR SUPPORT.
LADIES AND GENTLEMEN.
I GIVE YOU BATMAN, INCORPORATED!
BATMAN
INCORPORATED

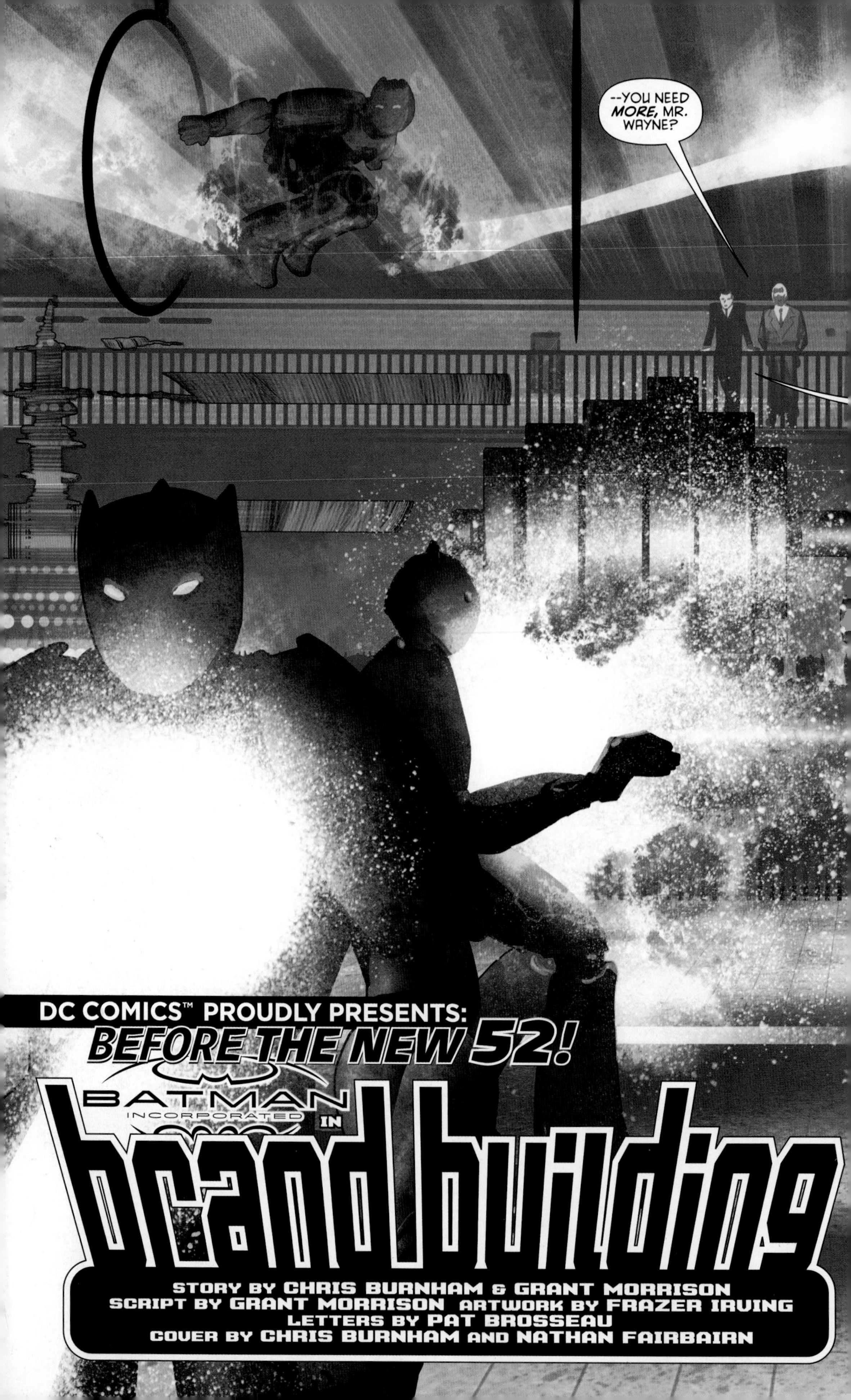
--YOU NEED MORE, MR. WAYNE?
DC COMICS™ PROUDLY PRESENTS:
BEFORE THE NEW 52!
BATMAN INCORPORATED IN
brand building
STORY BY CHRIS BURNHAM & GRANT MORRISON
SCRIPT BY GRANT MORRISON ARTWORK BY FRAZER IRVING
LETTERS BY PAT BROSSEAU
COVER BY CHRIS BURNHAM AND NATHAN FAIRBAIRN

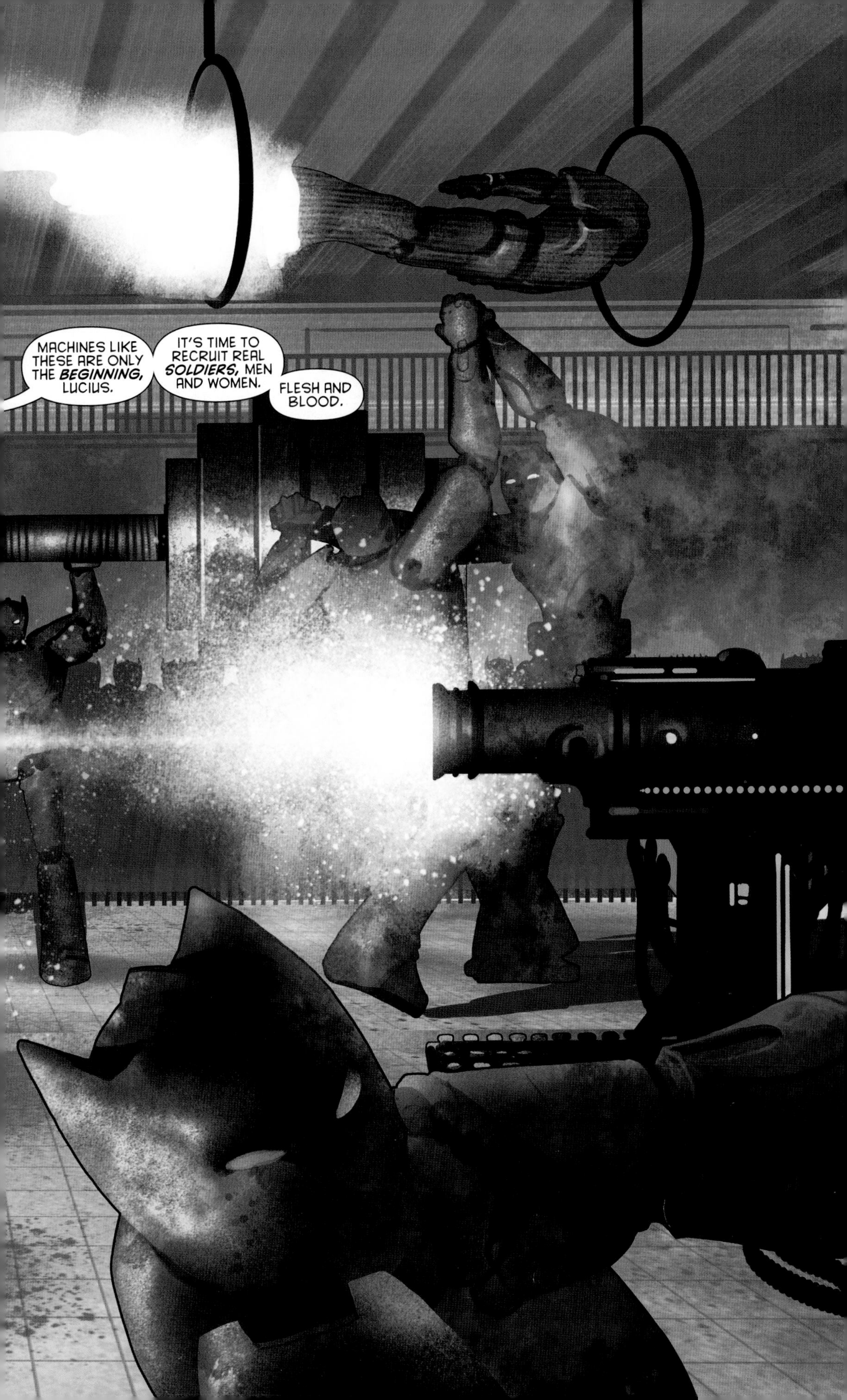
MACHINES LIKE THESE ARE ONLY THE BEGINNING, LUCIUS.
IT'S TIME TO RECRUIT REAL SOLDIERS, MEN AND WOMEN.
FLESH AND BLOOD.

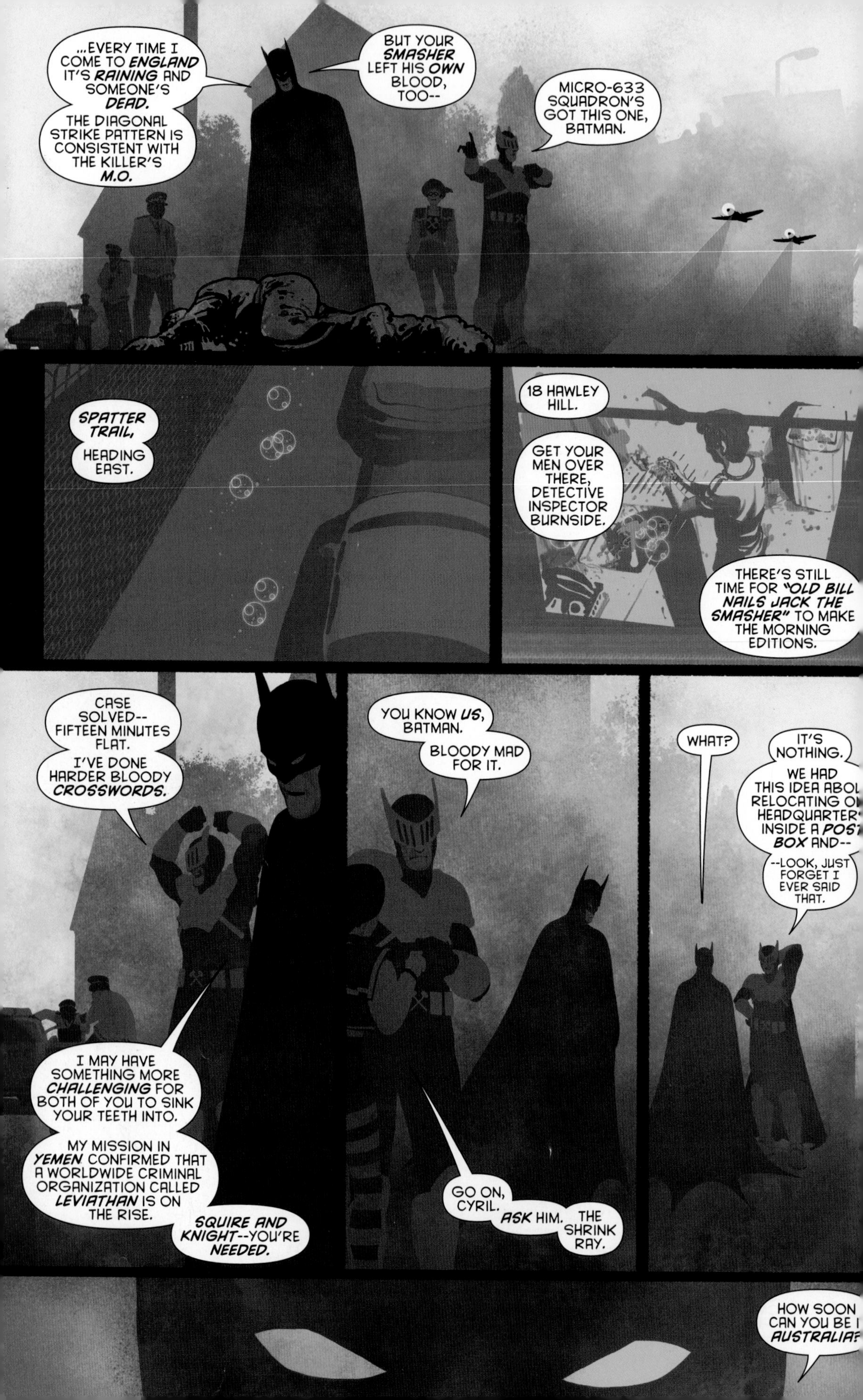
...EVERY TIME I COME TO ENGLAND IT'S RAINING AND SOMEONE'S DEAD.
THE DIAGONAL STRIKE PATTERN IS CONSISTENT WITH THE KILLER'S M.O.
BUT YOUR SMASHER LEFT HIS OWN BLOOD, TOO--
MICRO-633 SQUADRON'S GOT THIS ONE, BATMAN.
SPATTER TRAIL,
HEADING EAST.
18 HAWLEY HILL.
GET YOUR MEN OVER THERE, DETECTIVE INSPECTOR BURNSIDE.
THERE'S STILL TIME FOR "OLD BILL NAILS JACK THE SMASHER" TO MAKE THE MORNING EDITIONS.
CASE SOLVED-- FIFTEEN MINUTES FLAT.
I'VE DONE HARDER BLOODY CROSSWORDS.
I MAY HAVE SOMETHING MORE CHALLENGING FOR BOTH OF YOU TO SINK YOUR TEETH INTO.
MY MISSION IN YEMEN CONFIRMED THAT A WORLDWIDE CRIMINAL ORGANIZATION CALLED LEVIATHAN IS ON THE RISE.
SQUIRE AND KNIGHT--YOU'RE NEEDED.
YOU KNOW US, BATMAN.
BLOODY MAD FOR IT.
GO ON, CYRIL.
ASK HIM.
THE SHRINK RAY.
WHAT?
IT'S NOTHING.
--LOOK, JUST FORGET I EVER SAID THAT.

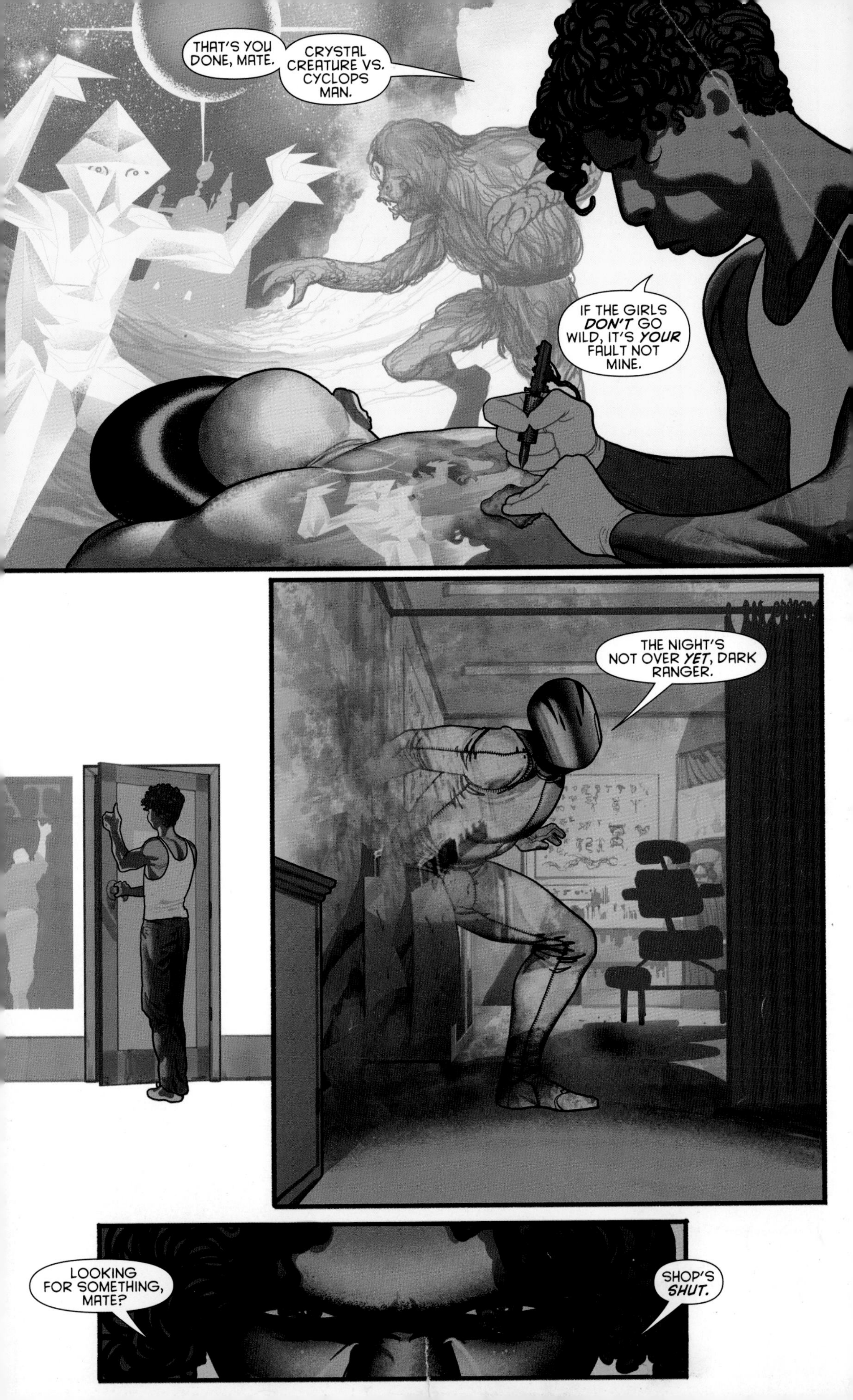
THAT'S YOU DONE, MATE.
CRYSTAL CREATURE VS. CYCLOPS MAN.
IF THE GIRLS DON'T GO WILD, IT'S YOUR FAULT NOT MINE.
THE NIGHT'S NOT OVER YET, DARK RANGER.
LOOKING FOR SOMETHING, MATE?
SHOP'S SHUT.

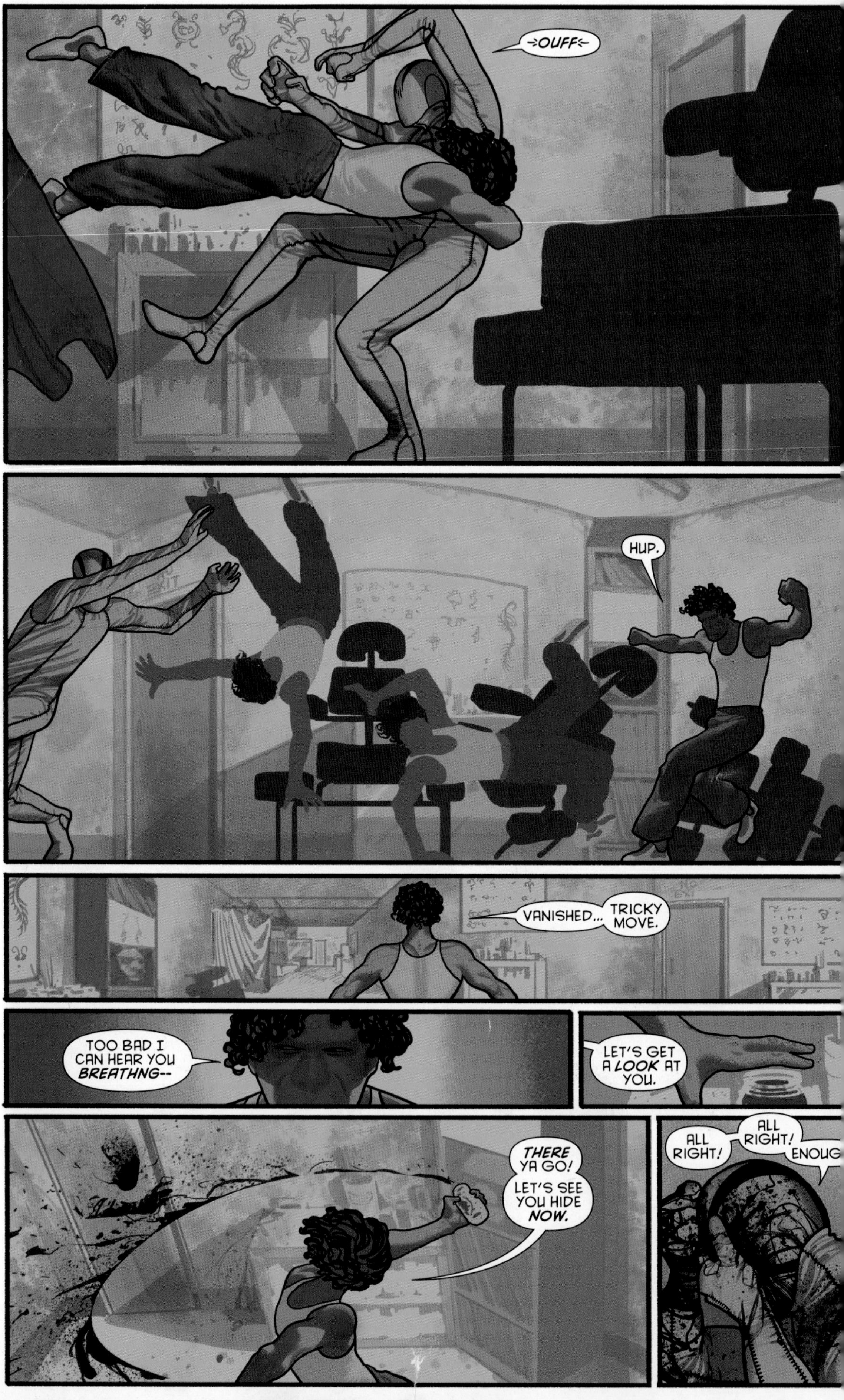
OUFF
HUP.
VANISHED...
TRICKY MOVE.
TOO BAD I CAN HEAR YOU BREATHNG--
LET'S GET A LOOK AT YOU.
THERE YA GO!
LET'S SEE YOU HIDE NOW.
ALL RIGHT!
ALL RIGHT!
ENOUG

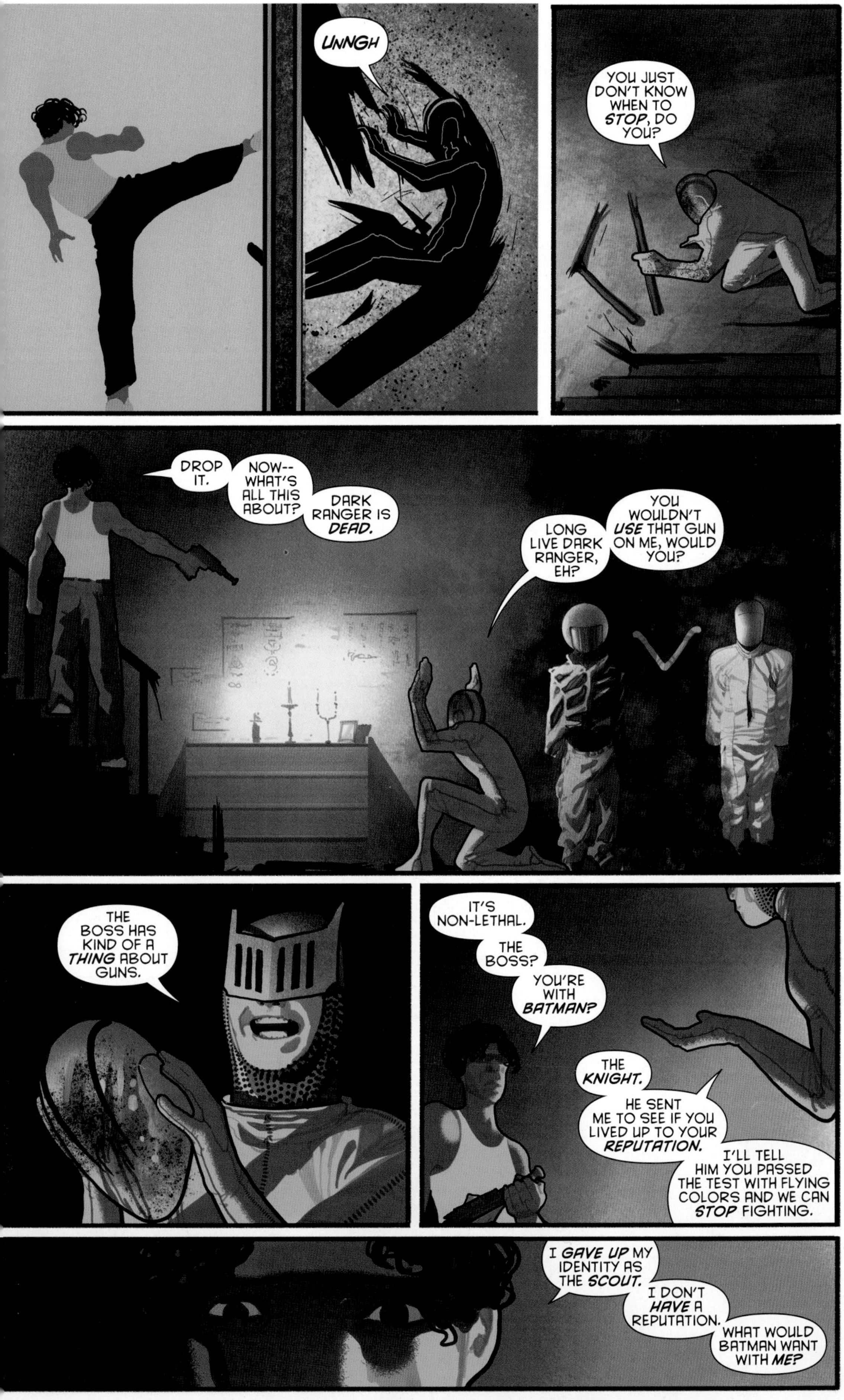
UNNGH
YOU JUST DON'T KNOW WHEN TO STOP, DO YOU?
DROP IT.
NOW-- WHAT'S ALL THIS ABOUT?
DARK RANGER IS DEAD.
LONG LIVE DARK RANGER, EH?
YOU WOULDN'T USE THAT GUN ON ME, WOULD YOU?
THE BOSS HAS KIND OF A THING ABOUT GUNS.
IT'S NON-LETHAL.
THE BOSS?
YOU'RE WITH BATMAN?
THE KNIGHT.
HE SENT ME TO SEE IF YOU LIVED UP TO YOUR REPUTATION.
I'LL TELL HIM YOU PASSED THE TEST WITH FLYING COLORS AND WE CAN STOP FIGHTING.
I GAVE UP MY IDENTITY AS THE SCOUT.
I DON'T HAVE A REPUTATION.
WHAT WOULD BATMAN WANT WITH ME?

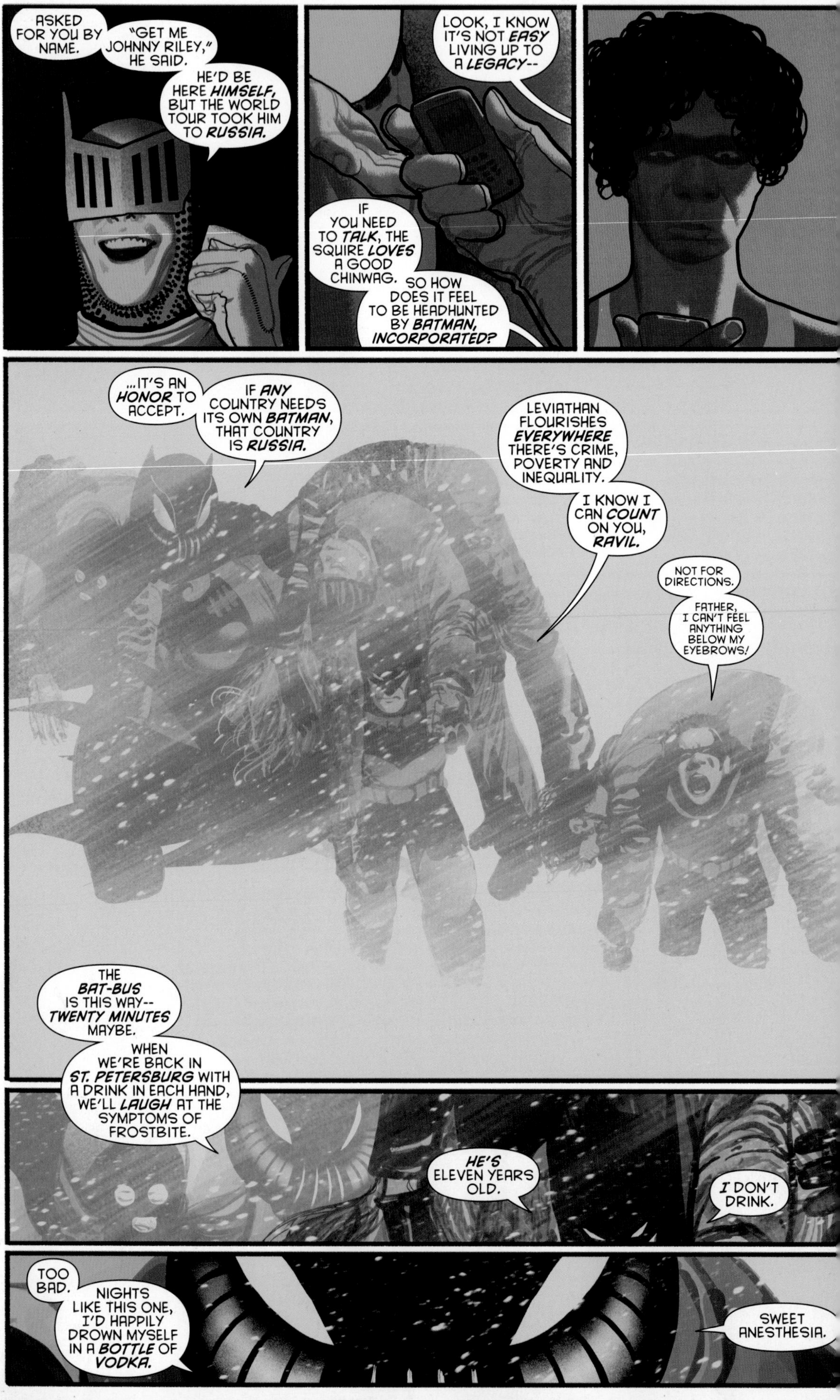
ASKED FOR YOU BY NAME.
"GET ME JOHNNY RILEY," HE SAID.
HE'D BE HERE HIMSELF, BUT THE WORLD TOUR TOOK HIM TO RUSSIA.
LOOK, I KNOW IT'S NOT EASY LIVING UP TO A LEGACY--
IF YOU NEED TO TALK, THE SQUIRE LOVES A GOOD CHINWAG.
SO HOW DOES IT FEEL TO BE HEADHUNTED BY BATMAN, INCORPORATED?
...IT'S AN HONOR TO ACCEPT.
IF ANY COUNTRY NEEDS ITS OWN BATMAN, THAT COUNTRY IS RUSSIA.
LEVIATHAN FLOURISHES EVERYWHERE THERE'S CRIME, POVERTY AND INEQUALITY.
I KNOW I CAN COUNT ON YOU, RAVIL.
NOT FOR DIRECTIONS.
FATHER, I CAN'T FEEL ANYTHING BELOW MY EYEBROWS!
THE BAT-BUS IS THIS WAY-- TWENTY MINUTES MAYBE.
WHEN WE'RE BACK IN ST. PETERSBURG WITH A DRINK IN EACH HAND, WE'LL LAUGH AT THE SYMPTOMS OF FROSTBITE.
HE'S ELEVEN YEARS OLD.
I DON'T DRINK.
TOO BAD.
NIGHTS LIKE THIS ONE, I'D HAPPILY DROWN MYSELF IN A BOTTLE OF VODKA.
SWEET ANESTHESIA.

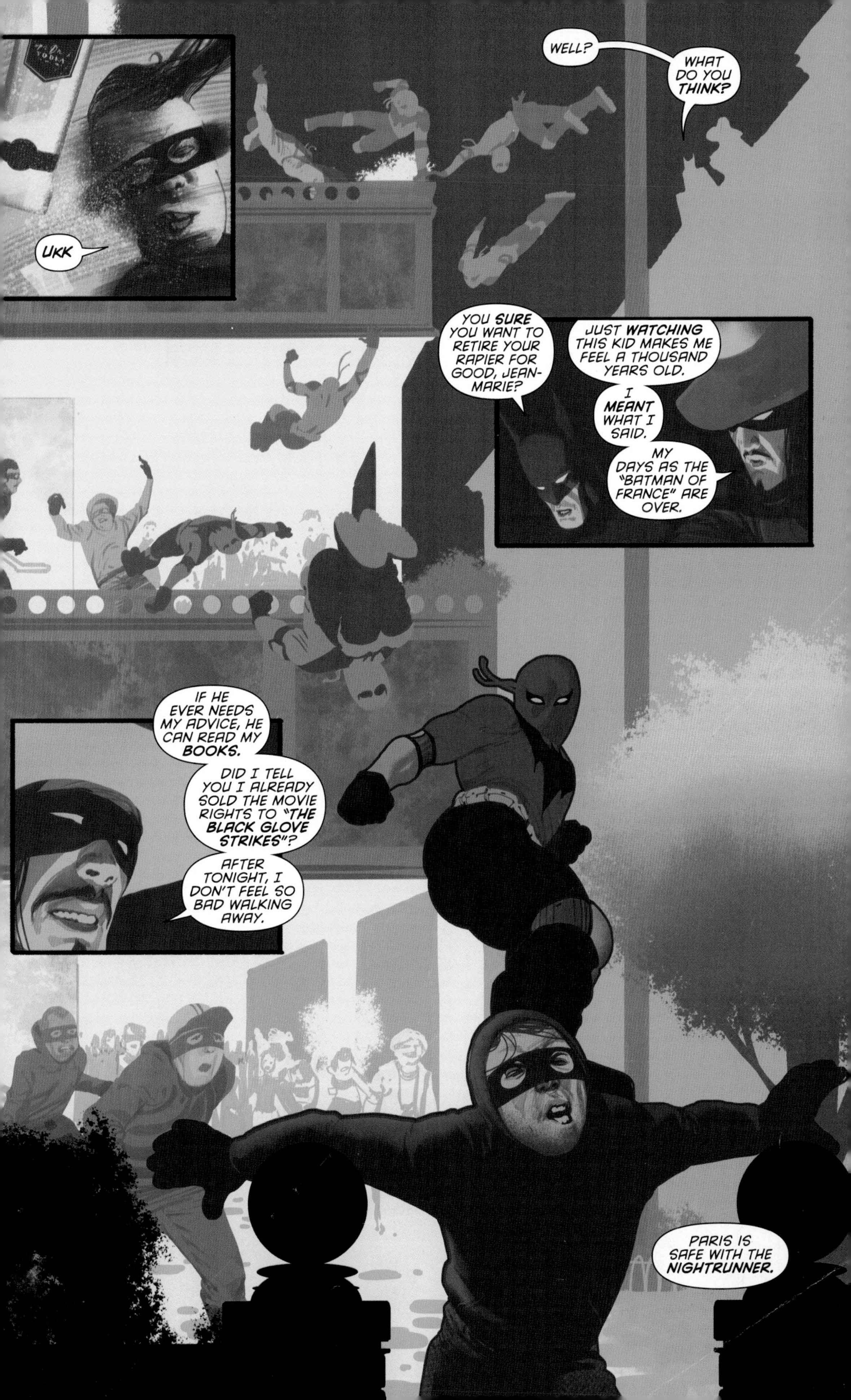
UKK
WELL?
WHAT DO YOU THINK?
YOU SURE YOU WANT TO RETIRE YOUR RAPIER FOR GOOD, JEAN-MARIE?
JUST WATCHING THIS KID MAKES ME FEEL A THOUSAND YEARS OLD.
I MEANT WHAT I SAID.
MY DAYS AS THE "BATMAN OF FRANCE" ARE OVER.
IF HE EVER NEEDS MY ADVICE, HE CAN READ MY BOOKS.
DID I TELL YOU I ALREADY SOLD THE MOVIE RIGHTS TO "THE BLACK GLOVE STRIKES"?
AFTER TONIGHT, I DON'T FEEL SO BAD WALKING AWAY.
PARIS IS SAFE WITH THE NIGHTRUNNER.

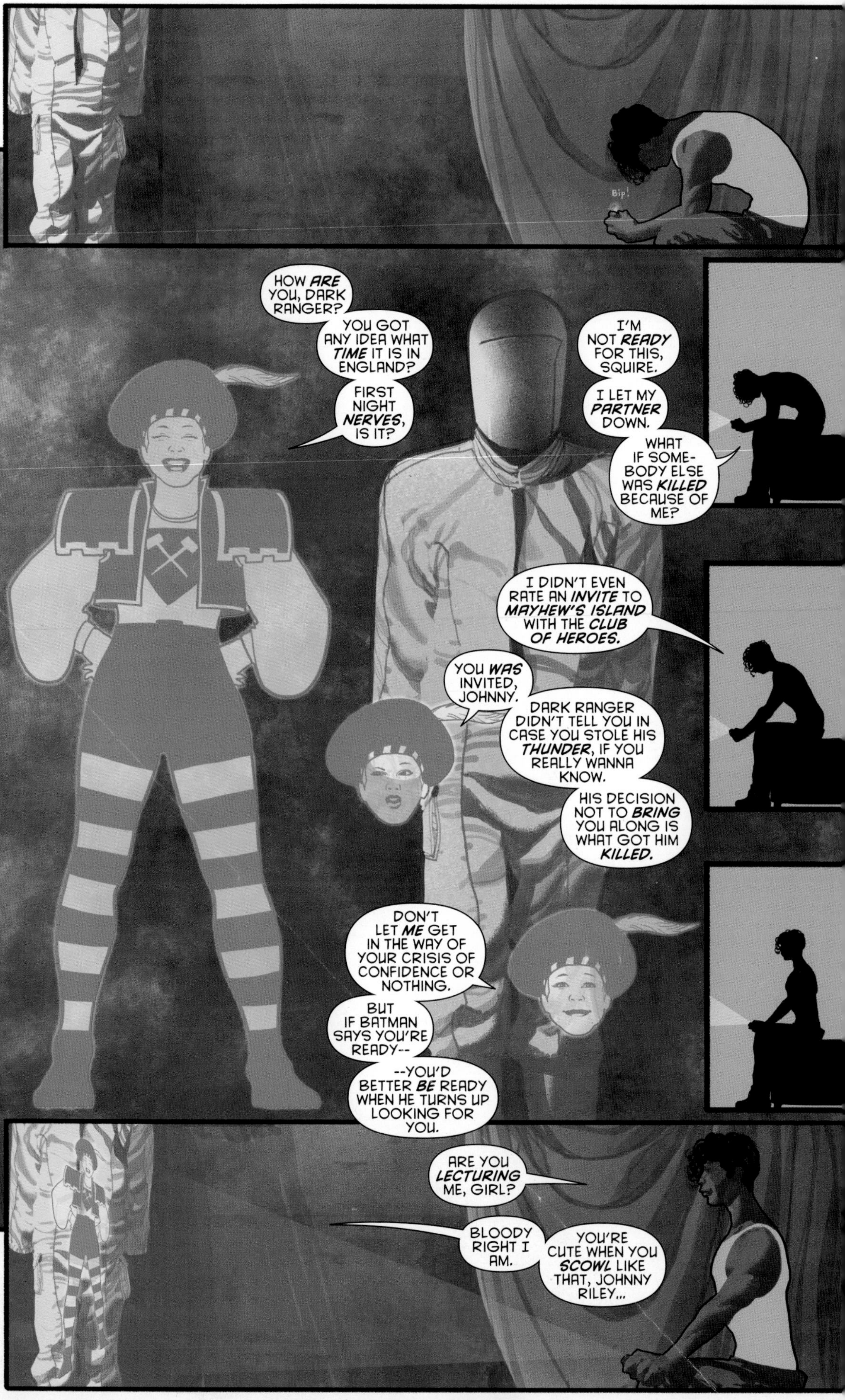

Bip!
HOW ARE YOU, DARK RANGER?
YOU GOT ANY IDEA WHAT TIME IT IS IN ENGLAND?
FIRST NIGHT NERVES, IS IT?
I'M NOT READY FOR THIS, SQUIRE.
I LET MY PARTNER DOWN.
WHAT IF SOMEBODY ELSE WAS KILLED BECAUSE OF ME?
I DIDN'T EVEN RATE AN INVITE TO MAYHEW'S ISLAND WITH THE CLUB OF HEROES.
YOU WAS INVITED, JOHNNY.
DARK RANGER DIDN'T TELL YOU IN CASE YOU STOLE HIS THUNDER, IF YOU REALLY WANNA KNOW.
HIS DECISION NOT TO BRING YOU ALONG IS WHAT GOT HIM KILLED.
DON'T LET ME GET IN THE WAY OF YOUR CRISIS OF CONFIDENCE OR NOTHING.
BUT IF BATMAN SAYS YOU'RE READY--
--YOU'D BETTER BE READY WHEN HE TURNS UP LOOKING FOR YOU.
ARE YOU LECTURING ME, GIRL?
BLOODY RIGHT I AM.
YOU'RE CUTE WHEN YOU SCOWL LIKE THAT, JOHNNY RILEY...

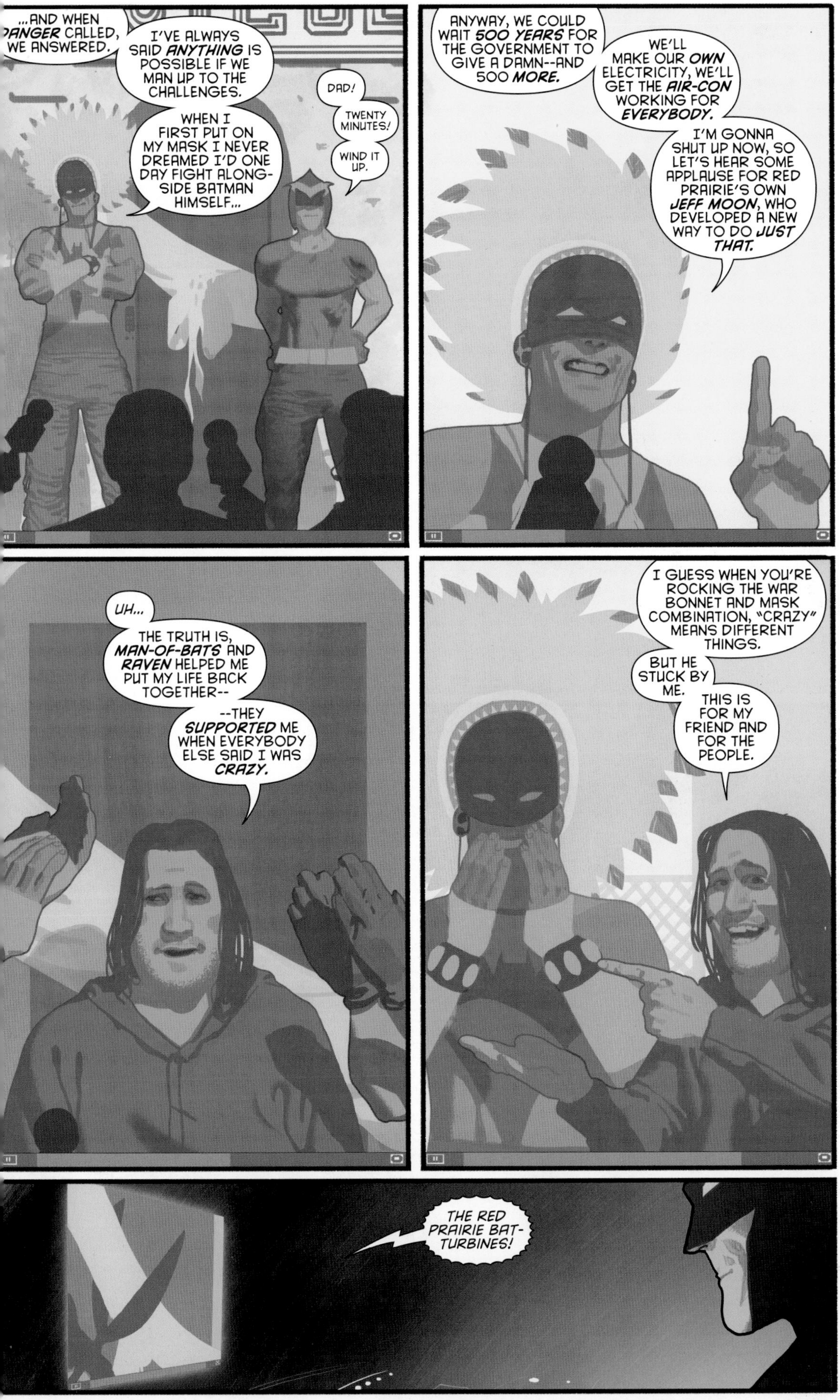
...AND WHEN DANGER CALLED, WE ANSWERED.
I'VE ALWAYS SAID ANYTHING IS POSSIBLE IF WE MAN UP TO THE CHALLENGES.
WHEN I FIRST PUT ON MY MASK I NEVER DREAMED I'D ONE DAY FIGHT ALONG-SIDE BATMAN HIMSELF...
DAD!
TWENTY MINUTES!
WIND IT UP.
ANYWAY, WE COULD WAIT 500 YEARS FOR THE GOVERNMENT TO GIVE A DAMN--AND 500 MORE.
WE'LL MAKE OUR OWN ELECTRICITY, WE'LL GET THE AIR-CON WORKING FOR EVERYBODY.
I'M GONNA SHUT UP NOW, SO LET'S HEAR SOME APPLAUSE FOR RED PRAIRIE'S OWN JEFF MOON, WHO DEVELOPED A NEW WAY TO DO JUST THAT.
UH...
THE TRUTH IS, MAN-OF-BATS AND RAVEN HELPED ME PUT MY LIFE BACK TOGETHER--
--THEY SUPPORTED ME WHEN EVERYBODY ELSE SAID I WAS CRAZY.
I GUESS WHEN YOU'RE ROCKING THE WAR BONNET AND MASK COMBINATION, "CRAZY" MEANS DIFFERENT THINGS.
BUT HE STUCK BY ME.
THIS IS FOR MY FRIEND AND FOR THE PEOPLE.
THE RED PRAIRIE BAT-TURBINES!

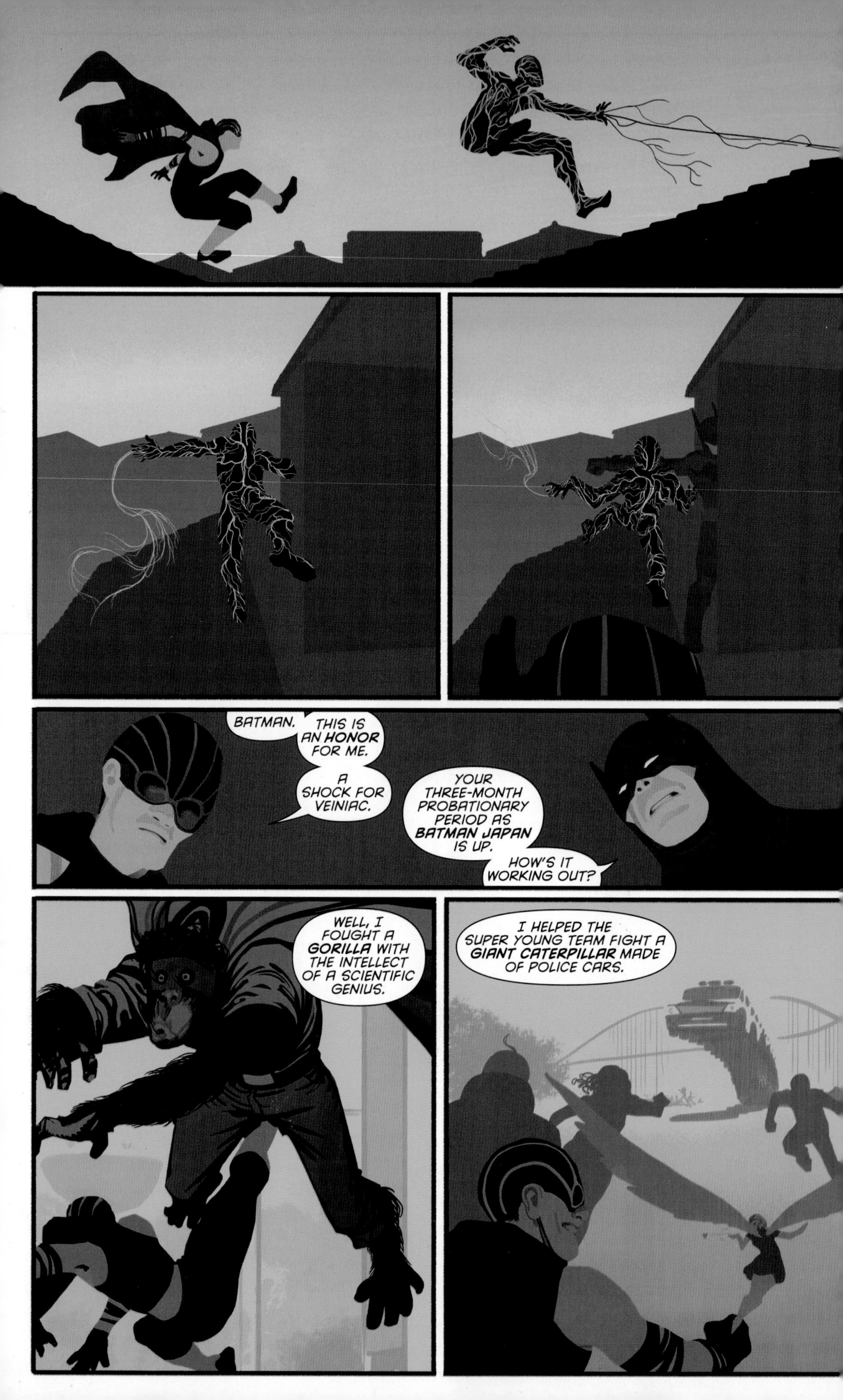
BATMAN.
THIS IS AN HONOR FOR ME.
A SHOCK FOR VEINIAC.
YOUR THREE-MONTH PROBATIONARY PERIOD AS BATMAN JAPAN IS UP.
HOW'S IT WORKING OUT?
WELL, I FOUGHT A GORILLA WITH THE INTELLECT OF A SCIENTIFIC GENIUS.
I HELPED THE SUPER YOUNG TEAM FIGHT A GIANT CATERPILLAR MADE OF POLICE CARS.

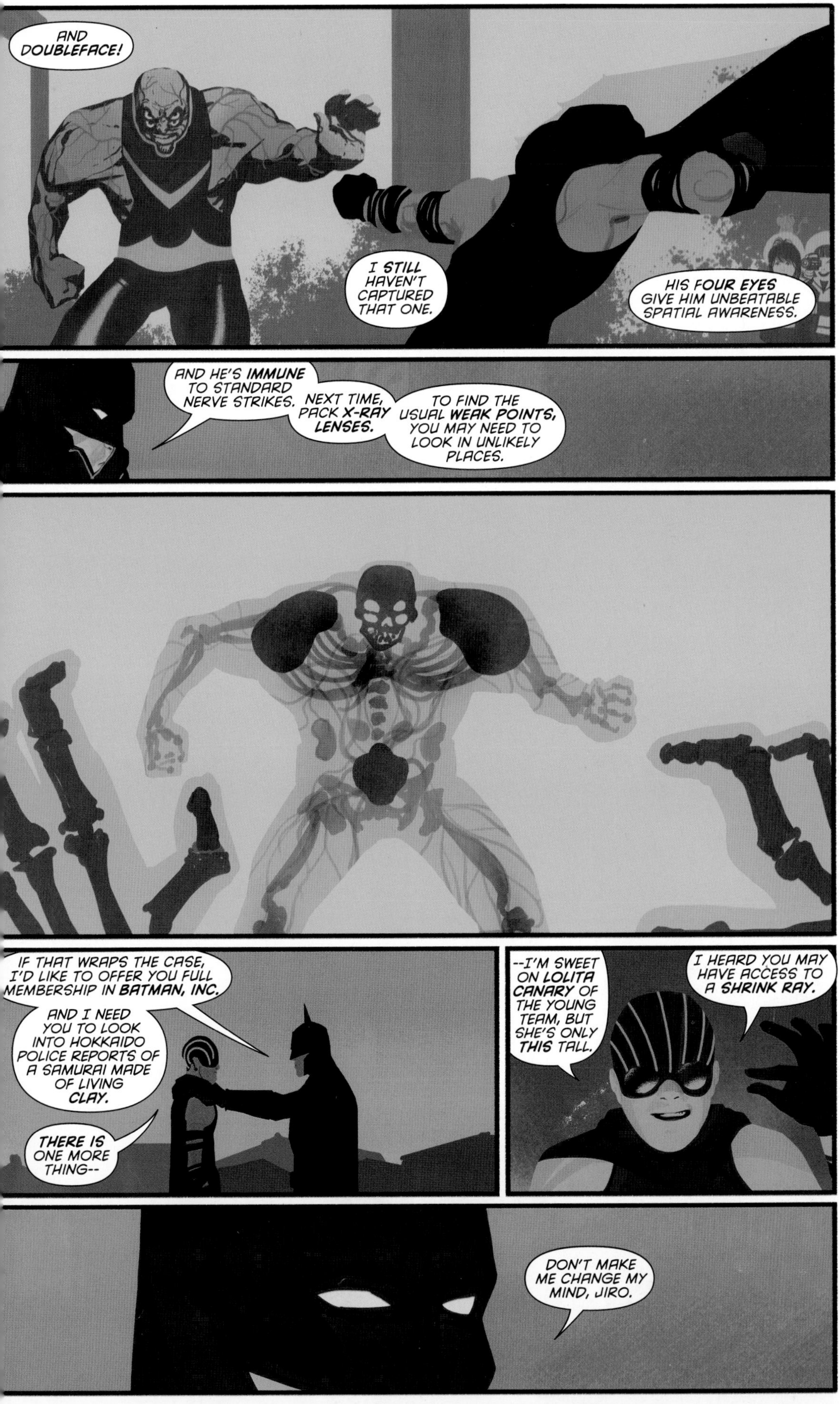
AND DOUBLEFACE!
I STILL HAVEN'T CAPTURED THAT ONE.
HIS FOUR EYES GIVE HIM UNBEATABLE SPATIAL AWARENESS.
AND HE'S IMMUNE TO STANDARD NERVE STRIKES.
NEXT TIME, PACK X-RAY LENSES.
TO FIND THE USUAL WEAK POINTS, YOU MAY NEED TO LOOK IN UNLIKELY PLACES.
IF THAT WRAPS THE CASE, I'D LIKE TO OFFER YOU FULL MEMBERSHIP IN BATMAN, INC.
AND I NEED YOU TO LOOK INTO HOKKAIDO POLICE REPORTS OF A SAMURAI MADE OF LIVING CLAY.
THERE IS ONE MORE THING--
--I'M SWEET ON LOLITA CANARY OF THE YOUNG TEAM, BUT SHE'S ONLY THIS TALL.
I HEARD YOU MAY HAVE ACCESS TO A SHRINK RAY.
DON'T MAKE ME CHANGE MY MIND, JIRO.

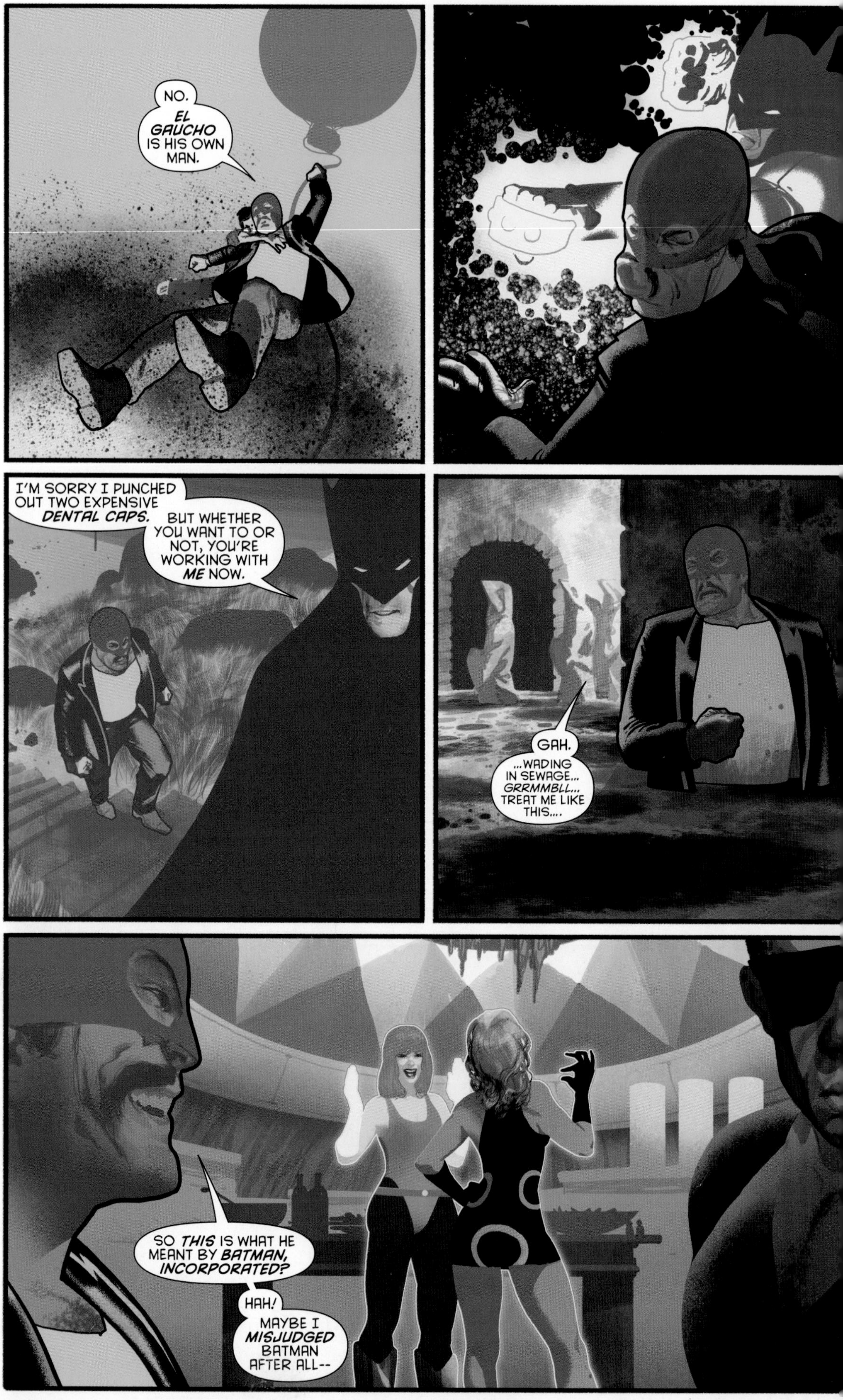
NO.
EL GAUCHO IS HIS OWN MAN.
I'M SORRY I PUNCHED OUT TWO EXPENSIVE DENTAL CAPS.
BUT WHETHER YOU WANT TO OR NOT, YOU'RE WORKING WITH ME NOW.
GAH.
...WADING IN SEWAGE... GRRMMBLL... TREAT ME LIKE THIS....
SO THIS IS WHAT HE MEANT BY BATMAN, INCORPORATED?
HAH!
MAYBE I MISJUDGED BATMAN AFTER ALL--

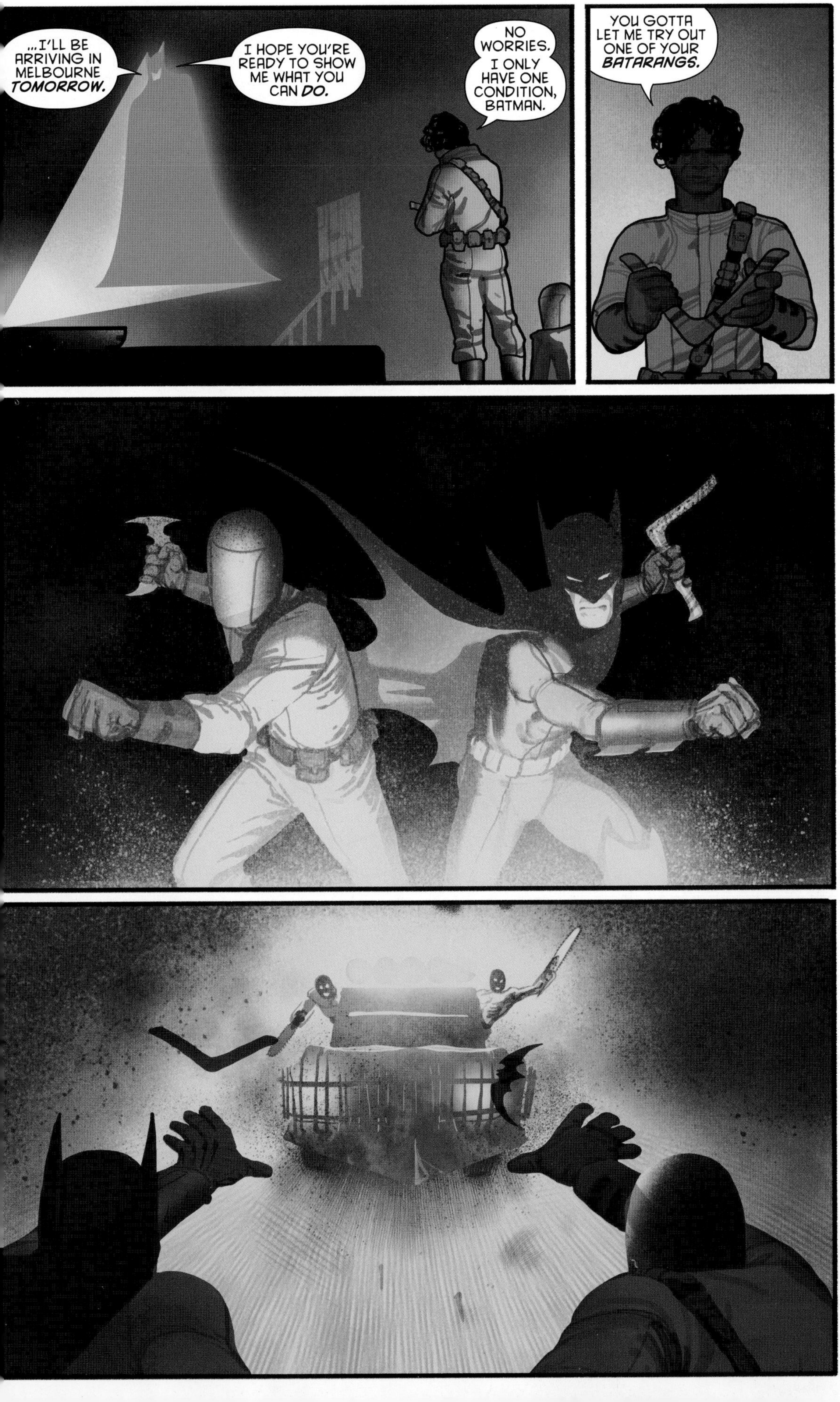
...I'LL BE ARRIVING IN MELBOURNE *TOMORROW.*
I HOPE YOU'RE READY TO SHOW ME WHAT YOU CAN *DO.*
NO WORRIES. I ONLY HAVE ONE CONDITION, BATMAN.
YOU GOTTA LET ME TRY OUT ONE OF YOUR *BATARANGS.*

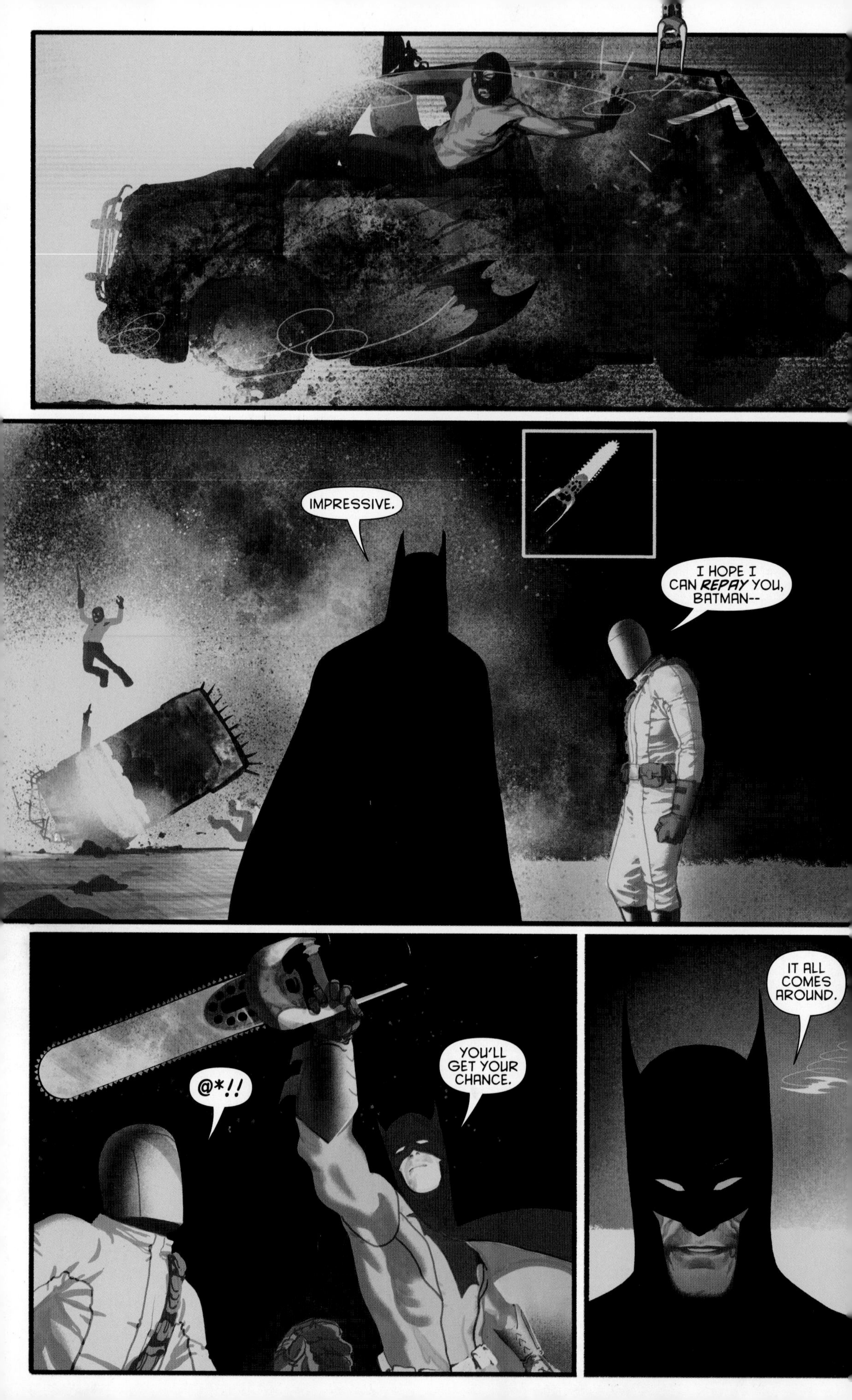
IMPRESSIVE.
I HOPE I CAN REPAY YOU, BATMAN--
@*!!
YOU'LL GET YOUR CHANCE.
IT ALL COMES AROUND.

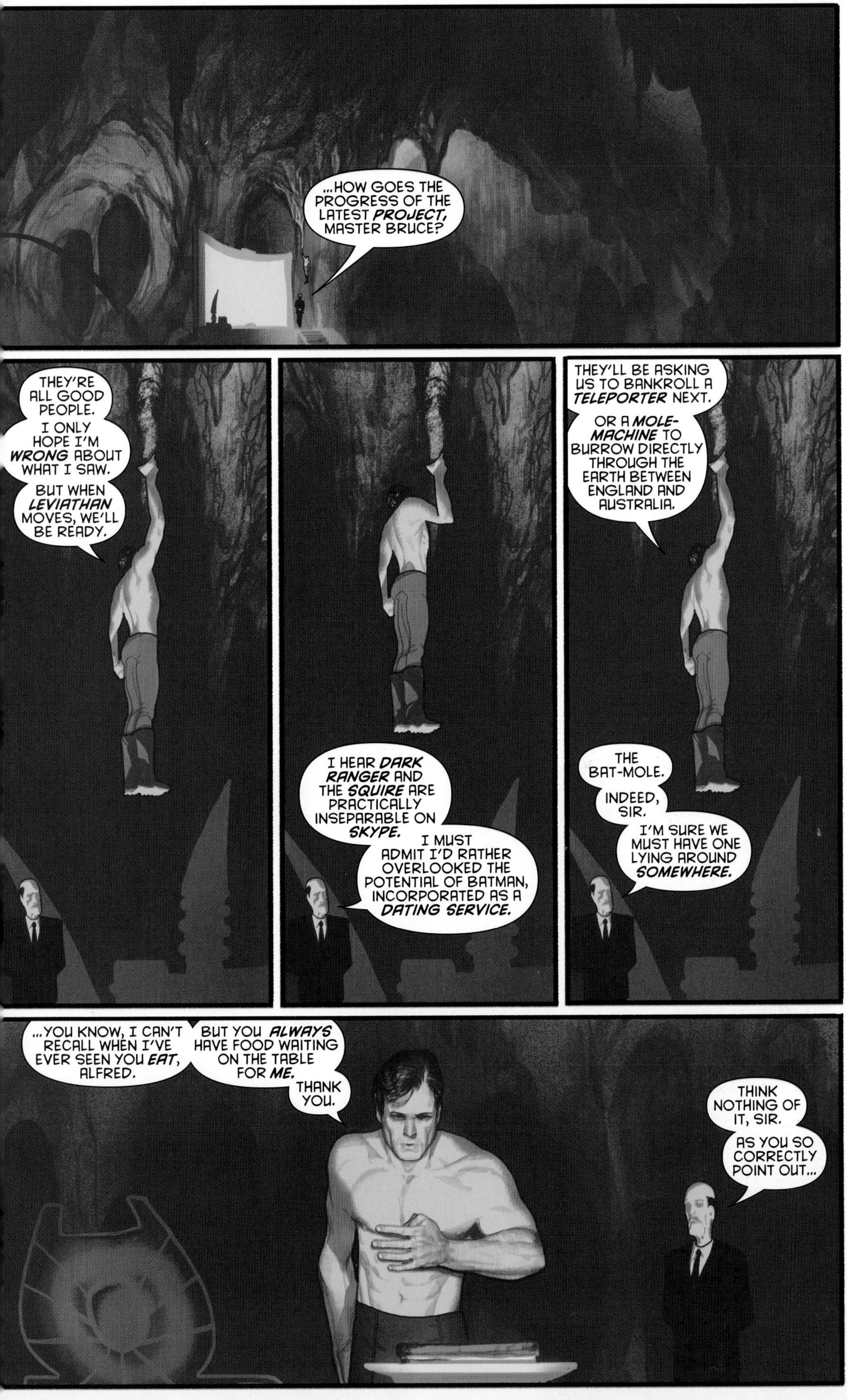
...HOW GOES THE PROGRESS OF THE LATEST *PROJECT,* MASTER BRUCE?
THEY'RE ALL GOOD PEOPLE.
I ONLY HOPE I'M *WRONG* ABOUT WHAT I SAW.
BUT WHEN *LEVIATHAN* MOVES, WE'LL BE READY.
I HEAR *DARK RANGER* AND THE *SQUIRE* ARE PRACTICALLY INSEPARABLE ON *SKYPE.*
I MUST ADMIT I'D RATHER OVERLOOKED THE POTENTIAL OF BATMAN, INCORPORATED AS A *DATING SERVICE.*
THEY'LL BE ASKING US TO BANKROLL A *TELEPORTER* NEXT.
OR A *MOLE-MACHINE* TO BURROW DIRECTLY THROUGH THE EARTH BETWEEN ENGLAND AND AUSTRALIA.
THE BAT-MOLE.
INDEED, SIR.
I'M SURE WE MUST HAVE ONE LYING AROUND *SOMEWHERE.*
...YOU KNOW, I CAN'T RECALL WHEN I'VE EVER SEEN YOU *EAT,* ALFRED.
BUT YOU *ALWAYS* HAVE FOOD WAITING ON THE TABLE FOR *ME.*
THANK YOU.
THINK NOTHING OF IT, SIR.
AS YOU SO CORRECTLY POINT OUT...

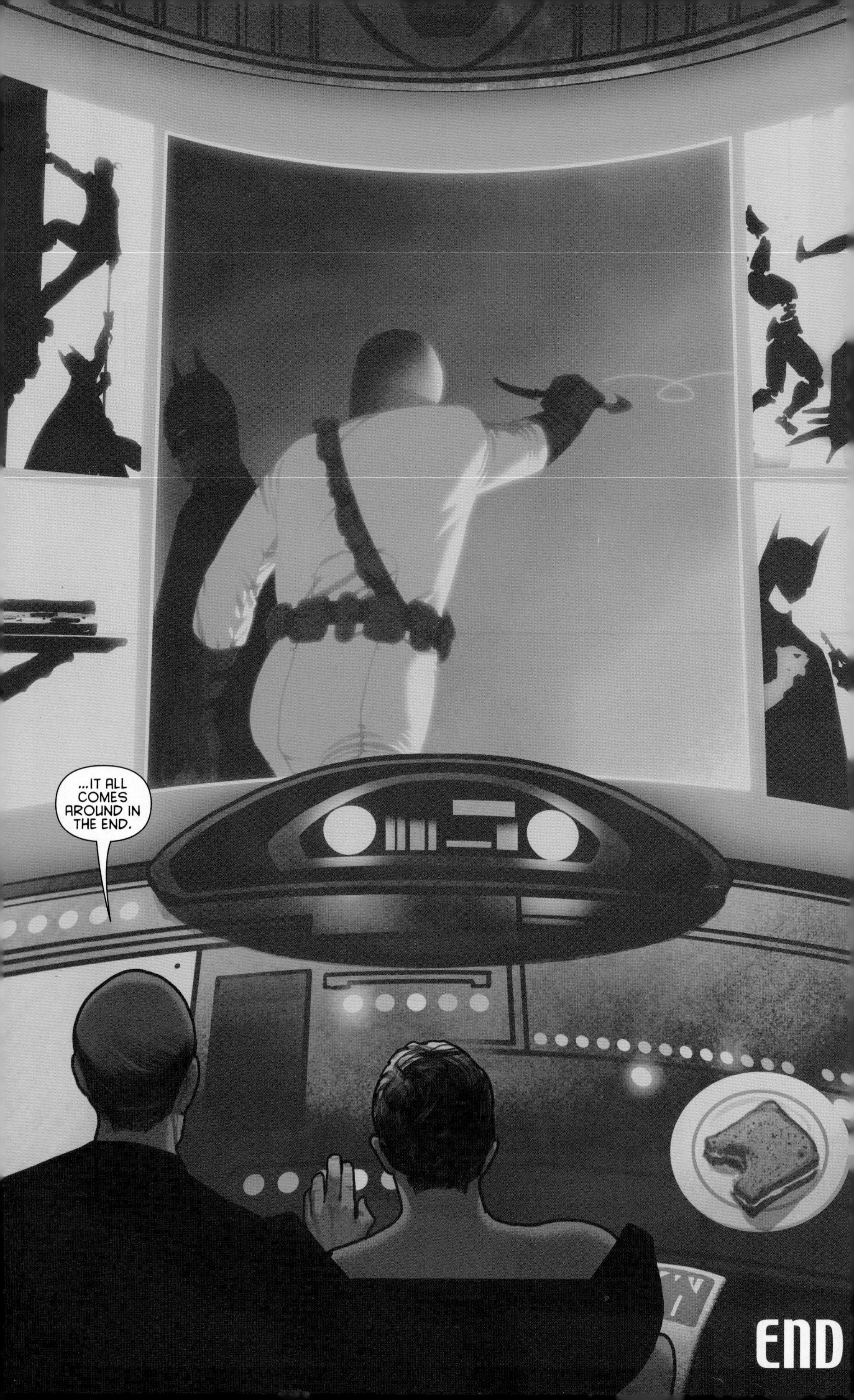
...IT ALL COMES AROUND IN THE END.
END

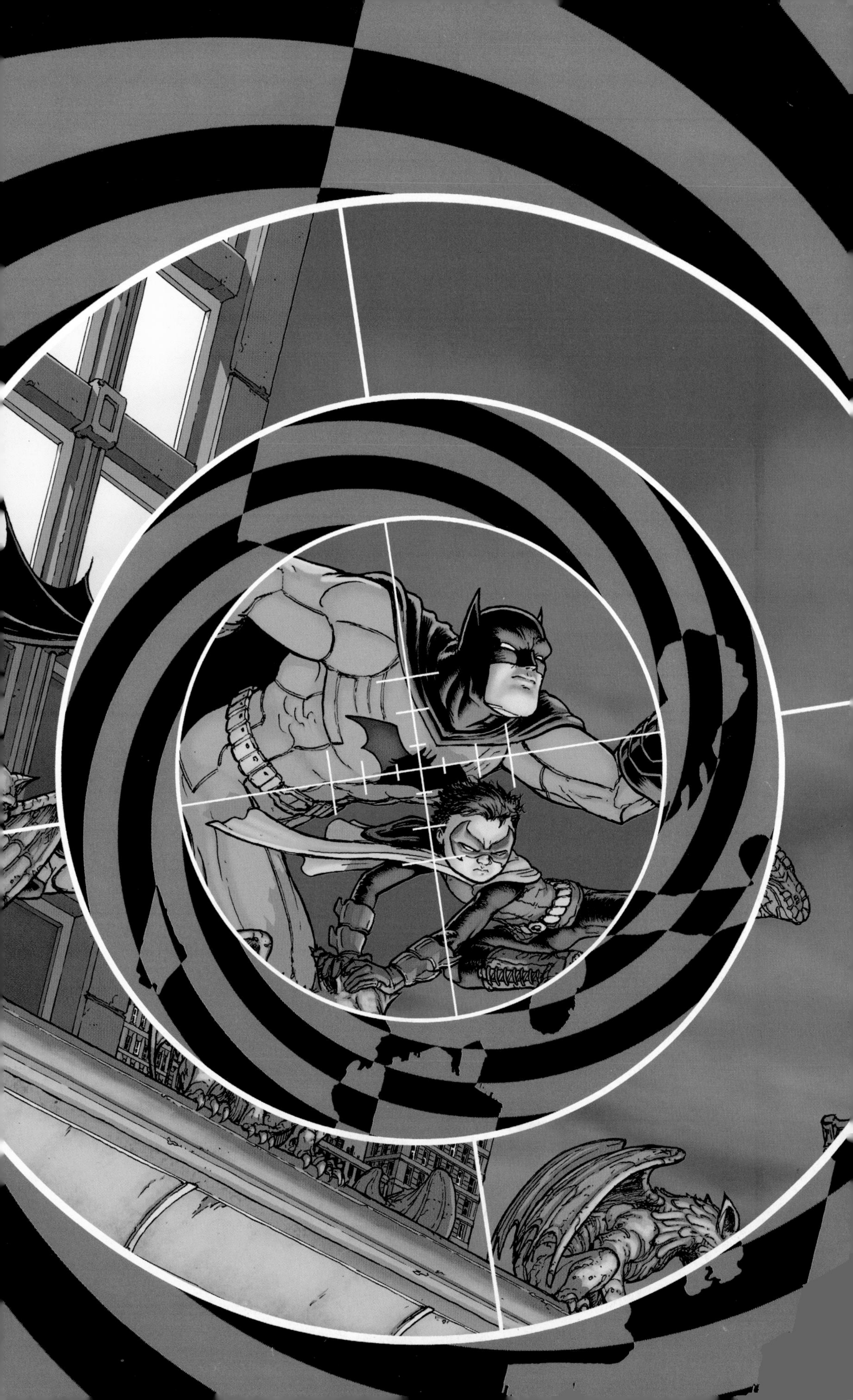

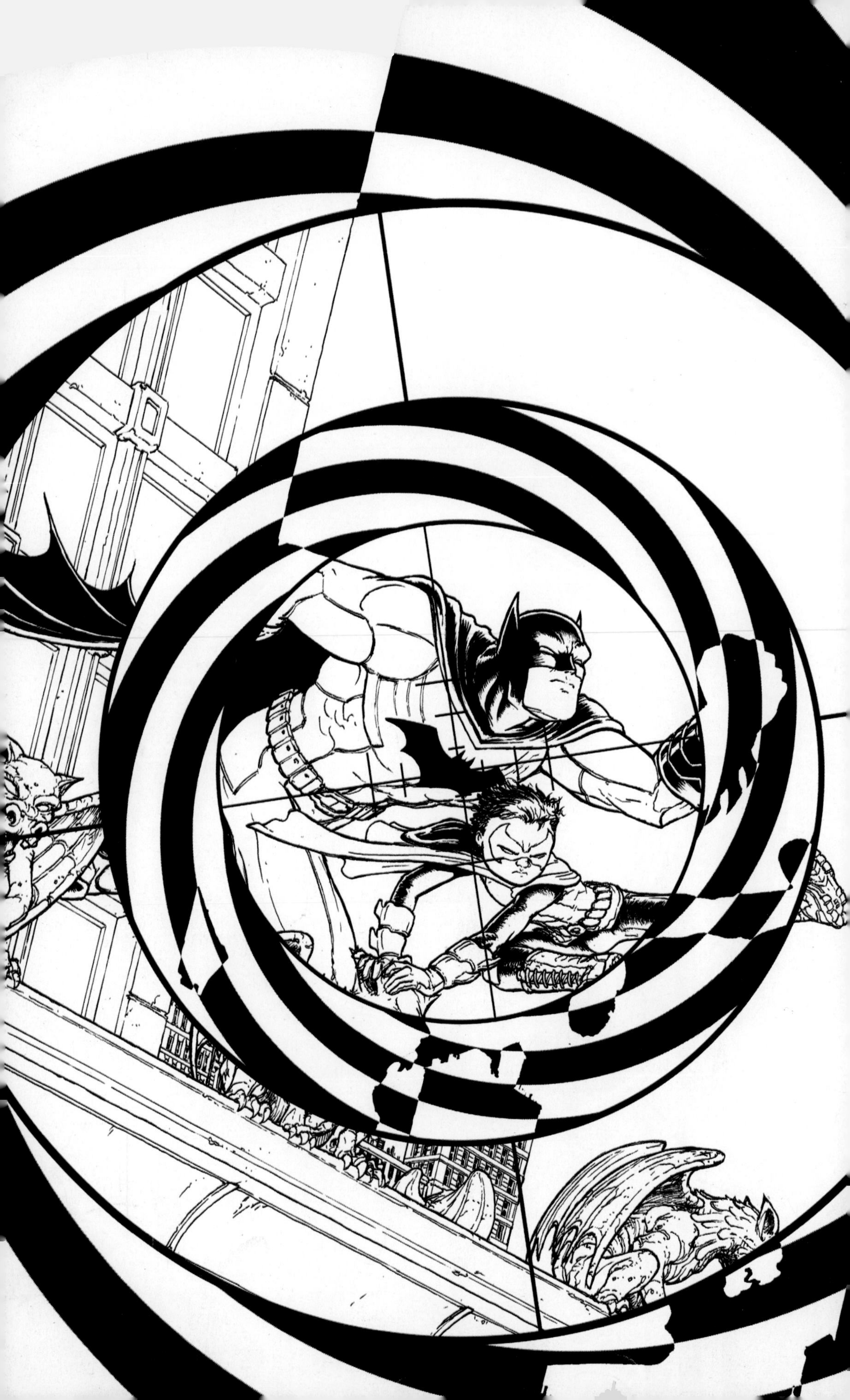

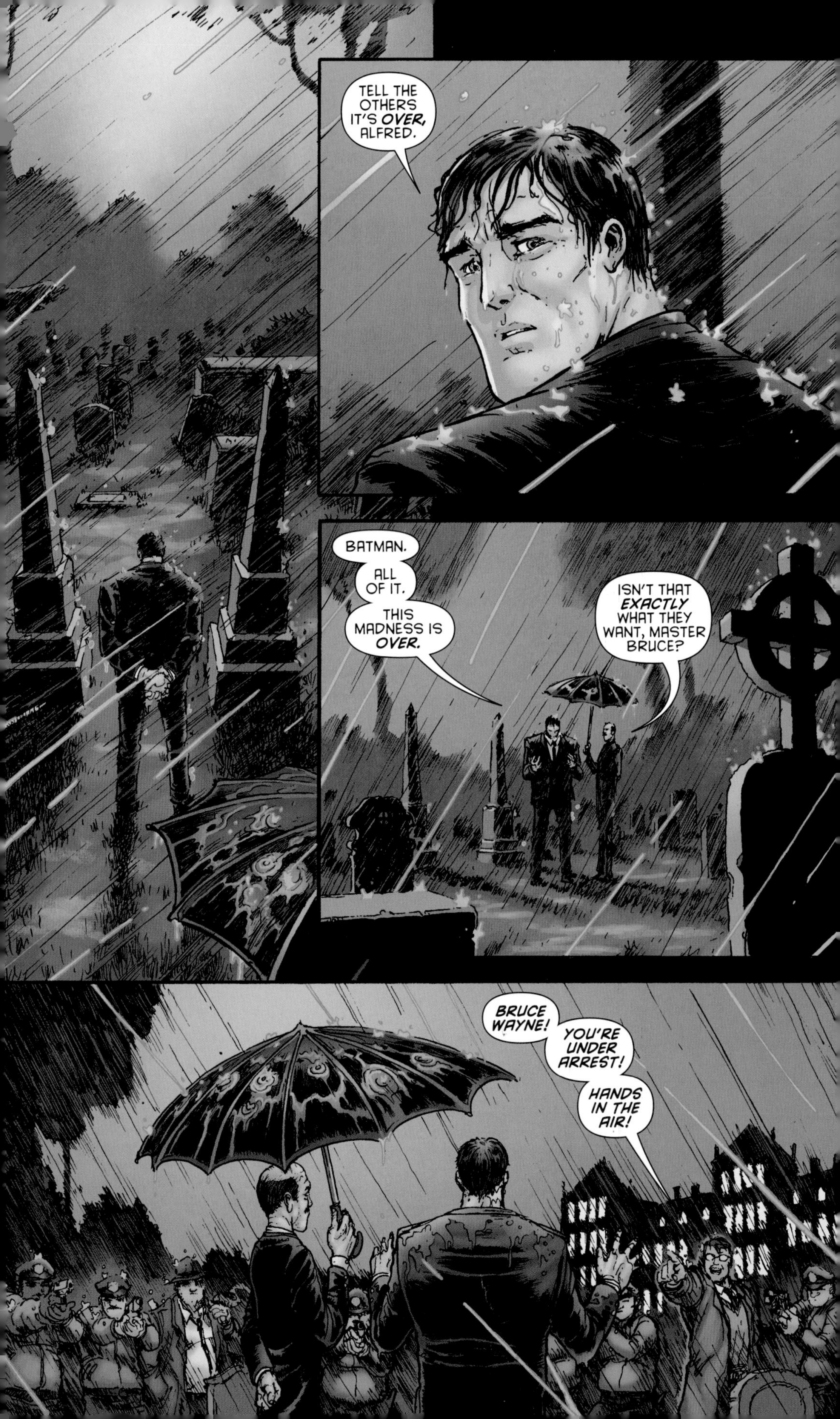

TELL THE OTHERS IT'S OVER, ALFRED.
BATMAN.
ALL OF IT.
THIS MADNESS IS OVER.
ISN'T THAT EXACTLY WHAT THEY WANT, MASTER BRUCE?
BRUCE WAYNE!
YOU'RE UNDER ARREST!
HANDS IN THE AIR!

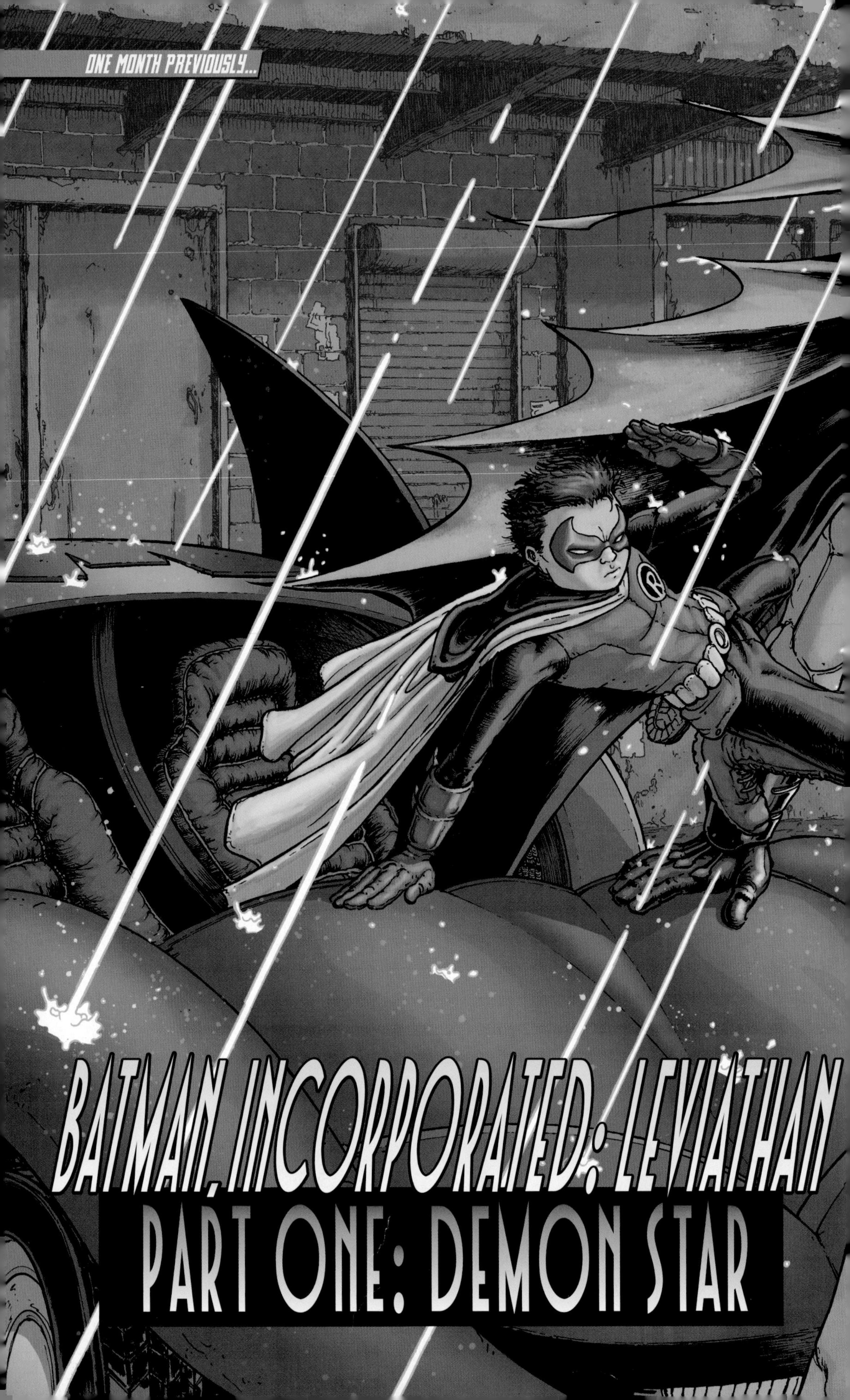
ONE MONTH PREVIOUSLY...
BATMAN, INCORPORATED: LEVIATHAN
PART ONE: DEMON STAR

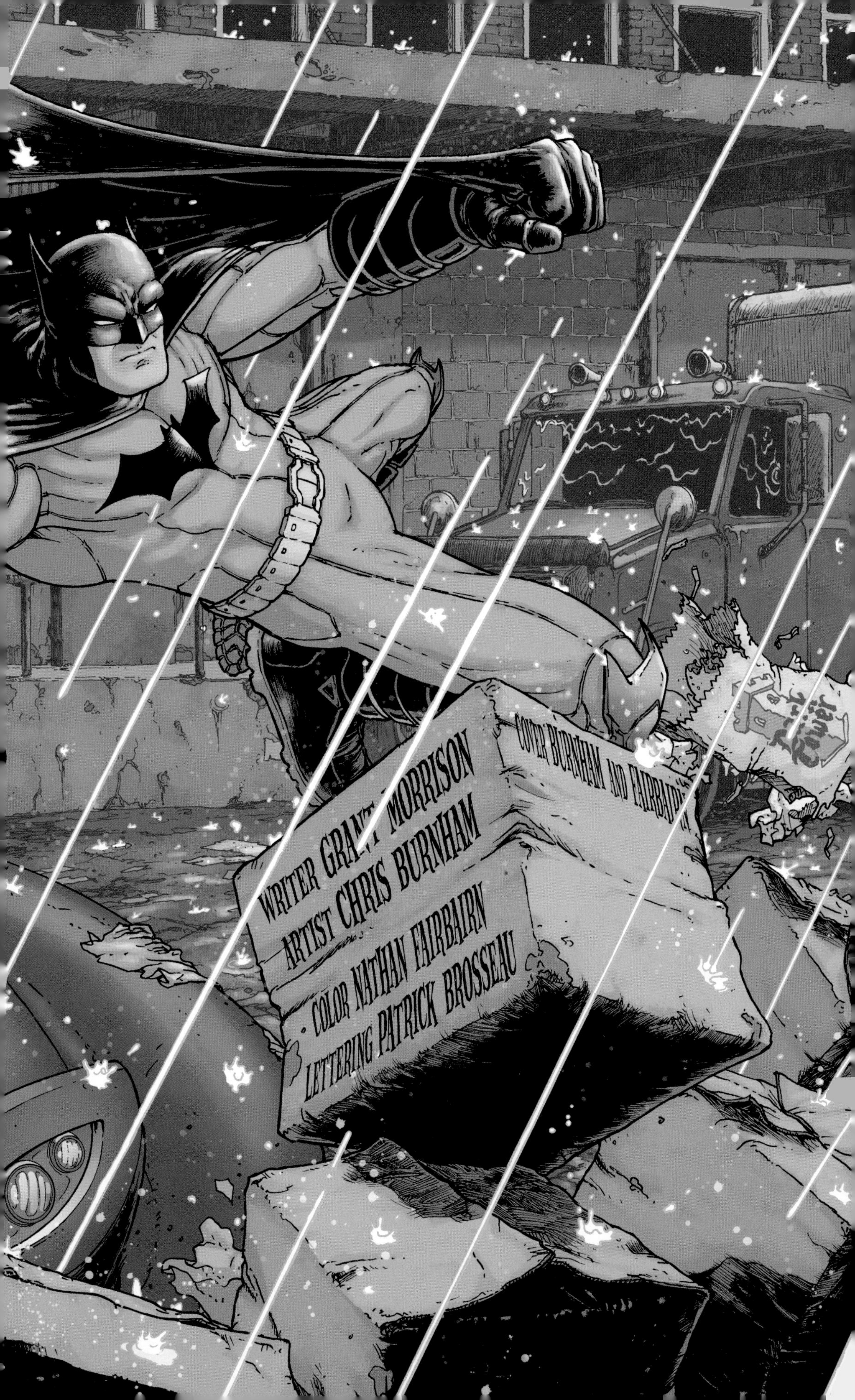
WRITER GRANT MORRISON
ARTIST CHRIS BURNHAM
COLOR NATHAN FAIRBAIRN
LETTERING PATRICK BROSSEAU
COVER BURNHAM AND FAIRBAIRN

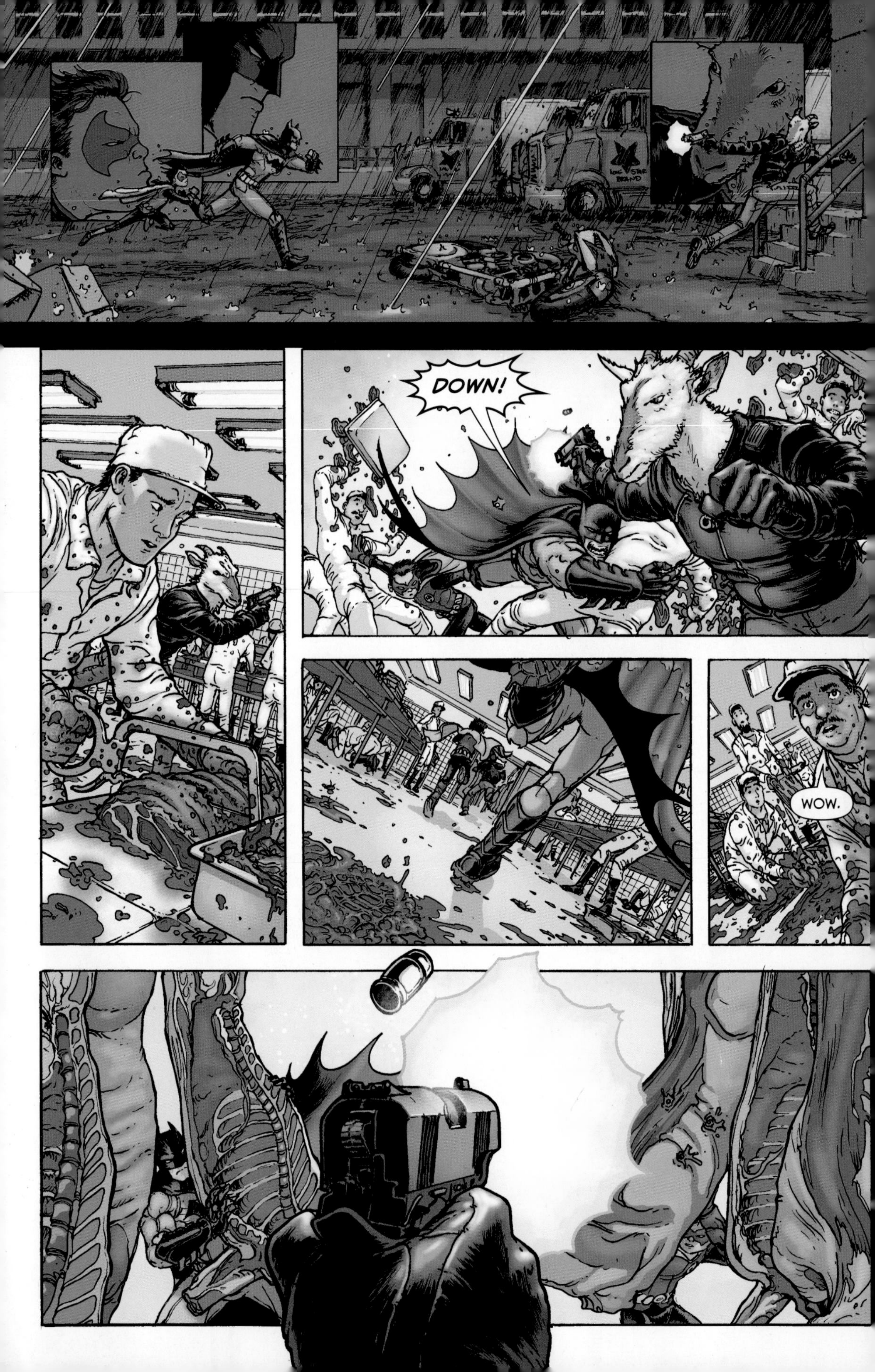
DOWN!
WOW.

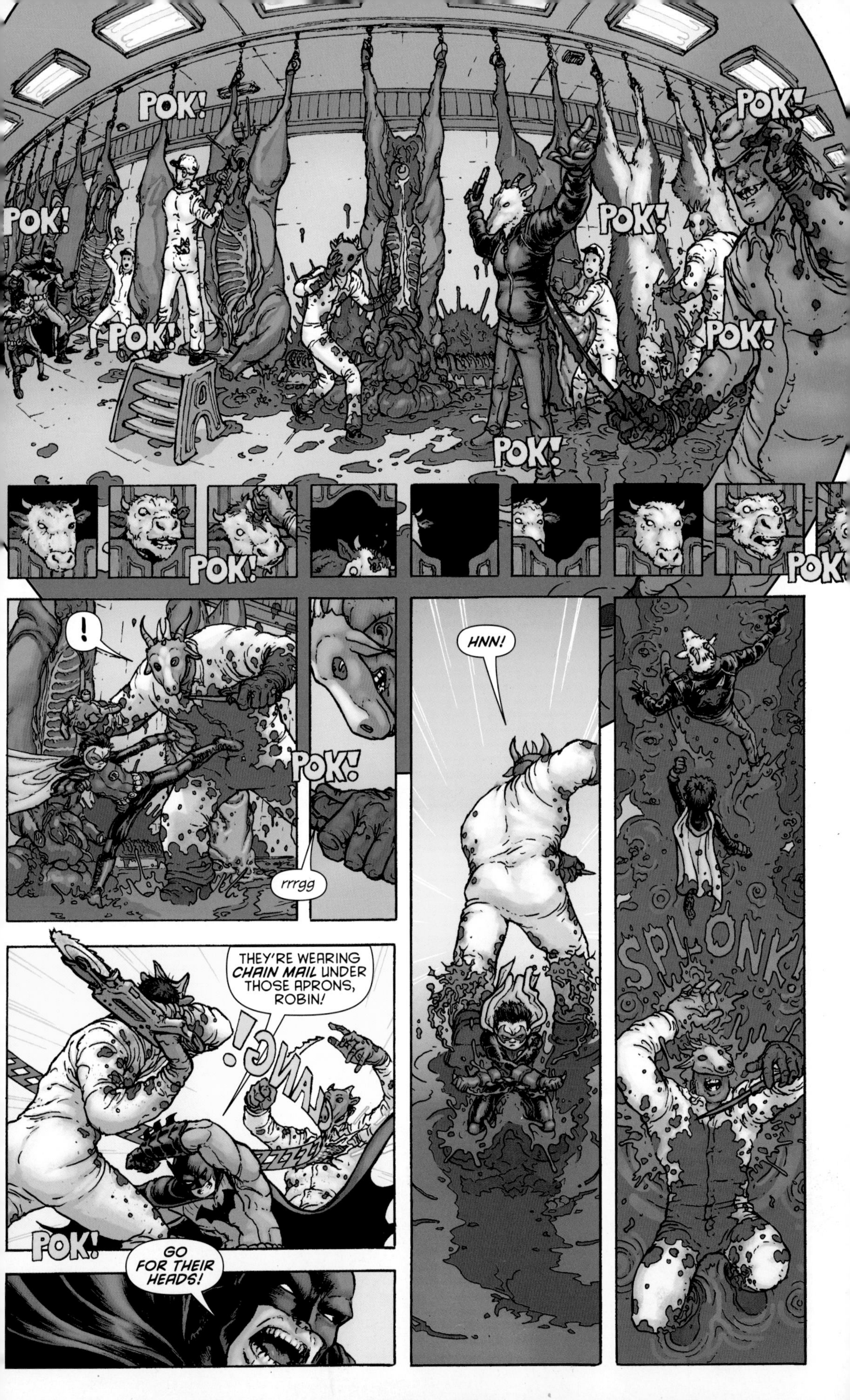
POK!
POK!
POK!
POK!
POK!
POK!
POK!
POK!
POK
!
POK!
rrrgg
HNN!
SPLONK!
THEY'RE WEARING CHAIN MAIL UNDER THOSE APRONS, ROBIN!
CLANG!
POK!
GO FOR THEIR HEADS!

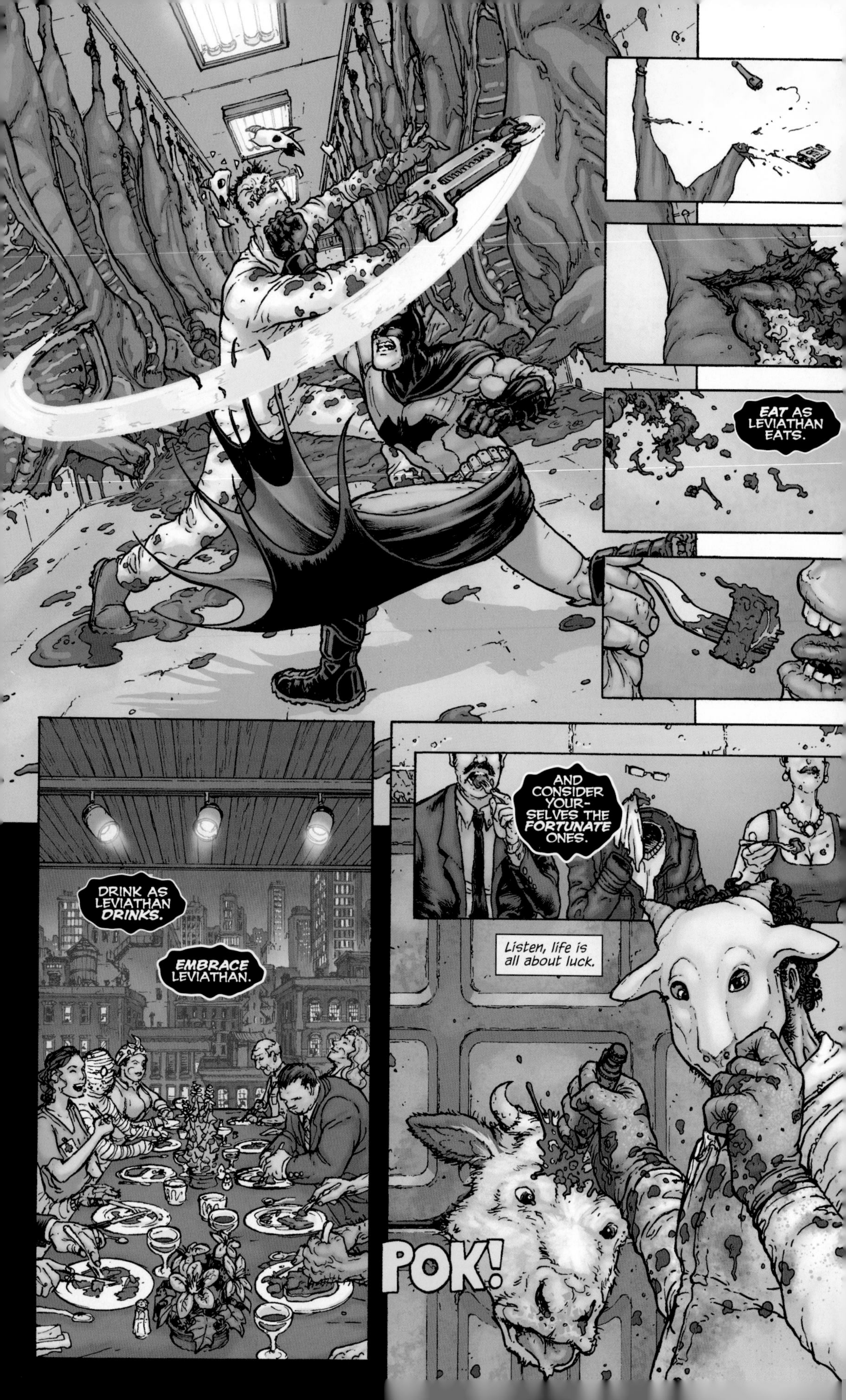
EAT AS LEVIATHAN EATS.
DRINK AS LEVIATHAN DRINKS.
EMBRACE LEVIATHAN.
AND CONSIDER YOUR-SELVES THE FORTUNATE ONES.
Listen, life is all about luck.
POK!

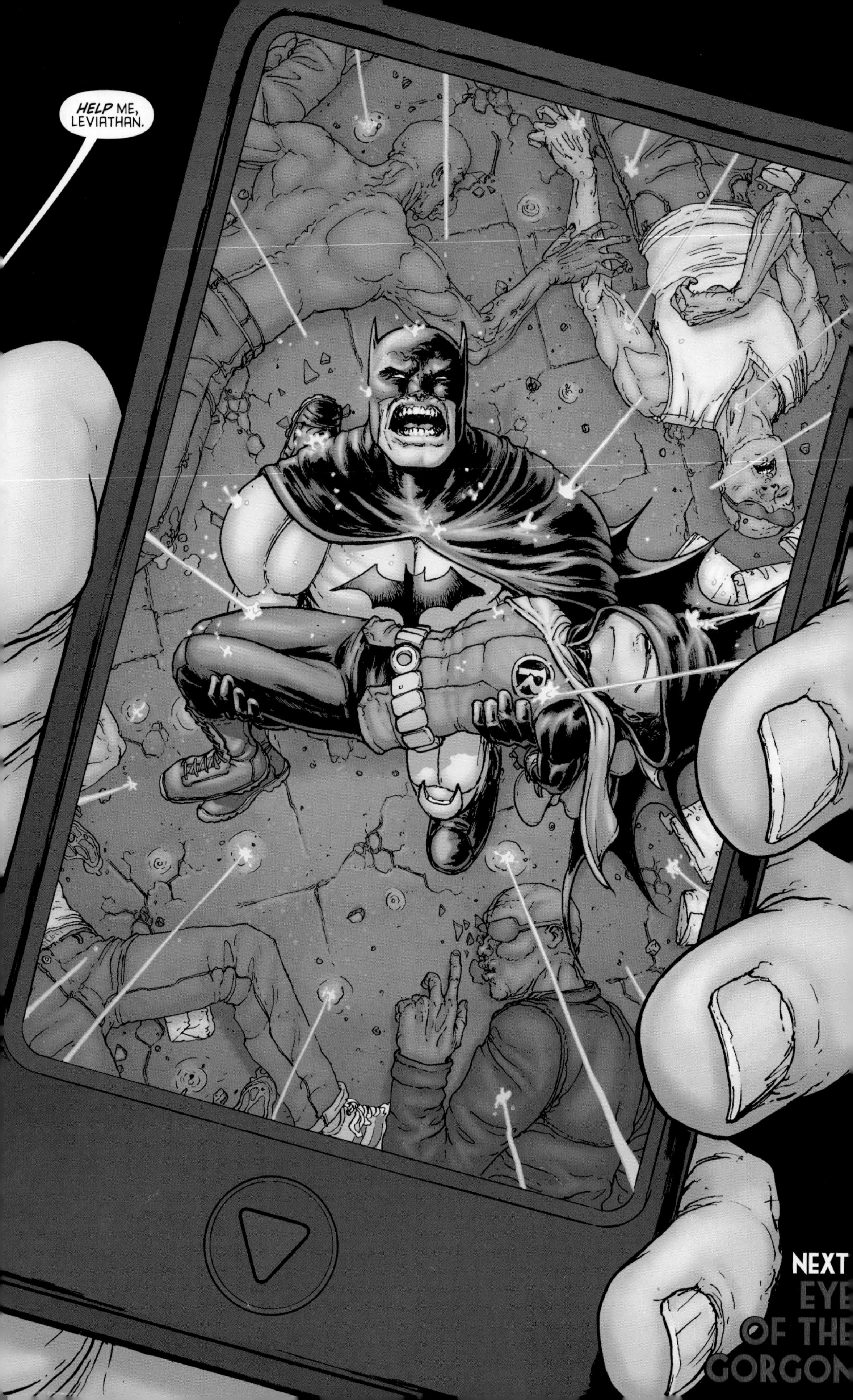
HELP ME, LEVIATHAN.
NEXT
EYE OF THE GORGON

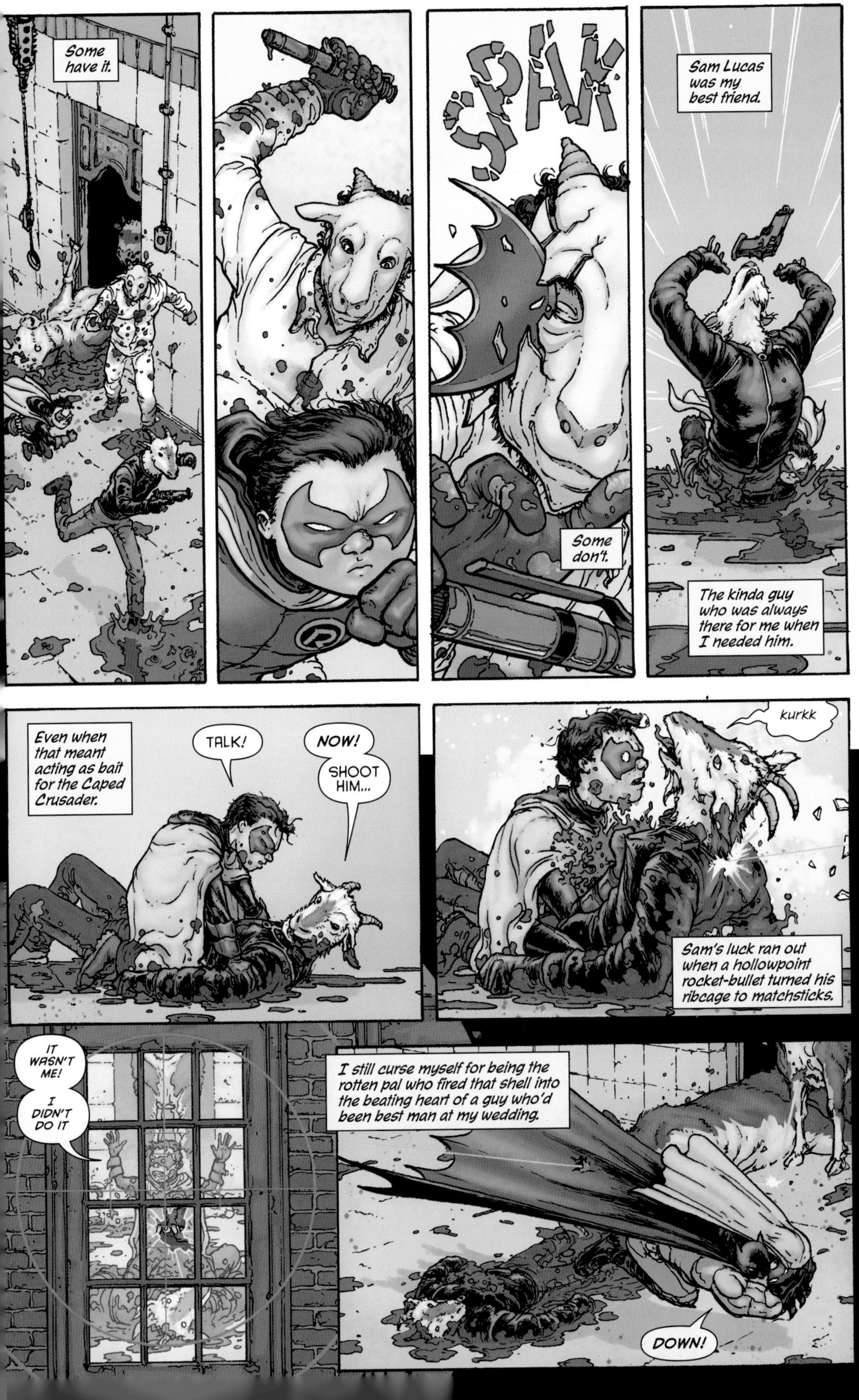
Some have it.
SPAK
Some don't.
Sam Lucas was my best friend.
The kinda guy who was always there for me when I needed him.
Even when that meant acting as bait for the Caped Crusader.
TALK!
NOW!
SHOOT HIM...
kurkk
Sam's luck ran out when a hollowpoint rocket-bullet turned his ribcage to matchsticks.
IT WASN'T ME!
I DIDN'T DO IT
I still curse myself for being the rotten pal who fired that shell into the beating heart of a guy who'd been best man at my wedding.
DOWN!

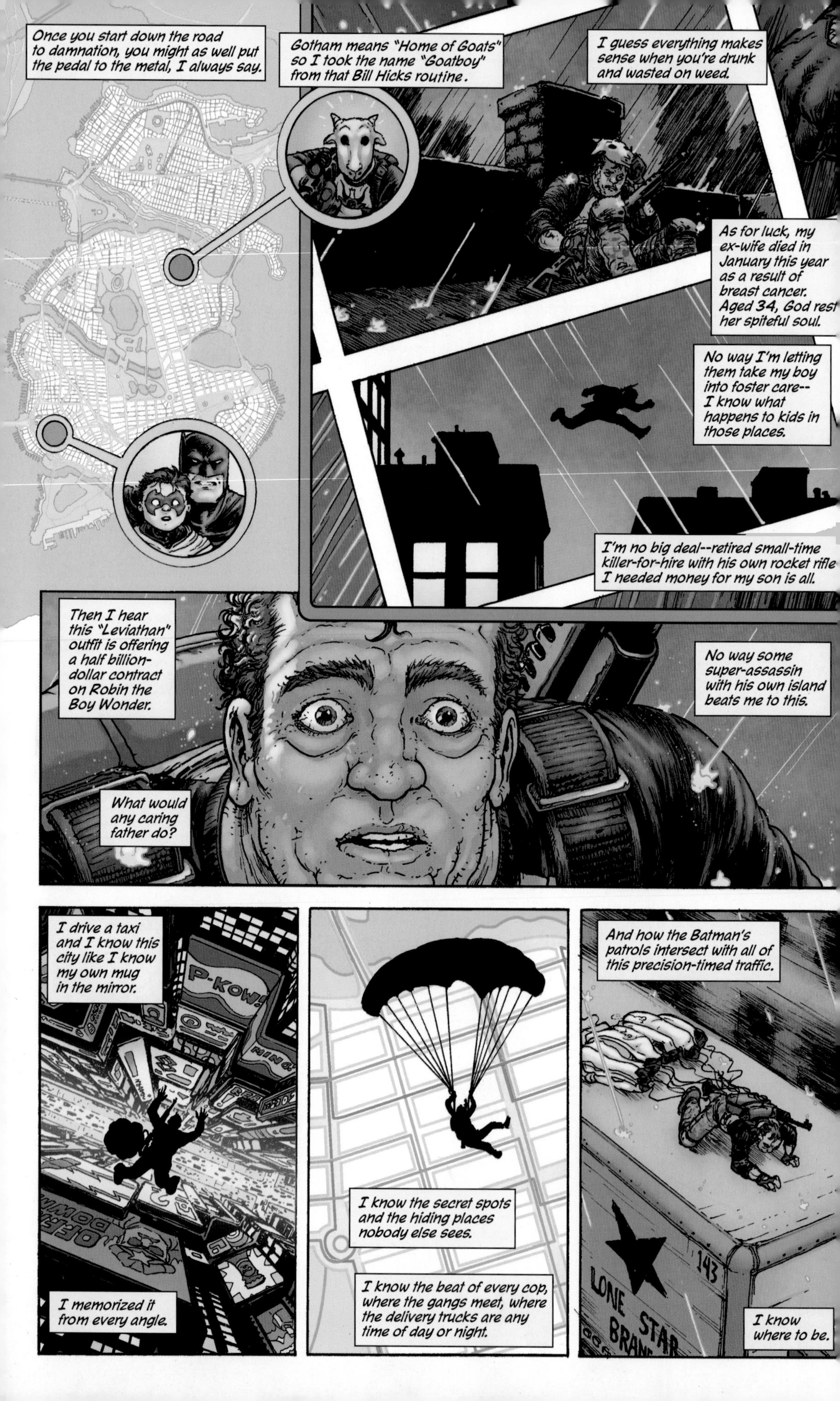

Once you start down the road to damnation, you might as well put the pedal to the metal, I always say.
Gotham means "Home of Goats" so I took the name "Goatboy" from that Bill Hicks routine.
I guess everything makes sense when you're drunk and wasted on weed.
As for luck, my ex-wife died in January this year as a result of breast cancer. Aged 34, God rest her spiteful soul.
No way I'm letting them take my boy into foster care-- I know what happens to kids in those places.
I'm no big deal--retired small-time killer-for-hire with his own rocket rifle I needed money for my son is all.
Then I hear this "Leviathan" outfit is offering a half billion-dollar contract on Robin the Boy Wonder.
No way some super-assassin with his own island beats me to this.
What would any caring father do?
I drive a taxi and I know this city like I know my own mug in the mirror.
P-KOW!
I memorized it from every angle.
I know the secret spots and the hiding places nobody else sees.
I know the beat of every cop, where the gangs meet, where the delivery trucks are any time of day or night.
And how the Batman's patrols intersect with all of this precision-timed traffic.
143
LONE STAR
I know where to be.

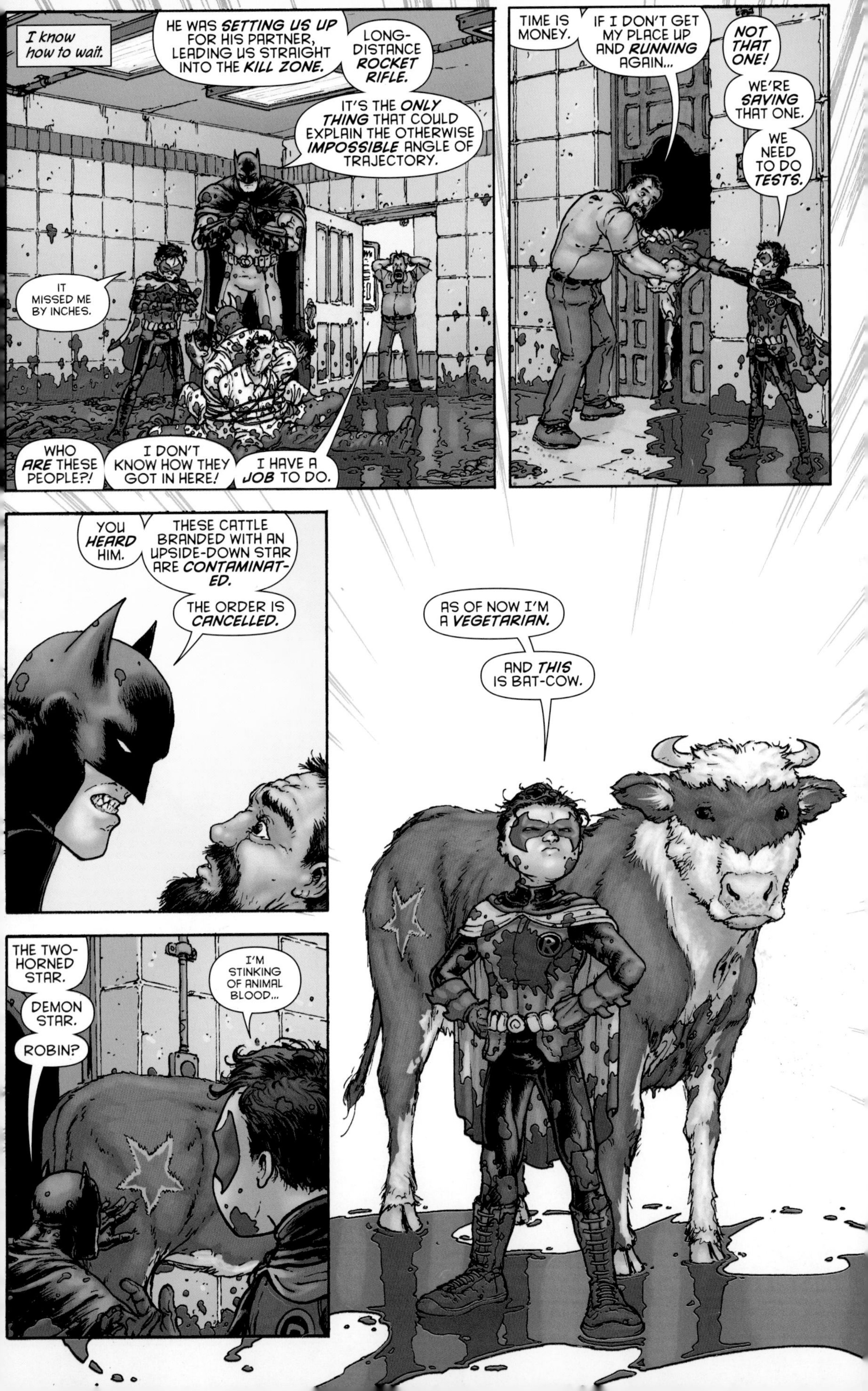
I know how to wait.
HE WAS SETTING US UP FOR HIS PARTNER, LEADING US STRAIGHT INTO THE KILL ZONE.
LONG-DISTANCE ROCKET RIFLE.
IT'S THE ONLY THING THAT COULD EXPLAIN THE OTHERWISE IMPOSSIBLE ANGLE OF TRAJECTORY.
IT MISSED ME BY INCHES.
WHO ARE THESE PEOPLE?!
I DON'T KNOW HOW THEY GOT IN HERE!
I HAVE A JOB TO DO.
TIME IS MONEY.
IF I DON'T GET MY PLACE UP AND RUNNING AGAIN...
NOT THAT ONE!
WE'RE SAVING THAT ONE.
WE NEED TO DO TESTS.
YOU HEARD HIM.
THESE CATTLE BRANDED WITH AN UPSIDE-DOWN STAR ARE CONTAMINAT-ED.
THE ORDER IS CANCELLED.
THE TWO-HORNED STAR.
DEMON STAR.
ROBIN?
I'M STINKING OF ANIMAL BLOOD...
AS OF NOW I'M A VEGETARIAN.
AND THIS IS BAT-COW.

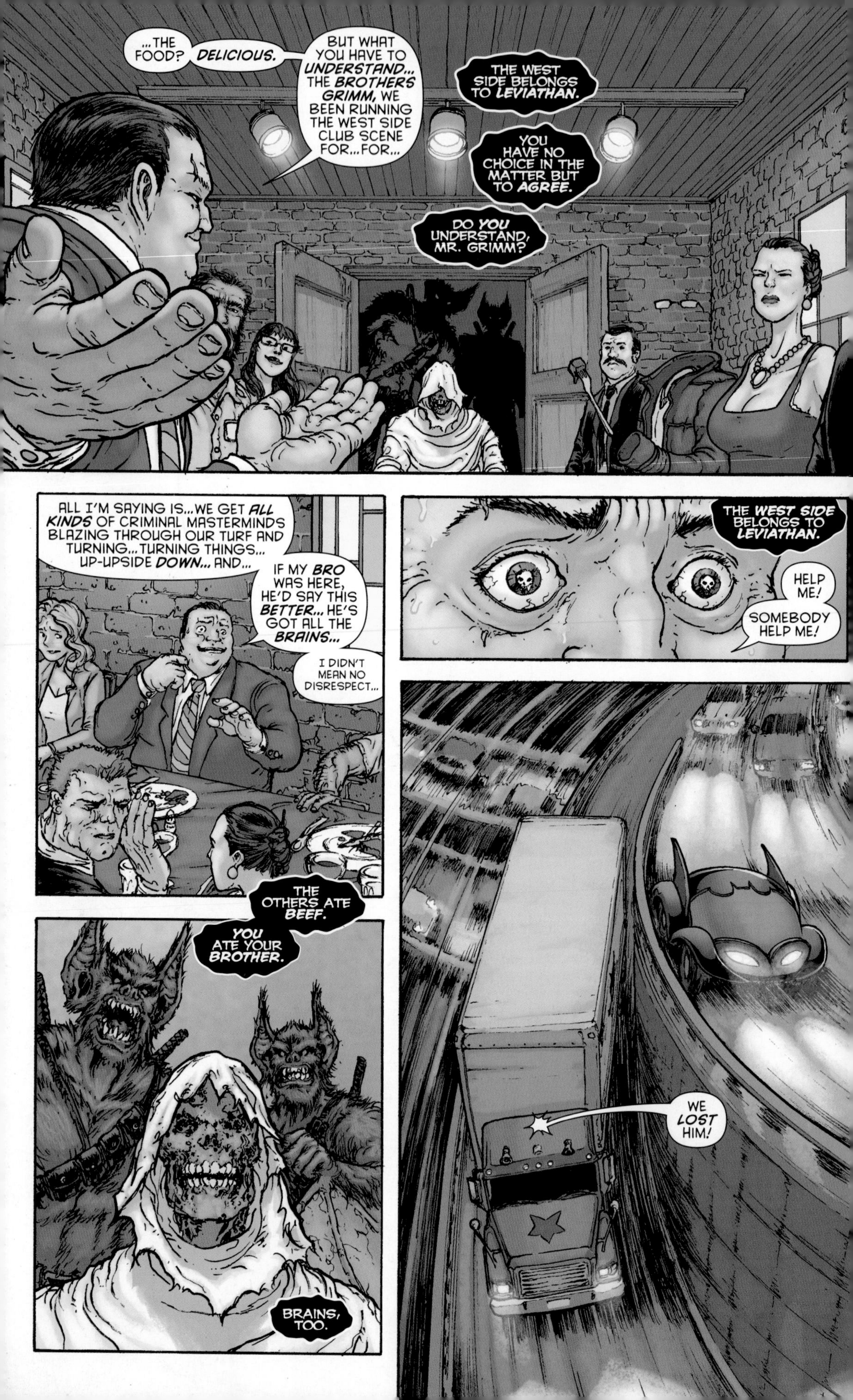
...THE FOOD? DELICIOUS.
BUT WHAT YOU HAVE TO UNDERSTAND... THE BROTHERS GRIMM, WE BEEN RUNNING THE WEST SIDE CLUB SCENE FOR...FOR...
THE WEST SIDE BELONGS TO LEVIATHAN.
YOU HAVE NO CHOICE IN THE MATTER BUT TO AGREE.
DO YOU UNDERSTAND, MR. GRIMM?
ALL I'M SAYING IS...WE GET ALL KINDS OF CRIMINAL MASTERMINDS BLAZING THROUGH OUR TURF AND TURNING...TURNING THINGS... UP-UPSIDE DOWN... AND...
IF MY BRO WAS HERE, HE'D SAY THIS BETTER... HE'S GOT ALL THE BRAINS...
I DIDN'T MEAN NO DISRESPECT...
THE OTHERS ATE BEEF.
YOU ATE YOUR BROTHER.
BRAINS, TOO.
THE WEST SIDE BELONGS TO LEVIATHAN.
HELP ME!
SOMEBODY HELP ME!
WE LOST HIM!

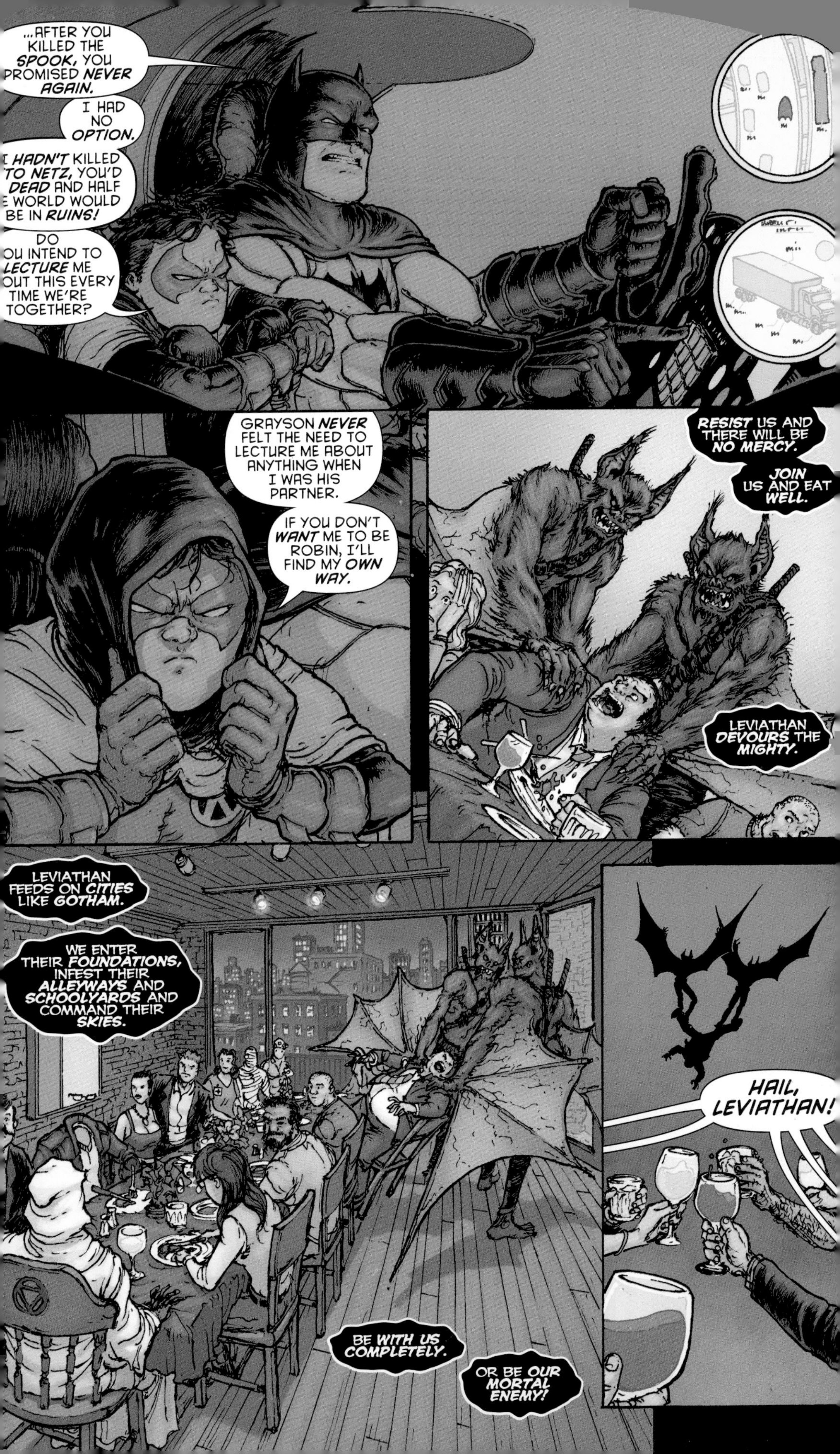

...AFTER YOU KILLED THE SPOOK, YOU PROMISED NEVER AGAIN.
I HAD NO OPTION.
I HADN'T KILLED TO NETZ, YOU'D DEAD AND HALF E WORLD WOULD BE IN RUINS!
DO OU INTEND TO LECTURE ME OUT THIS EVERY TIME WE'RE TOGETHER?
GRAYSON NEVER FELT THE NEED TO LECTURE ME ABOUT ANYTHING WHEN I WAS HIS PARTNER.
IF YOU DON'T WANT ME TO BE ROBIN, I'LL FIND MY OWN WAY.
RESIST US AND THERE WILL BE NO MERCY.
JOIN US AND EAT WELL.
LEVIATHAN DEVOURS THE MIGHTY.
LEVIATHAN FEEDS ON CITIES LIKE GOTHAM.
WE ENTER THEIR FOUNDATIONS, INFEST THEIR ALLEYWAYS AND SCHOOLYARDS AND COMMAND THEIR SKIES.
BE WITH US COMPLETELY.
OR BE OUR MORTAL ENEMY!
HAIL, LEVIATHAN!

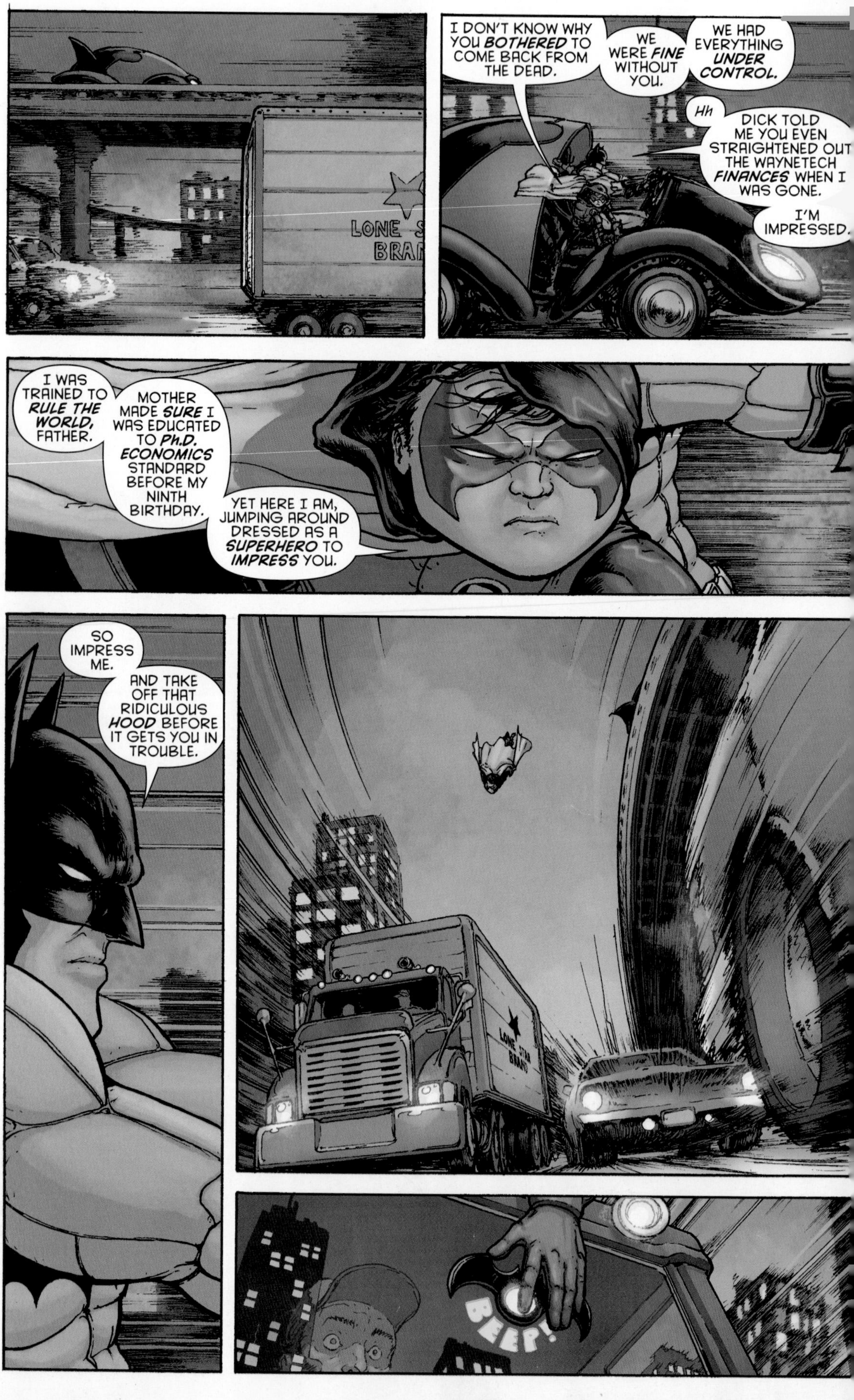

LONE STAR BRAN
I DON'T KNOW WHY YOU BOTHERED TO COME BACK FROM THE DEAD.
WE WERE FINE WITHOUT YOU.
WE HAD EVERYTHING UNDER CONTROL.
Hh
DICK TOLD ME YOU EVEN STRAIGHTENED OUT THE WAYNETECH FINANCES WHEN I WAS GONE.
I'M IMPRESSED.
I WAS TRAINED TO RULE THE WORLD, FATHER.
MOTHER MADE SURE I WAS EDUCATED TO Ph.D. ECONOMICS STANDARD BEFORE MY NINTH BIRTHDAY.
YET HERE I AM, JUMPING AROUND DRESSED AS A SUPERHERO TO IMPRESS YOU.
SO IMPRESS ME.
AND TAKE OFF THAT RIDICULOUS HOOD BEFORE IT GETS YOU IN TROUBLE.
BEEP!

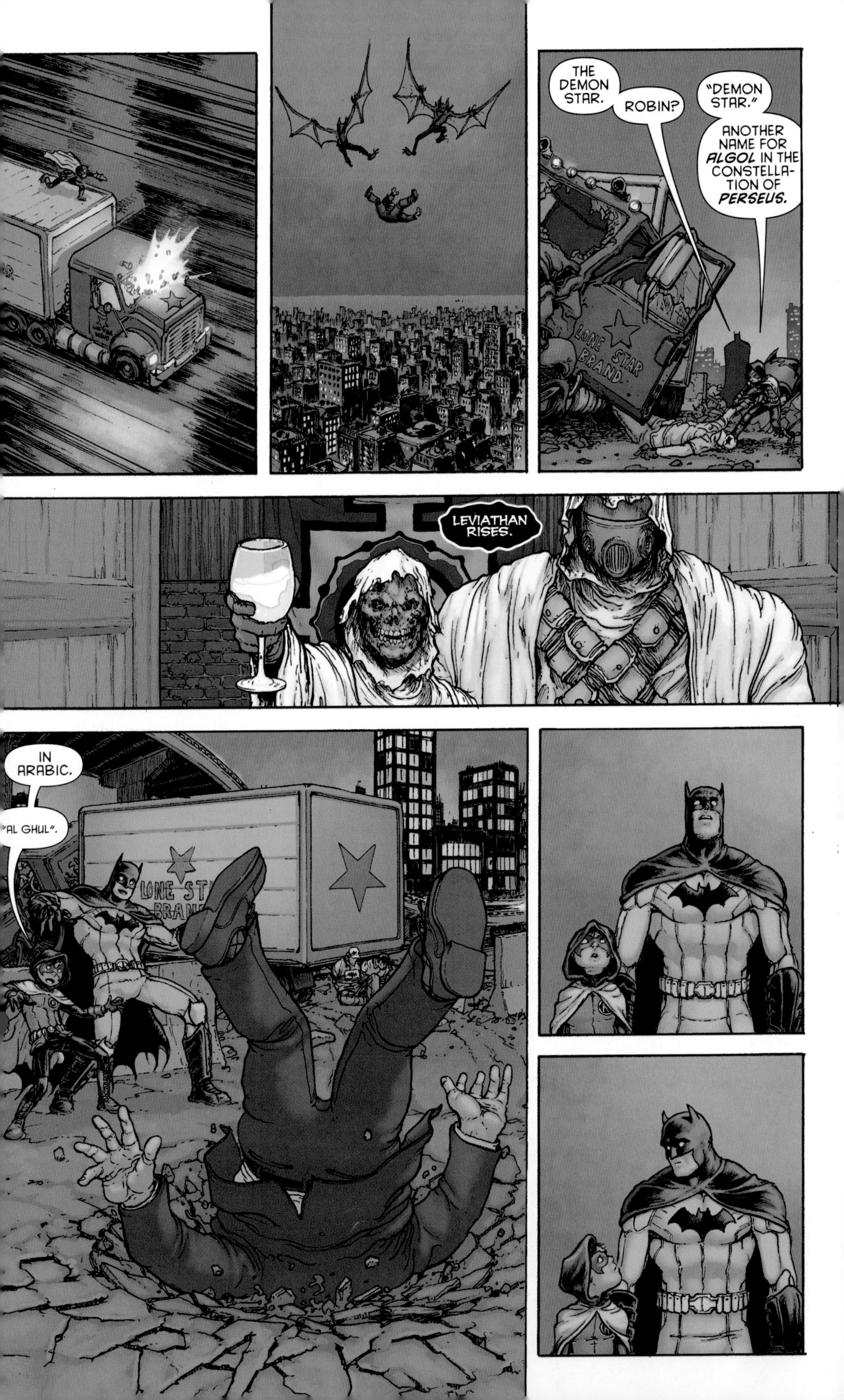
THE DEMON STAR.
ROBIN?
"DEMON STAR."
ANOTHER NAME FOR ALGOL IN THE CONSTELLATION OF PERSEUS.
LEVIATHAN RISES.
IN ARABIC.
"AL GHUL".
LONE STAR BRAND

SAN FRANCISCO.

ALL RIGHT, LUV?

JUST DROPPED IN TO SEE IF MY *PERV SUIT'S* TURNED UP.

THE OUTFIT YOU ORDERED IS *RIGHT HERE.*

♪

HM?

FANTASTIC.

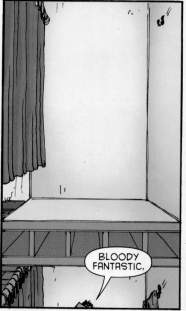

BLOODY FANTASTIC.

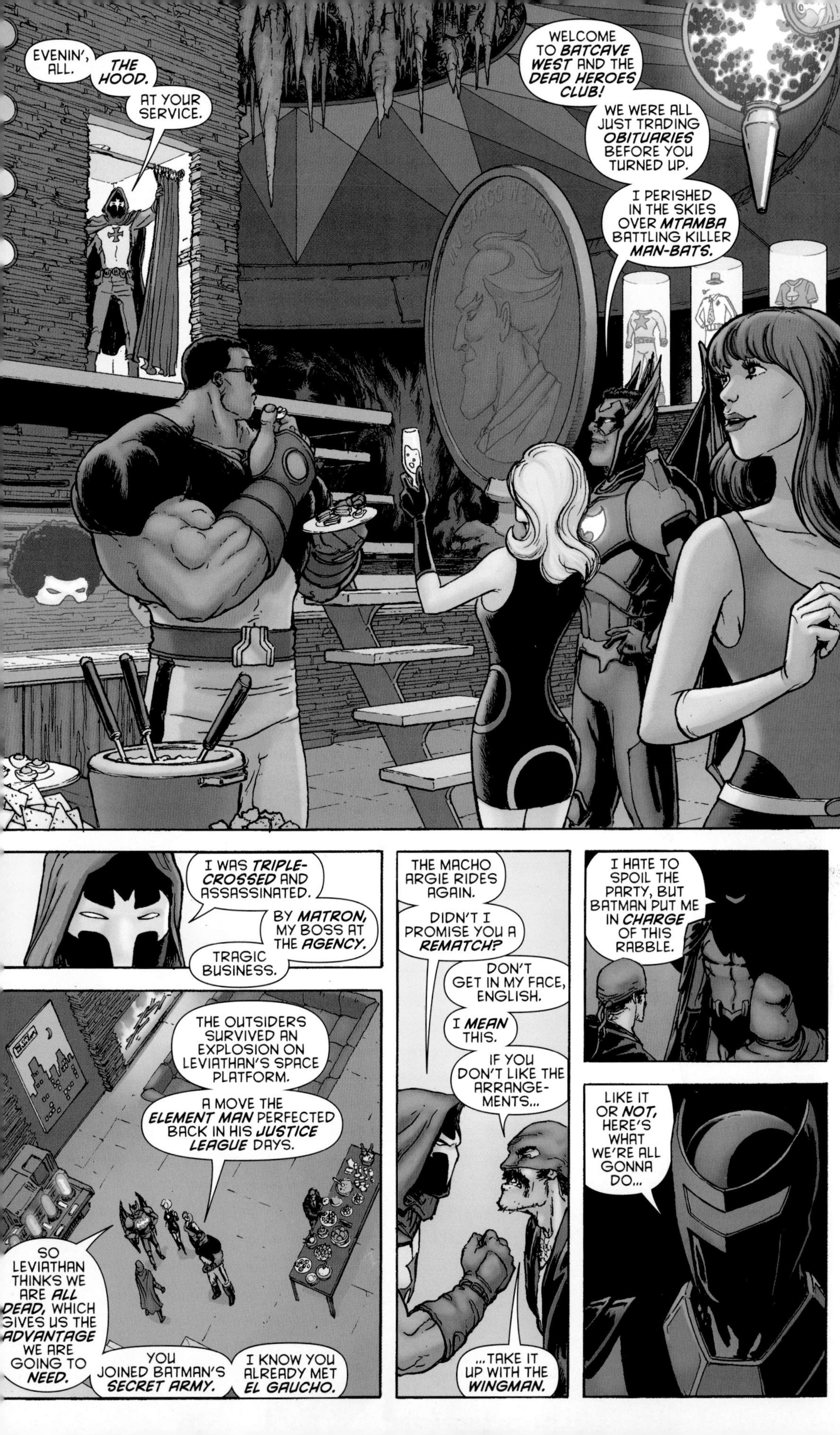
EVENIN', ALL.
THE HOOD.
AT YOUR SERVICE.
WELCOME TO BATCAVE WEST AND THE DEAD HEROES CLUB!
WE WERE ALL JUST TRADING OBITUARIES BEFORE YOU TURNED UP.
I PERISHED IN THE SKIES OVER MTAMBA BATTLING KILLER MAN-BATS.
I WAS TRIPLE-CROSSED AND ASSASSINATED.
BY MATRON, MY BOSS AT THE AGENCY.
TRAGIC BUSINESS.
THE OUTSIDERS SURVIVED AN EXPLOSION ON LEVIATHAN'S SPACE PLATFORM.
A MOVE THE ELEMENT MAN PERFECTED BACK IN HIS JUSTICE LEAGUE DAYS.
SO LEVIATHAN THINKS WE ARE ALL DEAD, WHICH GIVES US THE ADVANTAGE WE ARE GOING TO NEED.
YOU JOINED BATMAN'S SECRET ARMY.
I KNOW YOU ALREADY MET EL GAUCHO.
THE MACHO ARGIE RIDES AGAIN.
DIDN'T I PROMISE YOU A REMATCH?
DON'T GET IN MY FACE, ENGLISH.
I MEAN THIS.
IF YOU DON'T LIKE THE ARRANGE-MENTS...
...TAKE IT UP WITH THE WINGMAN.
I HATE TO SPOIL THE PARTY, BUT BATMAN PUT ME IN CHARGE OF THIS RABBLE.
LIKE IT OR NOT, HERE'S WHAT WE'RE ALL GONNA DO...

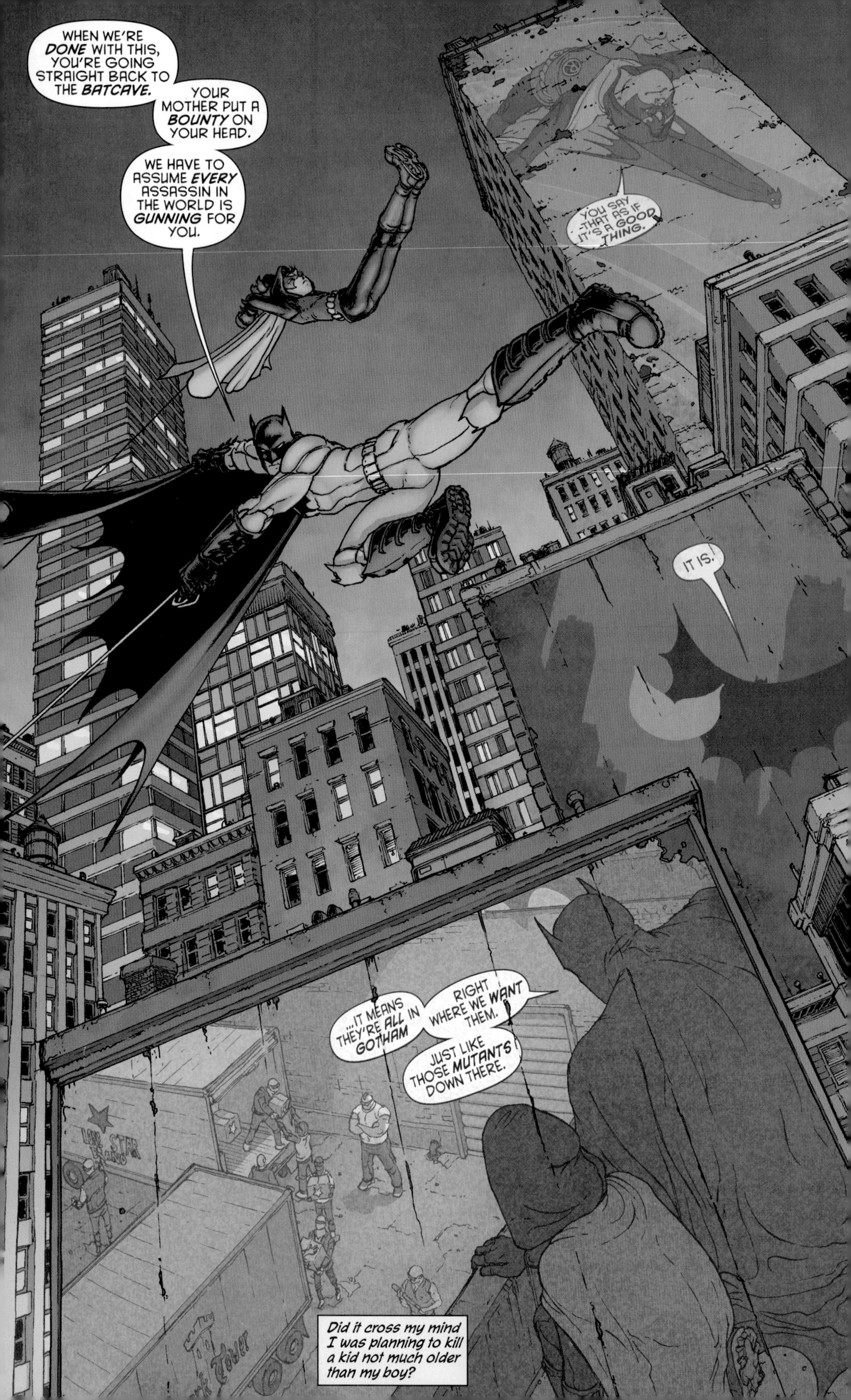
WHEN WE'RE DONE WITH THIS, YOU'RE GOING STRAIGHT BACK TO THE BATCAVE.
YOUR MOTHER PUT A BOUNTY ON YOUR HEAD.
WE HAVE TO ASSUME EVERY ASSASSIN IN THE WORLD IS GUNNING FOR YOU.
YOU SAY THAT AS IF IT'S A GOOD THING.
IT IS.
...IT MEANS THEY'RE ALL IN GOTHAM
RIGHT WHERE WE WANT THEM.
JUST LIKE THOSE MUTANTS DOWN THERE.
Did it cross my mind I was planning to kill a kid not much older than my boy?

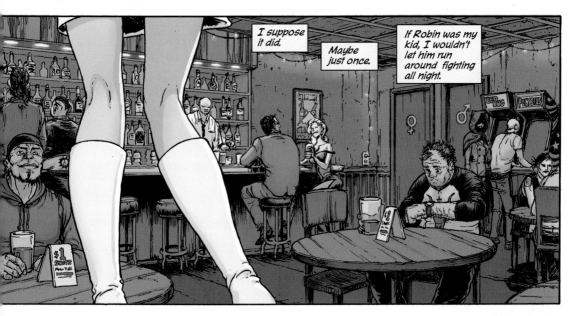

I suppose it did.

Maybe just once.

If Robin was my kid, I wouldn't let him run around fighting all night.

It wasn't my fault he was making himself a target.

Killing a kid like that's no different from any other hit.

All it takes is a little courage.

A creepy mask.

And the right place.

At the right time.

Goatboy takes aim.

MAKE WIF IT MUSCLE-STYLE, BRATTIES!

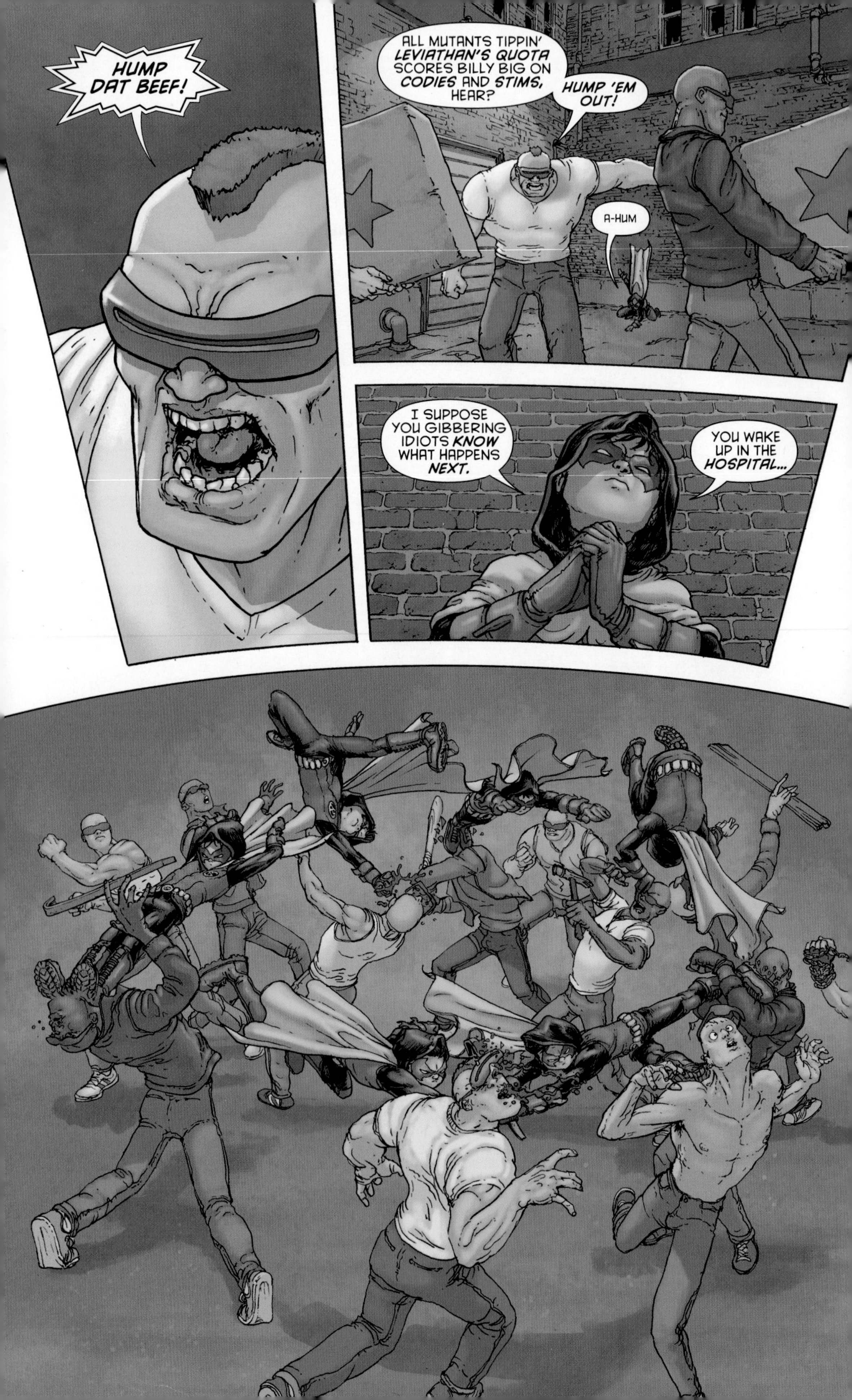
HUMP DAT BEEF!
ALL MUTANTS TIPPIN' LEVIATHAN'S QUOTA SCORES BILLY BIG ON CODIES AND STIMS, HEAR?
HUMP 'EM OUT!
A-HUM
I SUPPOSE YOU GIBBERING IDIOTS KNOW WHAT HAPPENS NEXT.
YOU WAKE UP IN THE HOSPITAL...

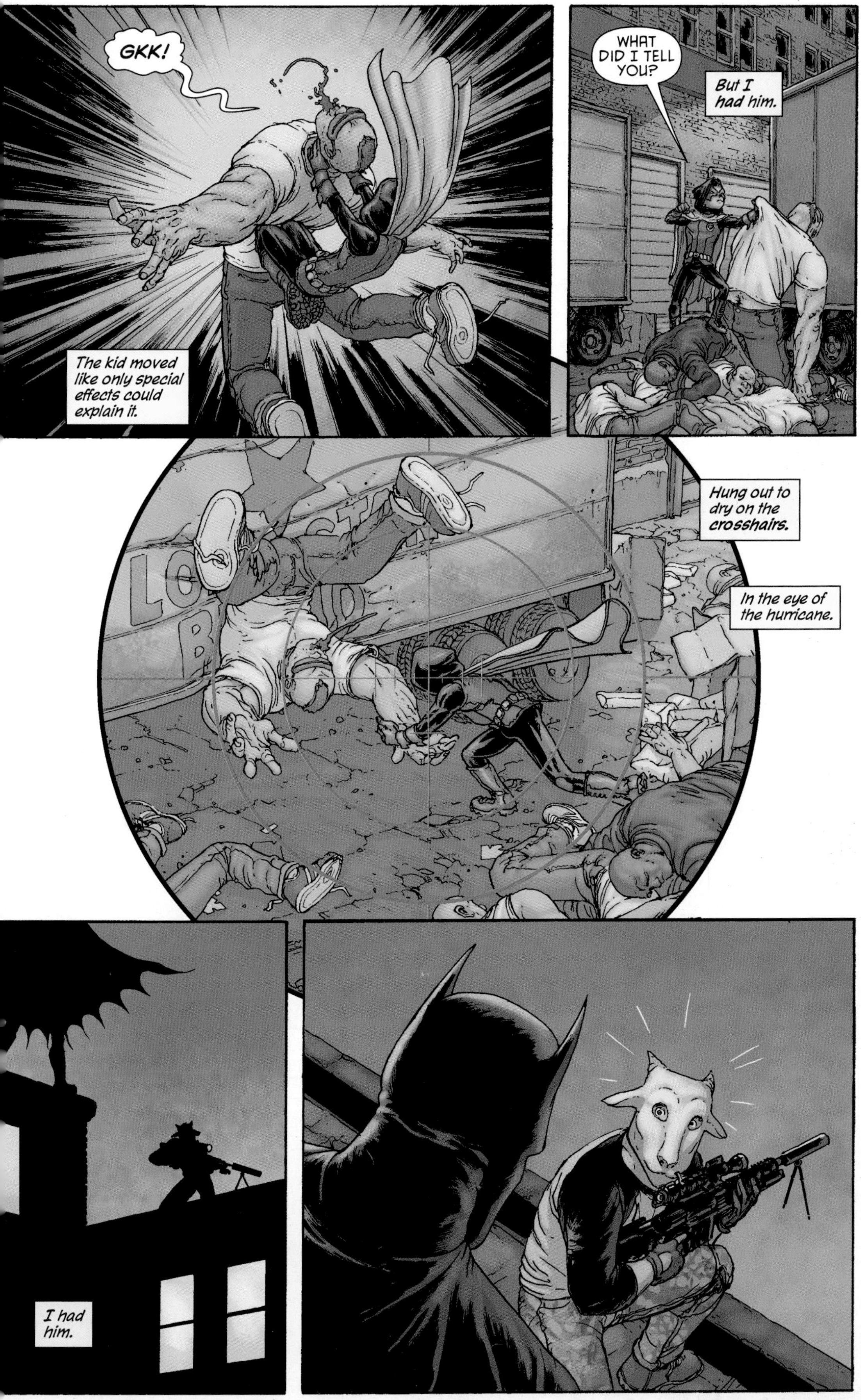
GKK!
The kid moved like only special effects could explain it.
WHAT DID I TELL YOU?
But I had him.
Hung out to dry on the crosshairs.
In the eye of the hurricane.
I had him.

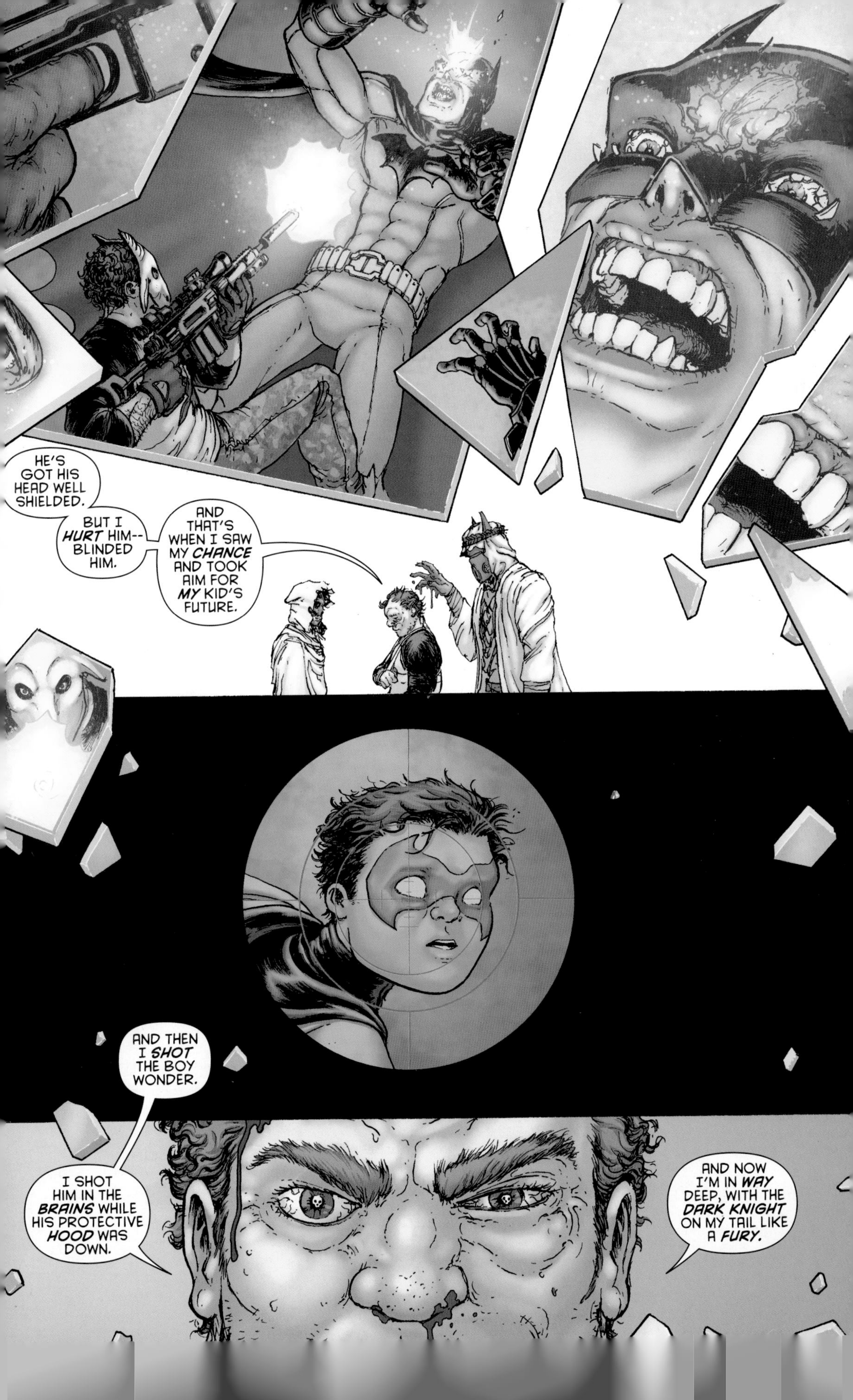
HE'S GOT HIS HEAD WELL SHIELDED.
BUT I *HURT* HIM-- BLINDED HIM.
AND THAT'S WHEN I SAW MY *CHANCE* AND TOOK AIM FOR *MY* KID'S FUTURE.
AND THEN I *SHOT* THE BOY WONDER.
I SHOT HIM IN THE *BRAINS* WHILE HIS PROTECTIVE *HOOD* WAS DOWN.
AND NOW I'M IN *WAY* DEEP, WITH THE *DARK KNIGHT* ON MY TAIL LIKE A *FURY.*

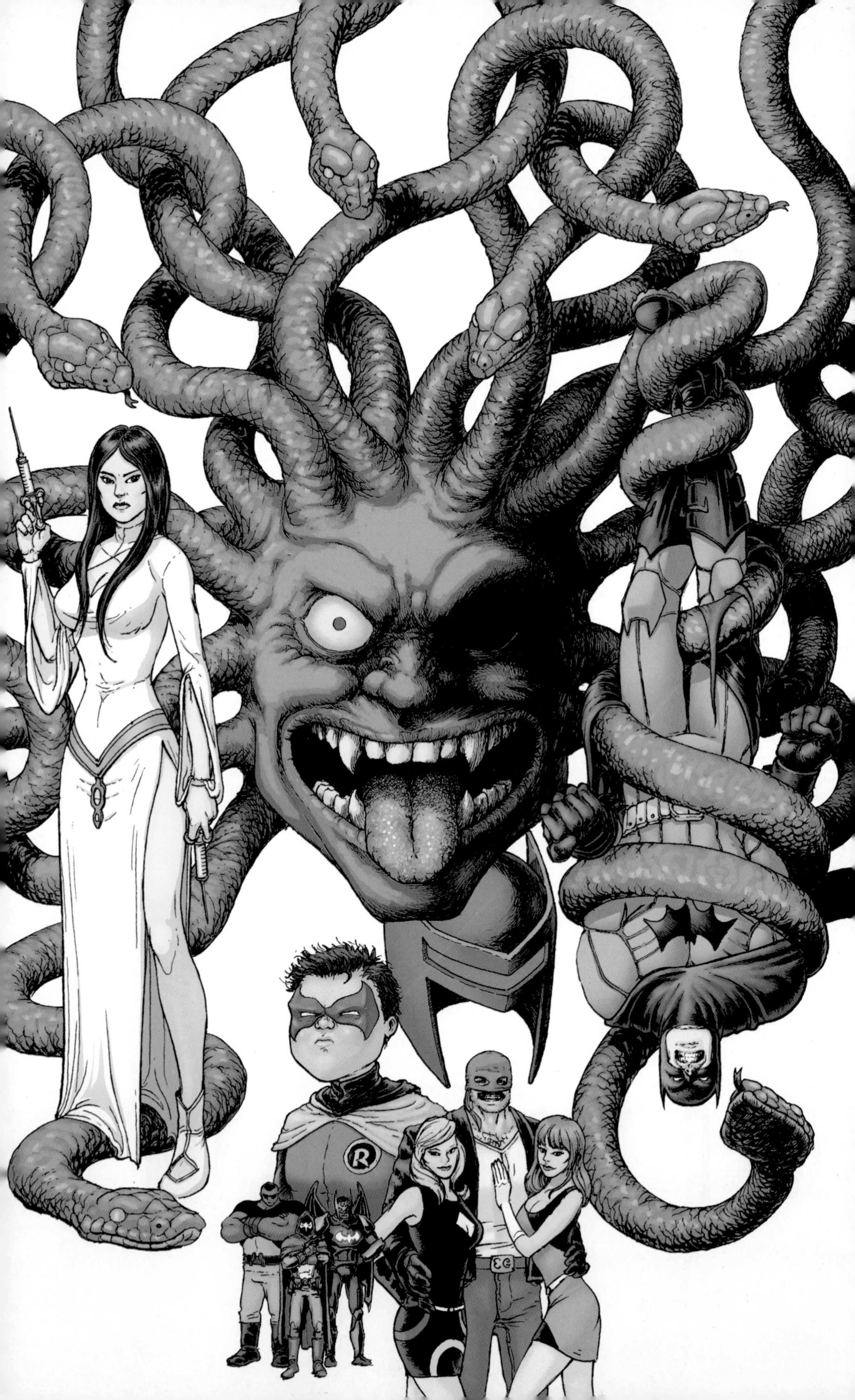

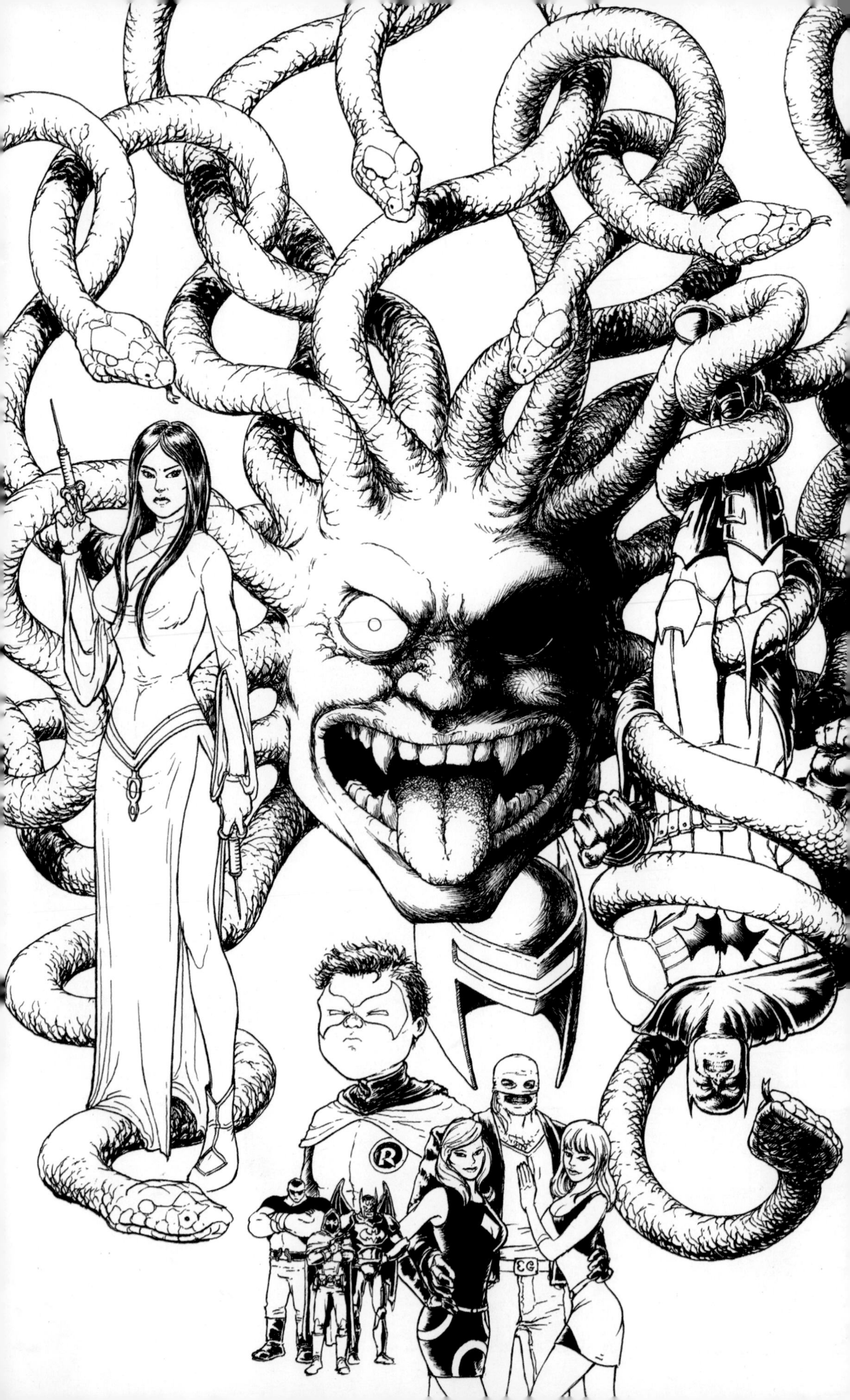

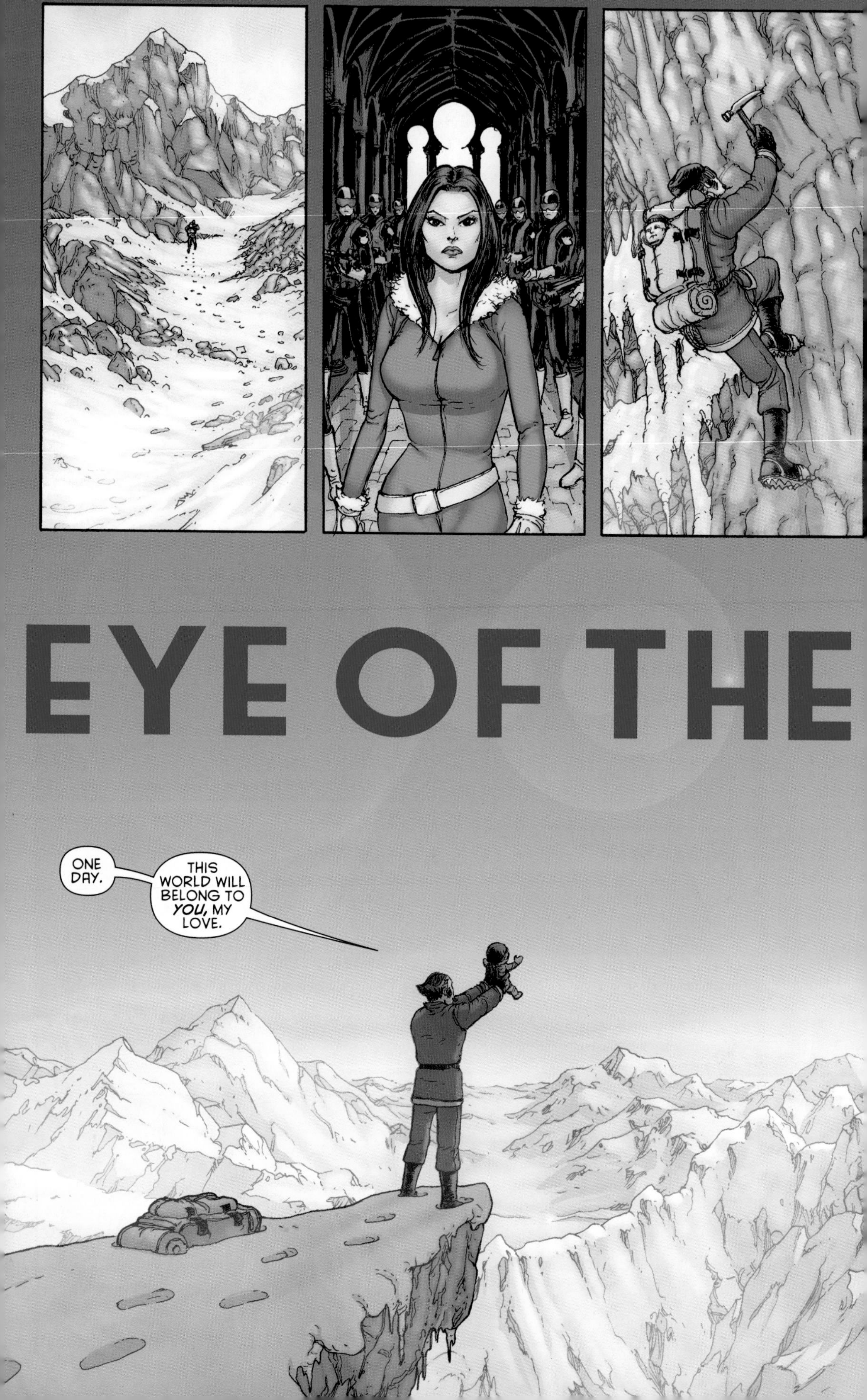
EYE OF THE
ONE DAY.
THIS WORLD WILL BELONG TO YOU, MY LOVE.

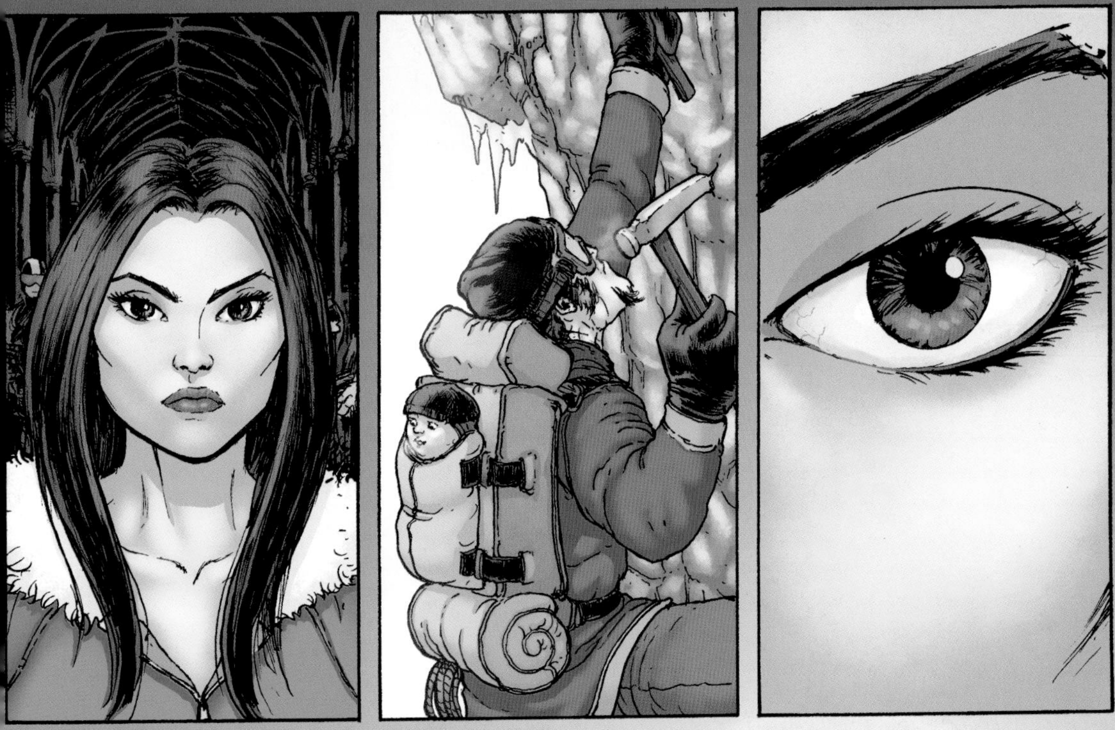

GORG N

WRITER GRANT MORRISON ARTIST CHRIS BURNHAM

COLOR NATHAN FAIRBAIRN LETTERING PATRICK BROSSEAU

COVER BURNHAM AND FAIRBAIRN

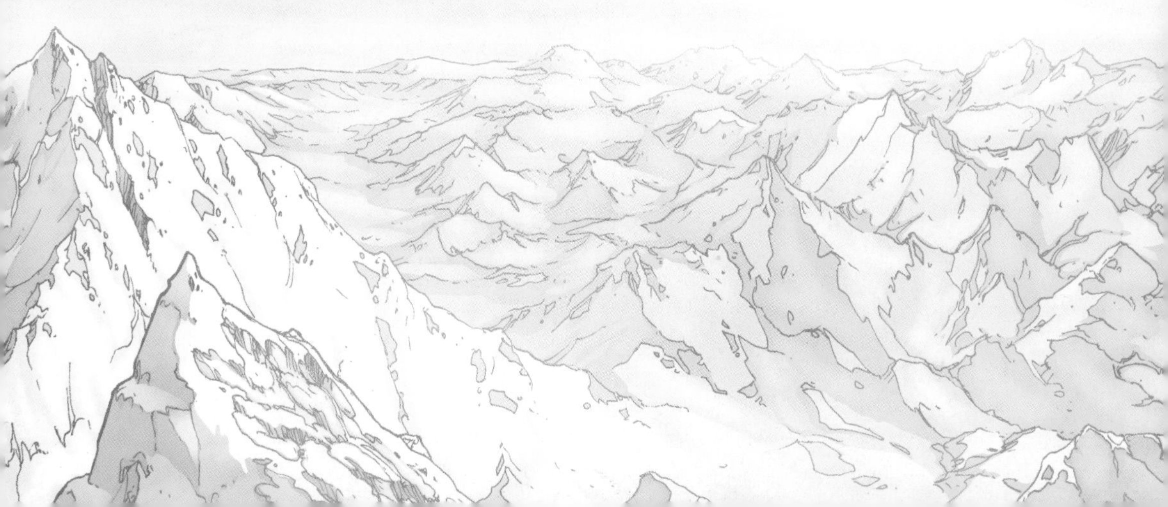

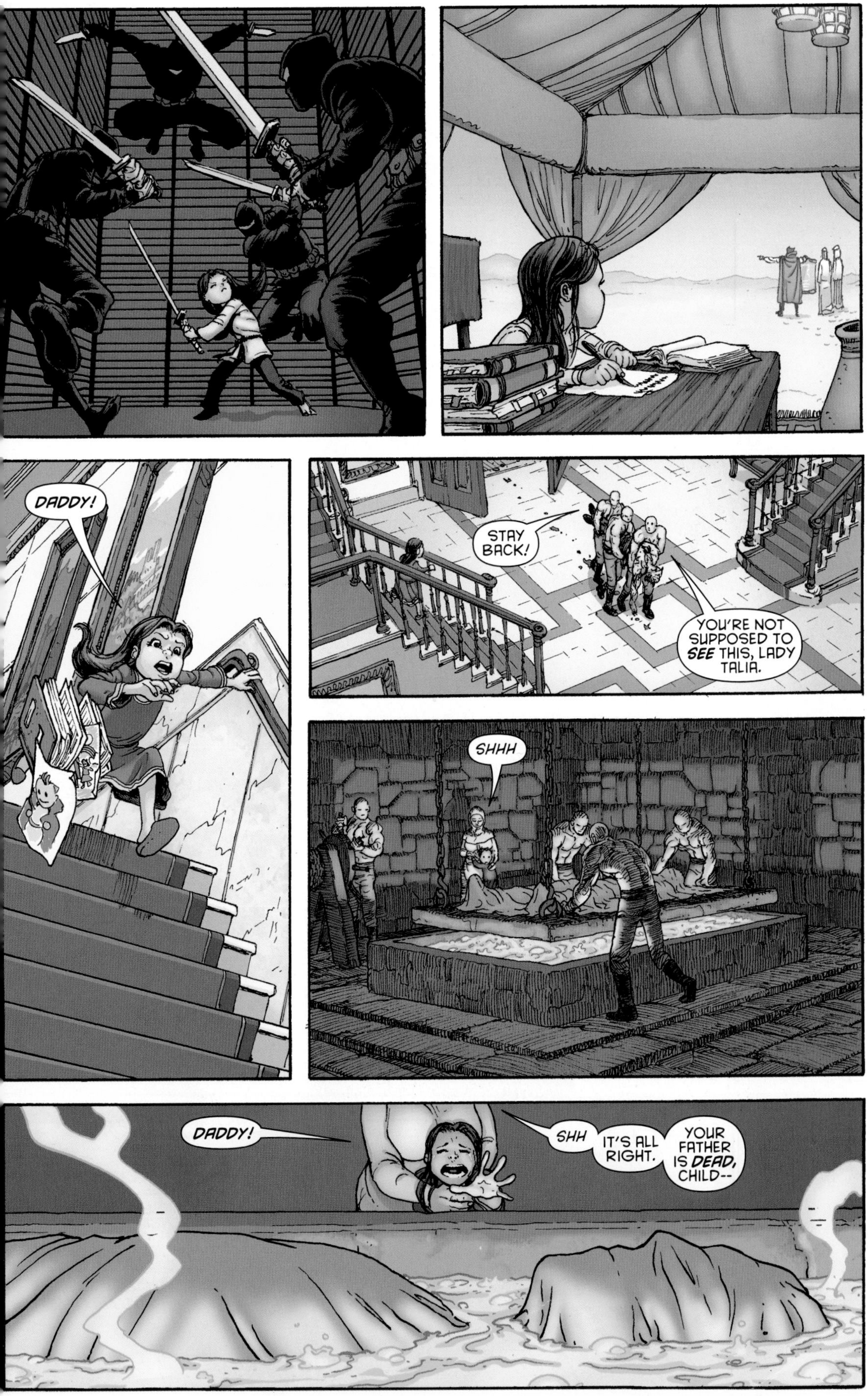
DADDY!
STAY BACK!
YOU'RE NOT SUPPOSED TO SEE THIS, LADY TALIA.
SHHH
DADDY!
SHH
IT'S ALL RIGHT.
YOUR FATHER IS DEAD, CHILD--

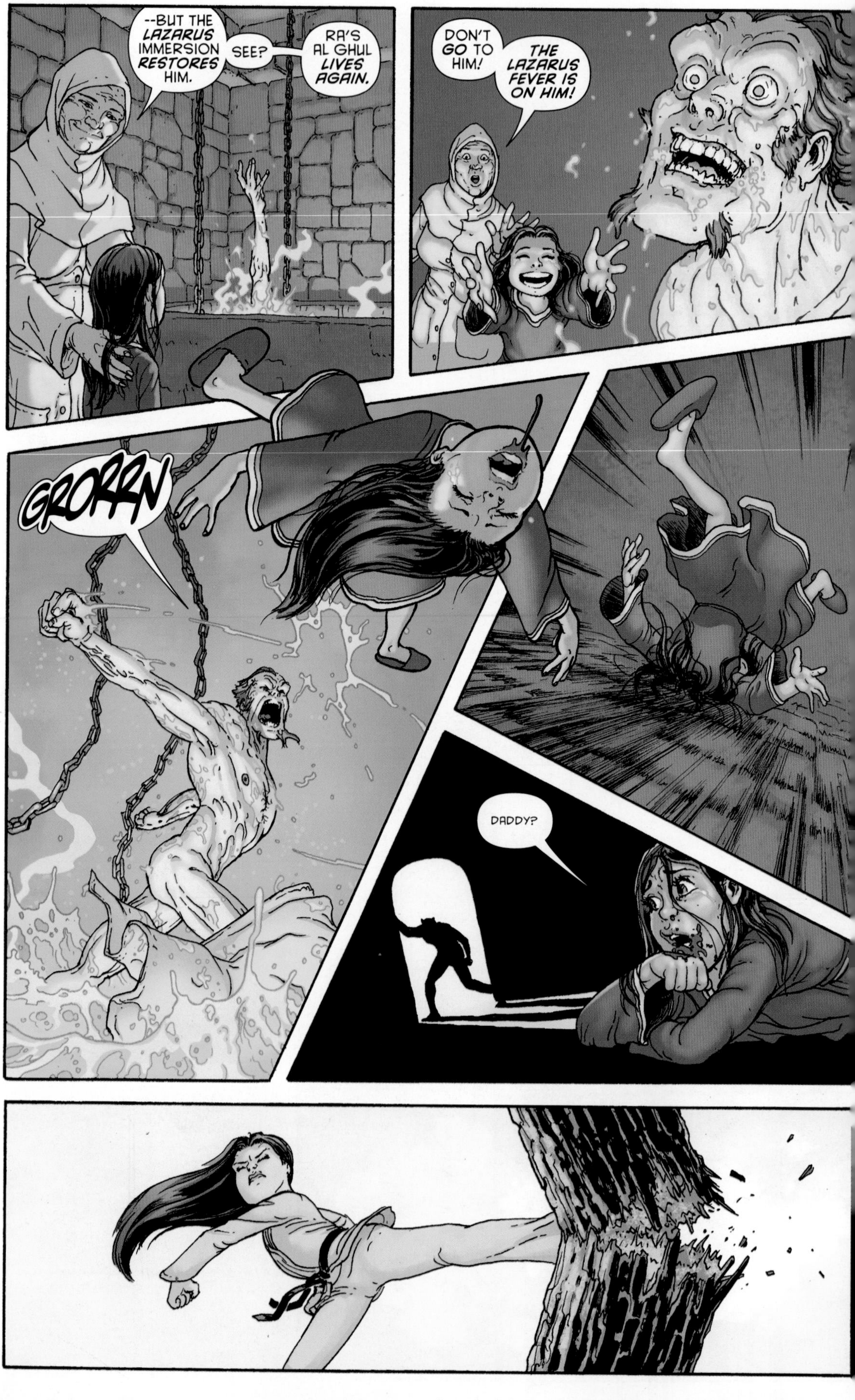
--BUT THE LAZARUS IMMERSION RESTORES HIM.
SEE?
RA'S AL GHUL LIVES AGAIN.
DON'T GO TO HIM!
THE LAZARUS FEVER IS ON HIM!
GRORRN
DADDY?

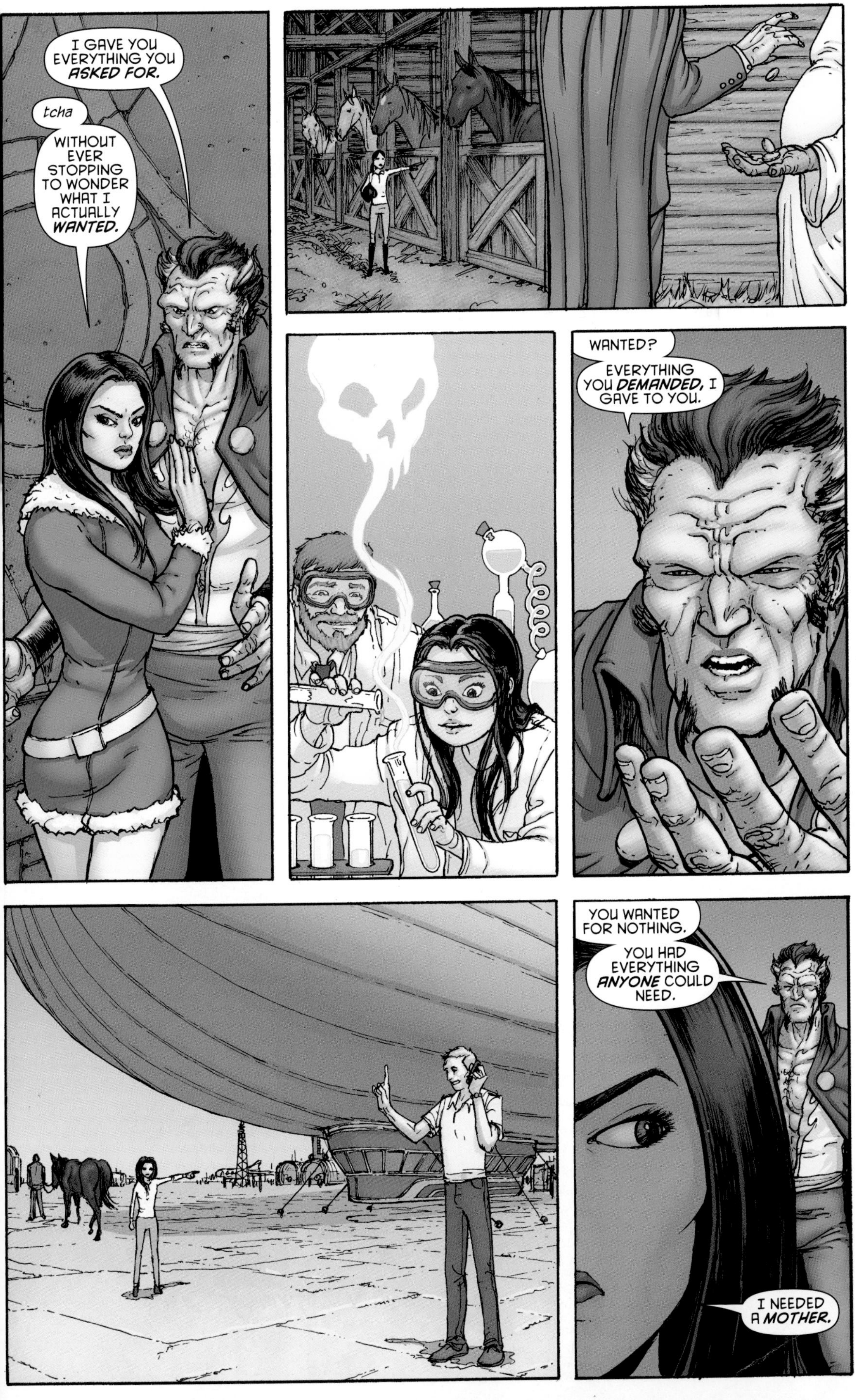
I GAVE YOU EVERYTHING YOU ASKED FOR.
tcha
WITHOUT EVER STOPPING TO WONDER WHAT I ACTUALLY WANTED.
WANTED?
EVERYTHING YOU DEMANDED, I GAVE TO YOU.
YOU WANTED FOR NOTHING.
YOU HAD EVERYTHING ANYONE COULD NEED.
I NEEDED A MOTHER.

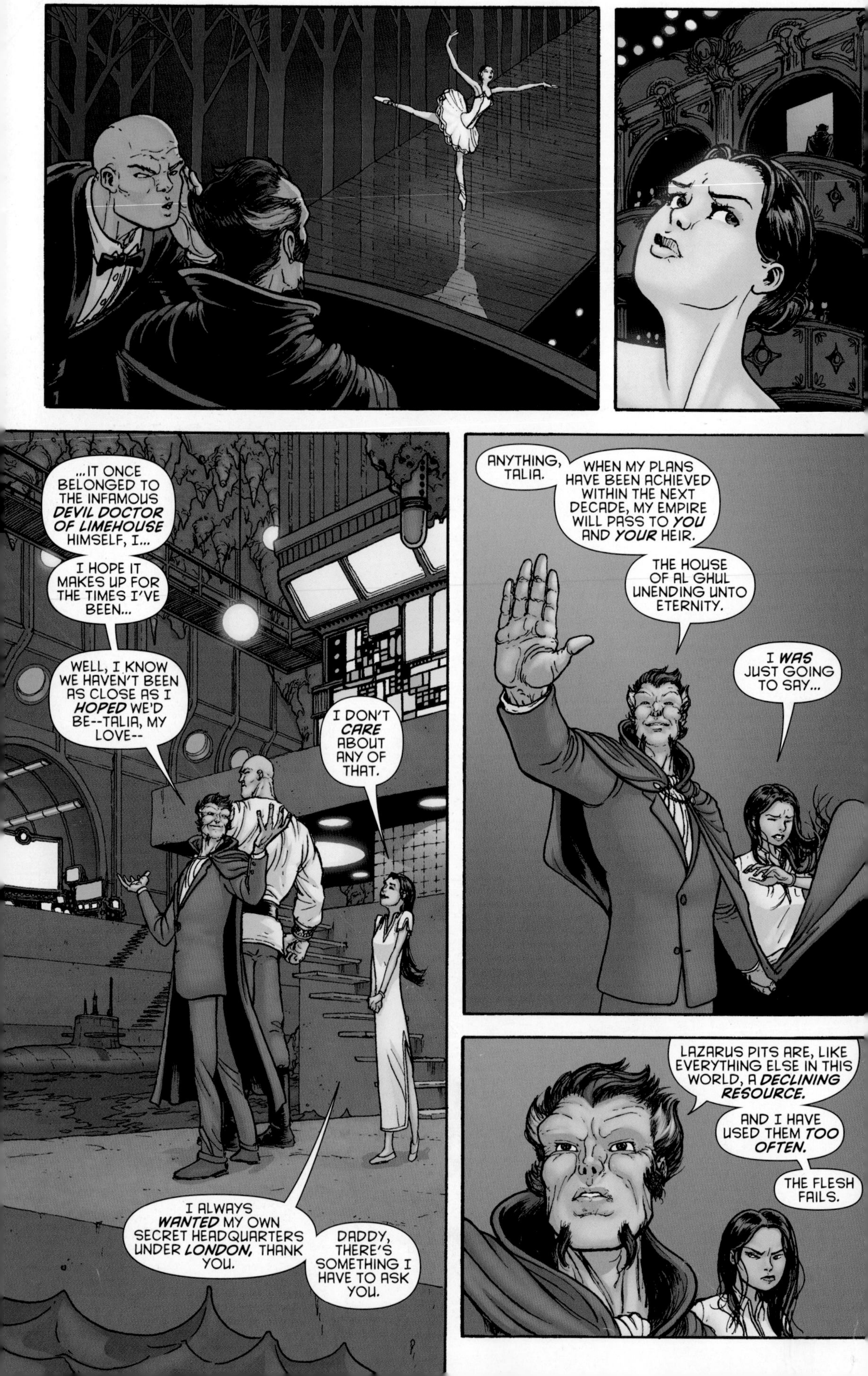
...IT ONCE BELONGED TO THE INFAMOUS DEVIL DOCTOR OF LIMEHOUSE HIMSELF, I...
I HOPE IT MAKES UP FOR THE TIMES I'VE BEEN...
WELL, I KNOW WE HAVEN'T BEEN AS CLOSE AS I HOPED WE'D BE--TALIA, MY LOVE--
I DON'T CARE ABOUT ANY OF THAT.
I ALWAYS WANTED MY OWN SECRET HEADQUARTERS UNDER LONDON, THANK YOU.
DADDY, THERE'S SOMETHING I HAVE TO ASK YOU.
ANYTHING, TALIA.
WHEN MY PLANS HAVE BEEN ACHIEVED WITHIN THE NEXT DECADE, MY EMPIRE WILL PASS TO YOU AND YOUR HEIR.
THE HOUSE OF AL GHUL UNENDING UNTO ETERNITY.
I WAS JUST GOING TO SAY...
LAZARUS PITS ARE, LIKE EVERYTHING ELSE IN THIS WORLD, A DECLINING RESOURCE.
AND I HAVE USED THEM TOO OFTEN.
THE FLESH FAILS.

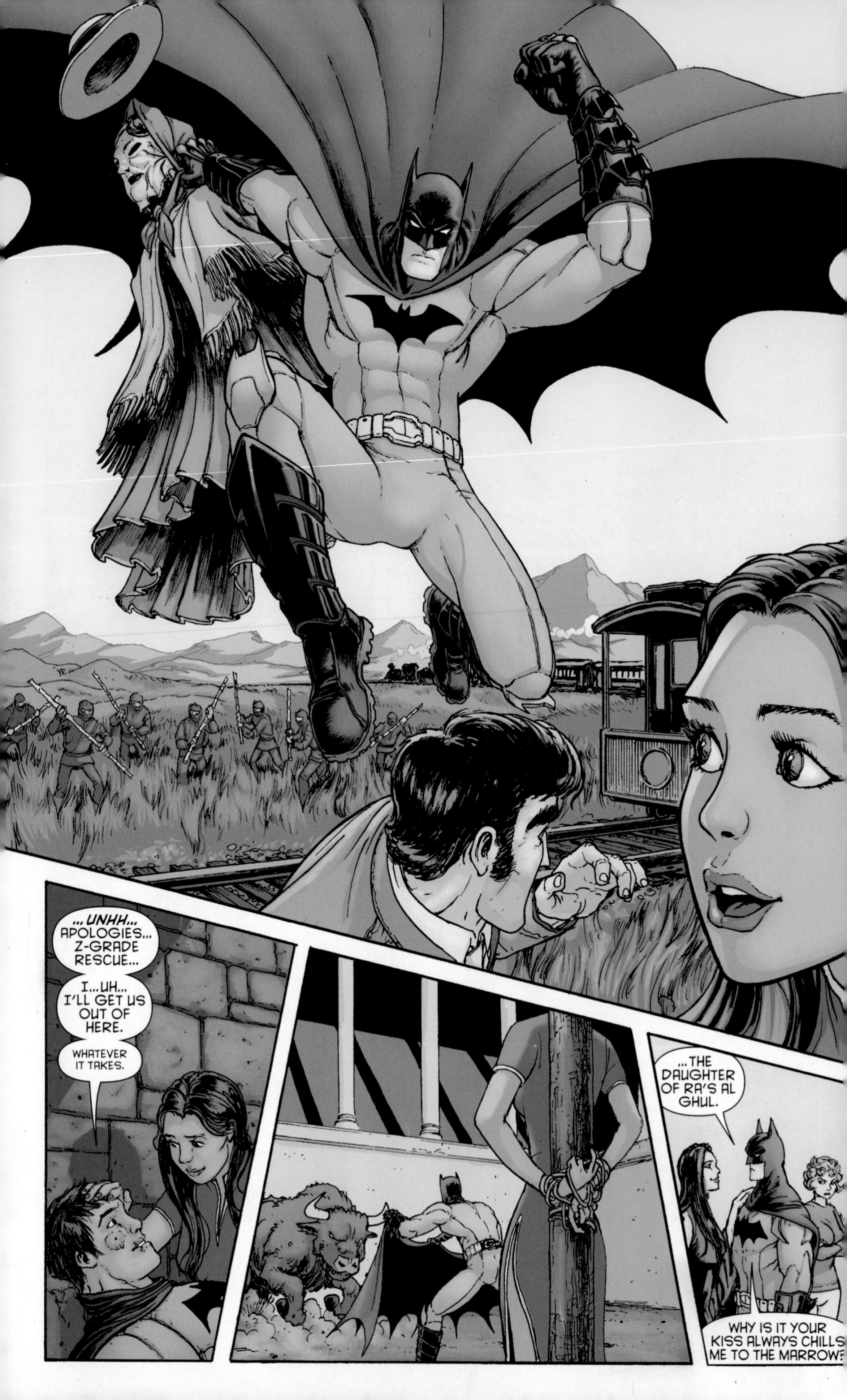
...UNHH... APOLOGIES... Z-GRADE RESCUE...
I...UH... I'LL GET US OUT OF HERE.
WHATEVER IT TAKES.
...THE DAUGHTER OF RA'S AL GHUL.
WHY IS IT YOUR KISS ALWAYS CHILLS ME TO THE MARROW?

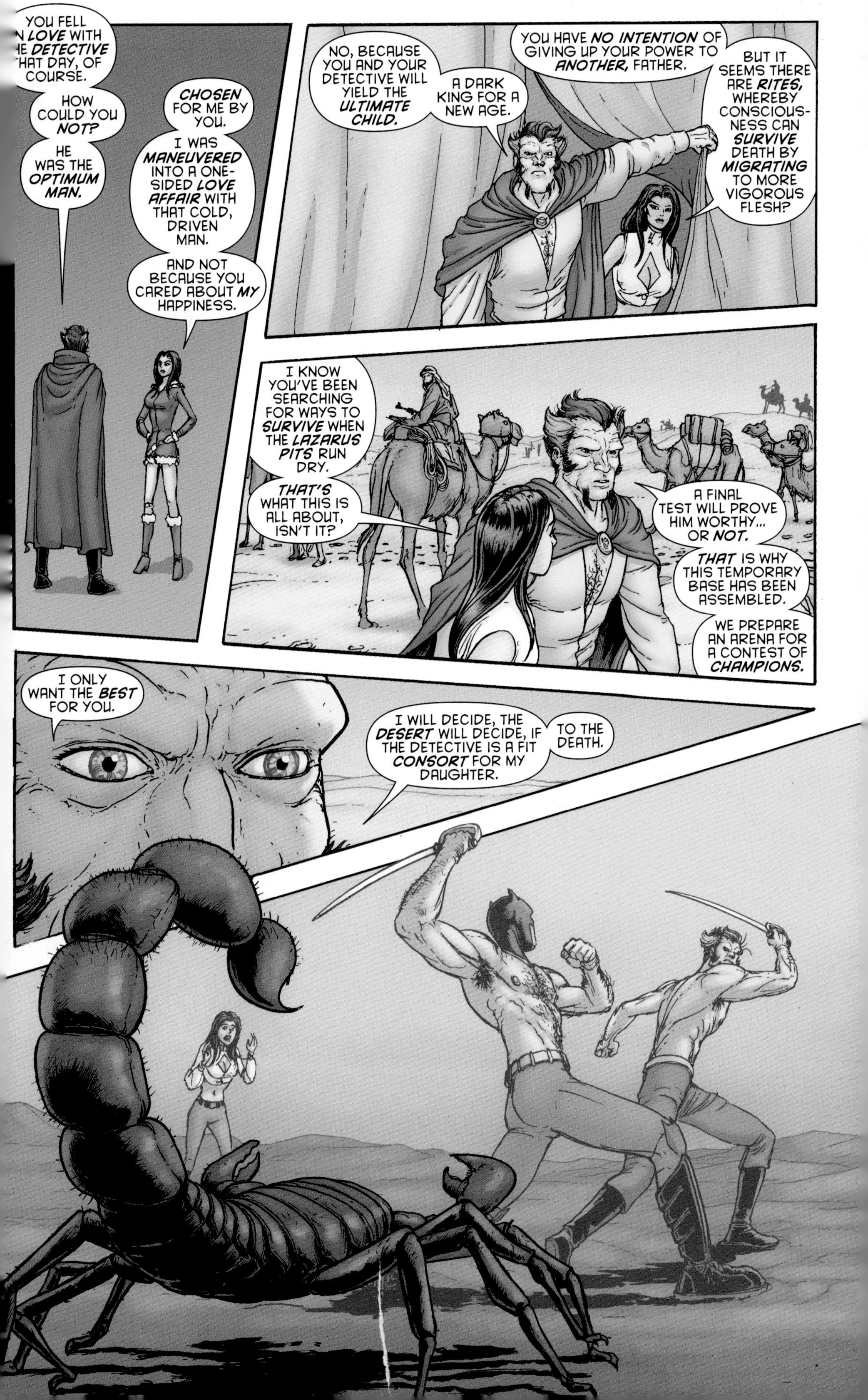

YOU FELL
N LOVE WITH
HE DETECTIVE
THAT DAY, OF COURSE.
HOW COULD YOU NOT?
HE WAS THE OPTIMUM MAN.
CHOSEN FOR ME BY YOU.
I WAS MANEUVERED INTO A ONE-SIDED LOVE AFFAIR WITH THAT COLD, DRIVEN MAN.
AND NOT BECAUSE YOU CARED ABOUT MY HAPPINESS.
NO, BECAUSE YOU AND YOUR DETECTIVE WILL YIELD THE ULTIMATE CHILD.
A DARK KING FOR A NEW AGE.
YOU HAVE NO INTENTION OF GIVING UP YOUR POWER TO ANOTHER, FATHER.
BUT IT SEEMS THERE ARE RITES, WHEREBY CONSCIOUS-NESS CAN SURVIVE DEATH BY MIGRATING TO MORE VIGOROUS FLESH?
I KNOW YOU'VE BEEN SEARCHING FOR WAYS TO SURVIVE WHEN THE LAZARUS PITS RUN DRY.
THAT'S WHAT THIS IS ALL ABOUT, ISN'T IT?
A FINAL TEST WILL PROVE HIM WORTHY... OR NOT.
THAT IS WHY THIS TEMPORARY BASE HAS BEEN ASSEMBLED.
WE PREPARE AN ARENA FOR A CONTEST OF CHAMPIONS.
I ONLY WANT THE BEST FOR YOU.
I WILL DECIDE, THE DESERT WILL DECIDE, IF THE DETECTIVE IS A FIT CONSORT FOR MY DAUGHTER.
TO THE DEATH.

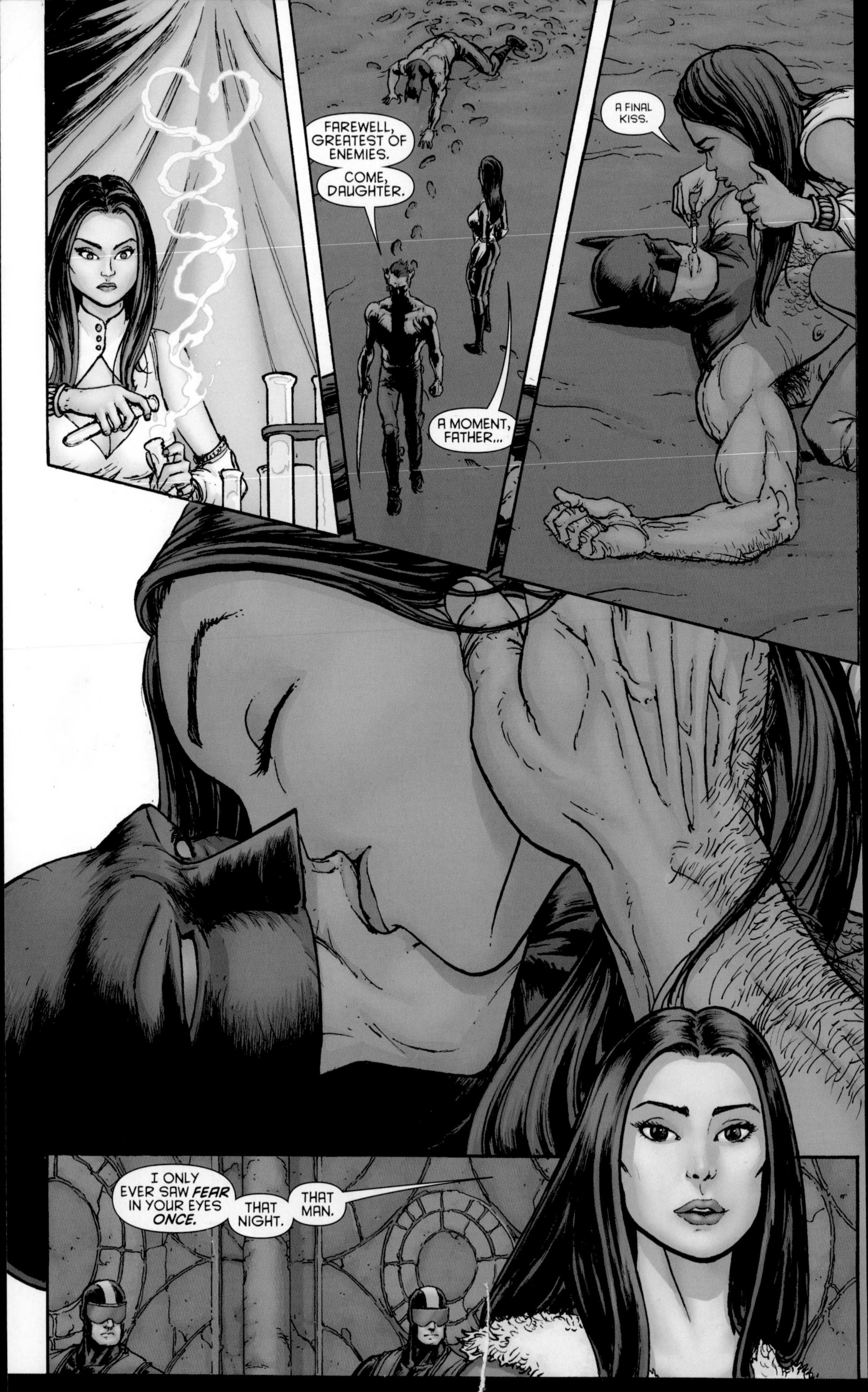
FAREWELL, GREATEST OF ENEMIES.
COME, DAUGHTER.
A MOMENT, FATHER...
A FINAL KISS.
I ONLY EVER SAW FEAR IN YOUR EYES ONCE.
THAT NIGHT.
THAT MAN.

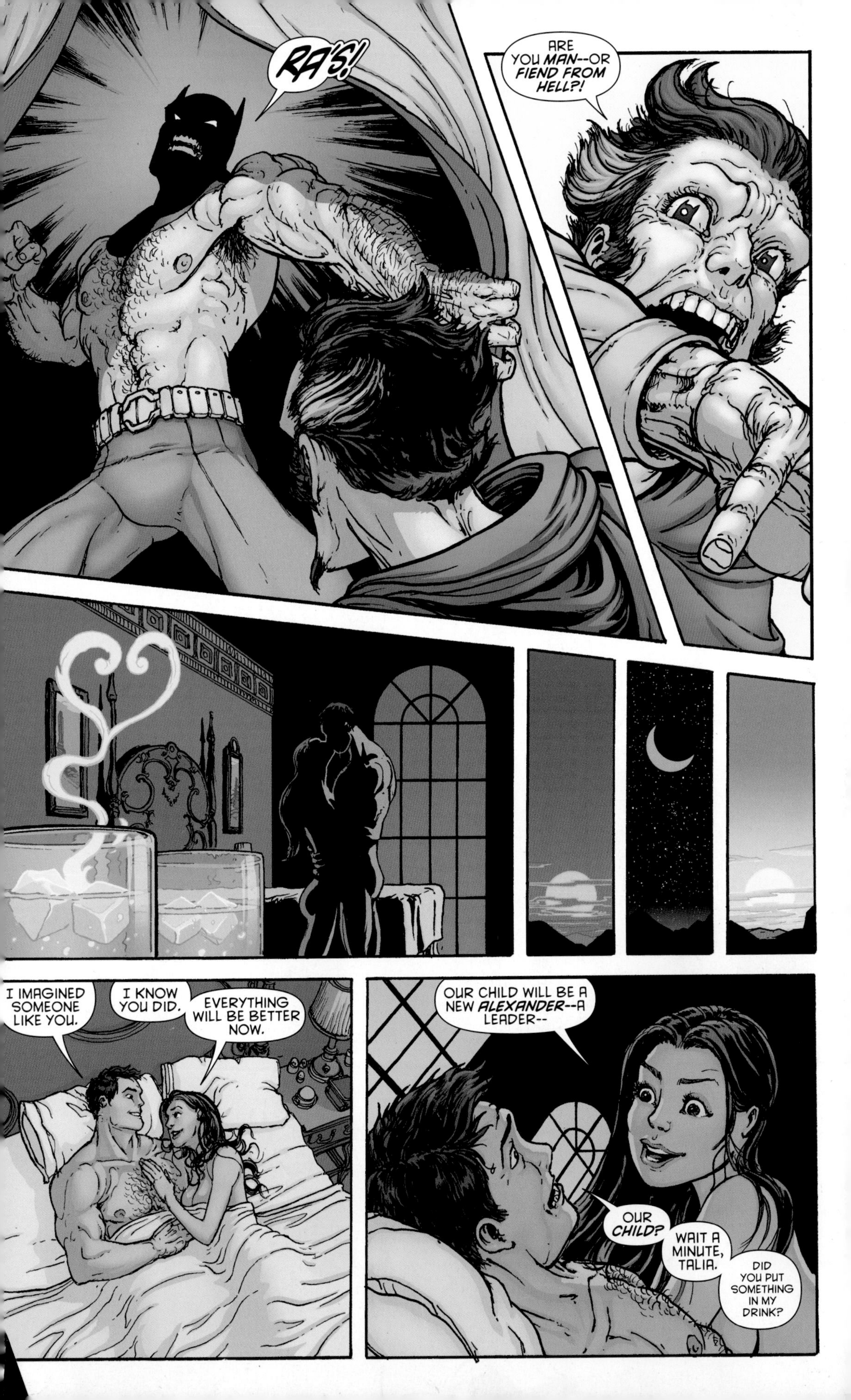
RA'S!
ARE YOU MAN--OR FIEND FROM HELL?!
I IMAGINED SOMEONE LIKE YOU.
I KNOW YOU DID.
EVERYTHING WILL BE BETTER NOW.
OUR CHILD WILL BE A NEW ALEXANDER--A LEADER--
OUR CHILD?
WAIT A MINUTE, TALIA.
DID YOU PUT SOMETHING IN MY DRINK?

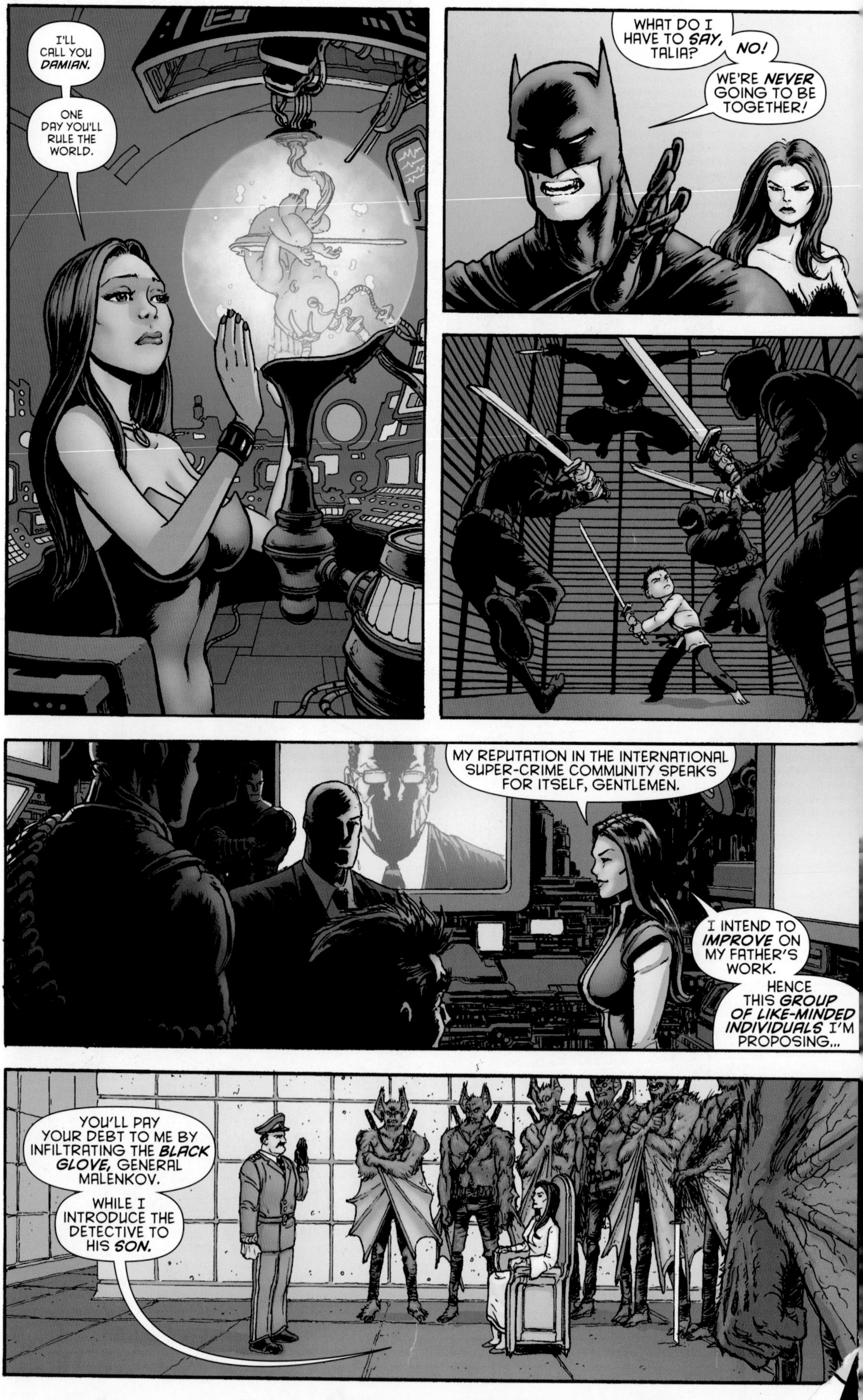

I'LL CALL YOU DAMIAN.
ONE DAY YOU'LL RULE THE WORLD.
WHAT DO I HAVE TO SAY, TALIA?
NO!
WE'RE NEVER GOING TO BE TOGETHER!
MY REPUTATION IN THE INTERNATIONAL SUPER-CRIME COMMUNITY SPEAKS FOR ITSELF, GENTLEMEN.
I INTEND TO IMPROVE ON MY FATHER'S WORK.
HENCE THIS GROUP OF LIKE-MINDED INDIVIDUALS I'M PROPOSING...
YOU'LL PAY YOUR DEBT TO ME BY INFILTRATING THE BLACK GLOVE, GENERAL MALENKOV.
WHILE I INTRODUCE THE DETECTIVE TO HIS SON.

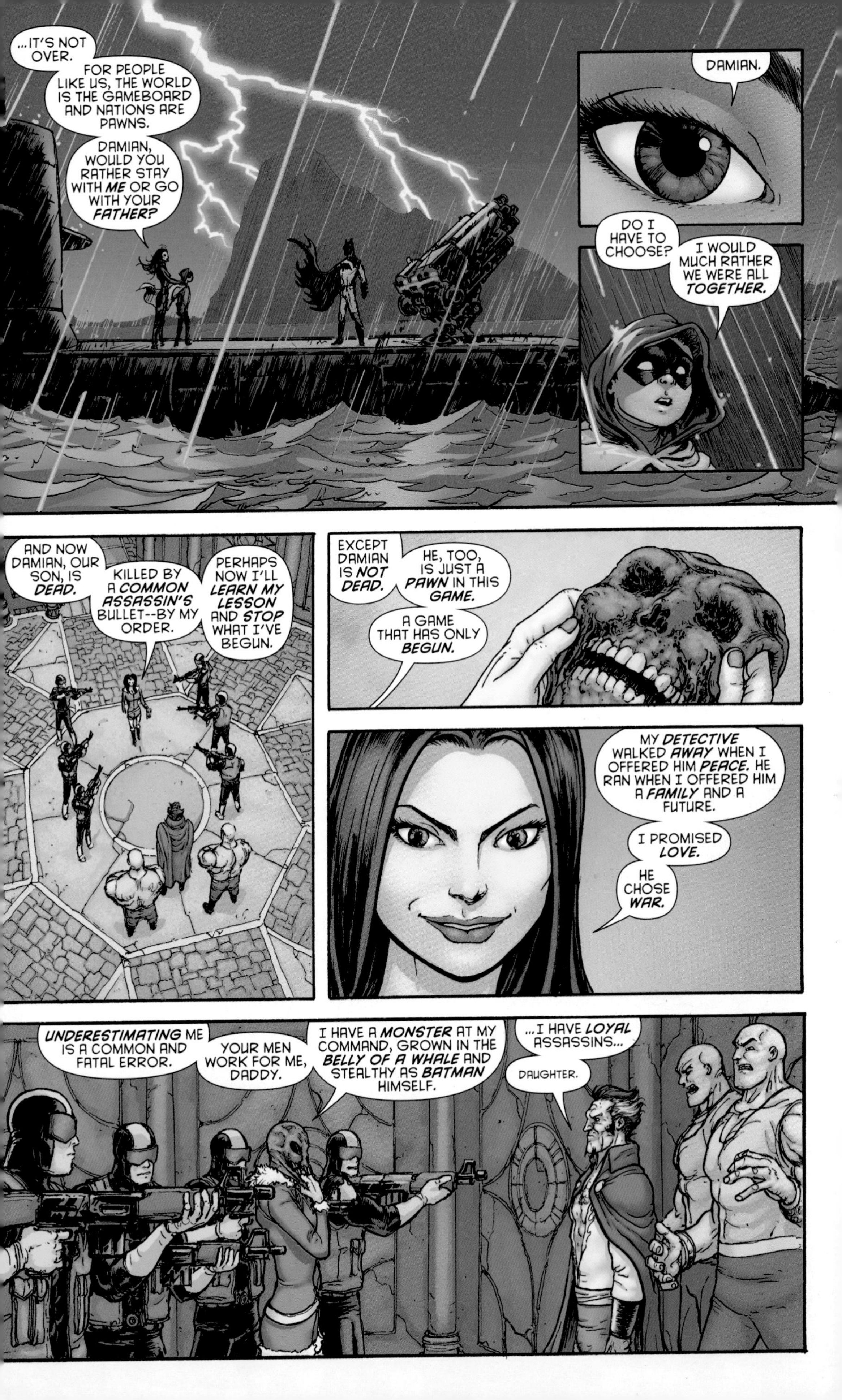
...IT'S NOT OVER.
FOR PEOPLE LIKE US, THE WORLD IS THE GAMEBOARD AND NATIONS ARE PAWNS.
DAMIAN, WOULD YOU RATHER STAY WITH ME OR GO WITH YOUR FATHER?
DAMIAN.
DO I HAVE TO CHOOSE?
I WOULD MUCH RATHER WE WERE ALL TOGETHER.
AND NOW DAMIAN, OUR SON, IS DEAD.
KILLED BY A COMMON ASSASSIN'S BULLET--BY MY ORDER.
PERHAPS NOW I'LL LEARN MY LESSON AND STOP WHAT I'VE BEGUN.
EXCEPT DAMIAN IS NOT DEAD.
HE, TOO, IS JUST A PAWN IN THIS GAME.
A GAME THAT HAS ONLY BEGUN.
MY DETECTIVE WALKED AWAY WHEN I OFFERED HIM PEACE. HE RAN WHEN I OFFERED HIM A FAMILY AND A FUTURE.
I PROMISED LOVE.
HE CHOSE WAR.
UNDERESTIMATING ME IS A COMMON AND FATAL ERROR.
YOUR MEN WORK FOR ME, DADDY.
I HAVE A MONSTER AT MY COMMAND, GROWN IN THE BELLY OF A WHALE AND STEALTHY AS BATMAN HIMSELF.
...I HAVE LOYAL ASSASSINS...
DAUGHTER.

NEXT

the Resurrection of MaTches Malone!

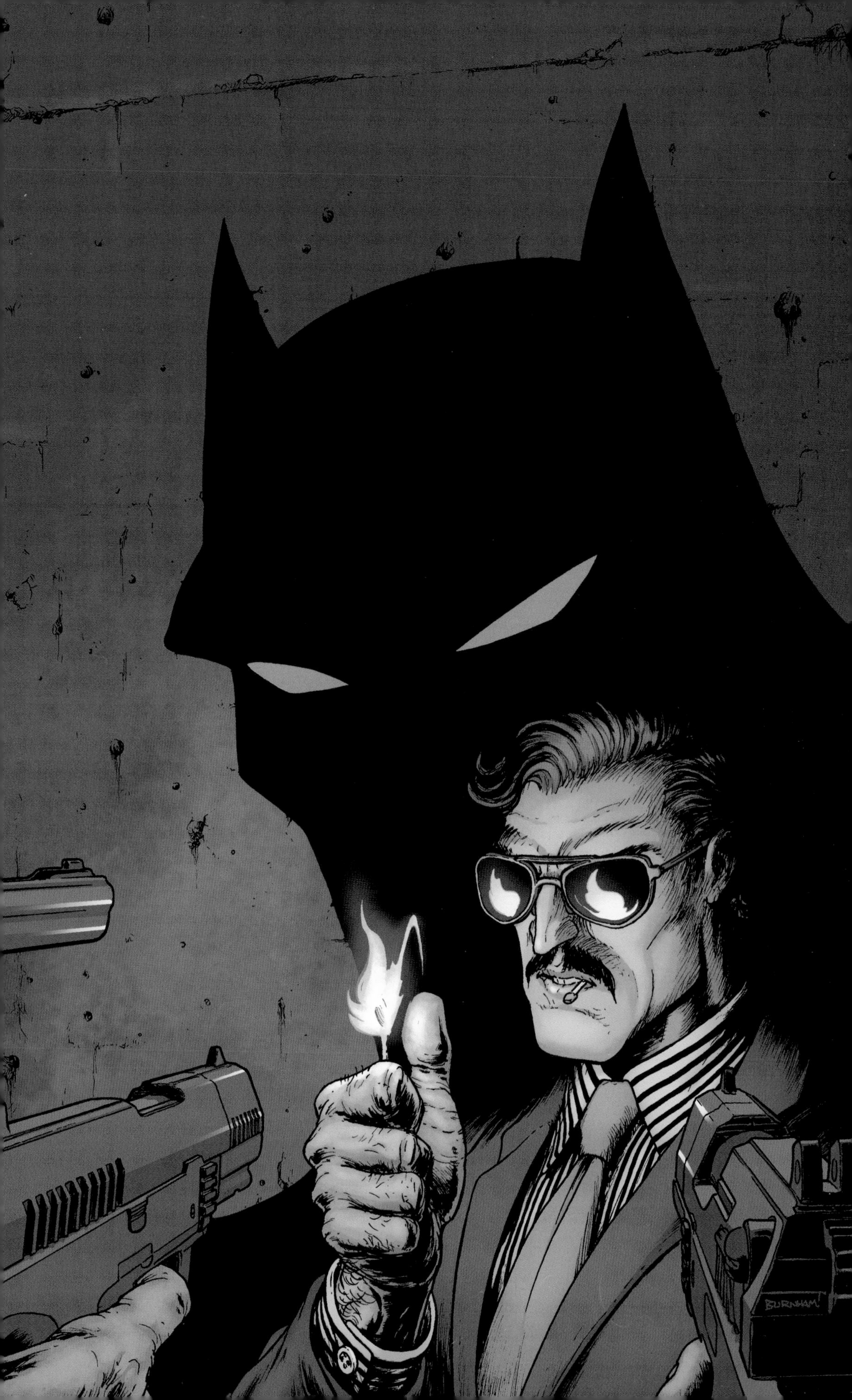
BURNHAM

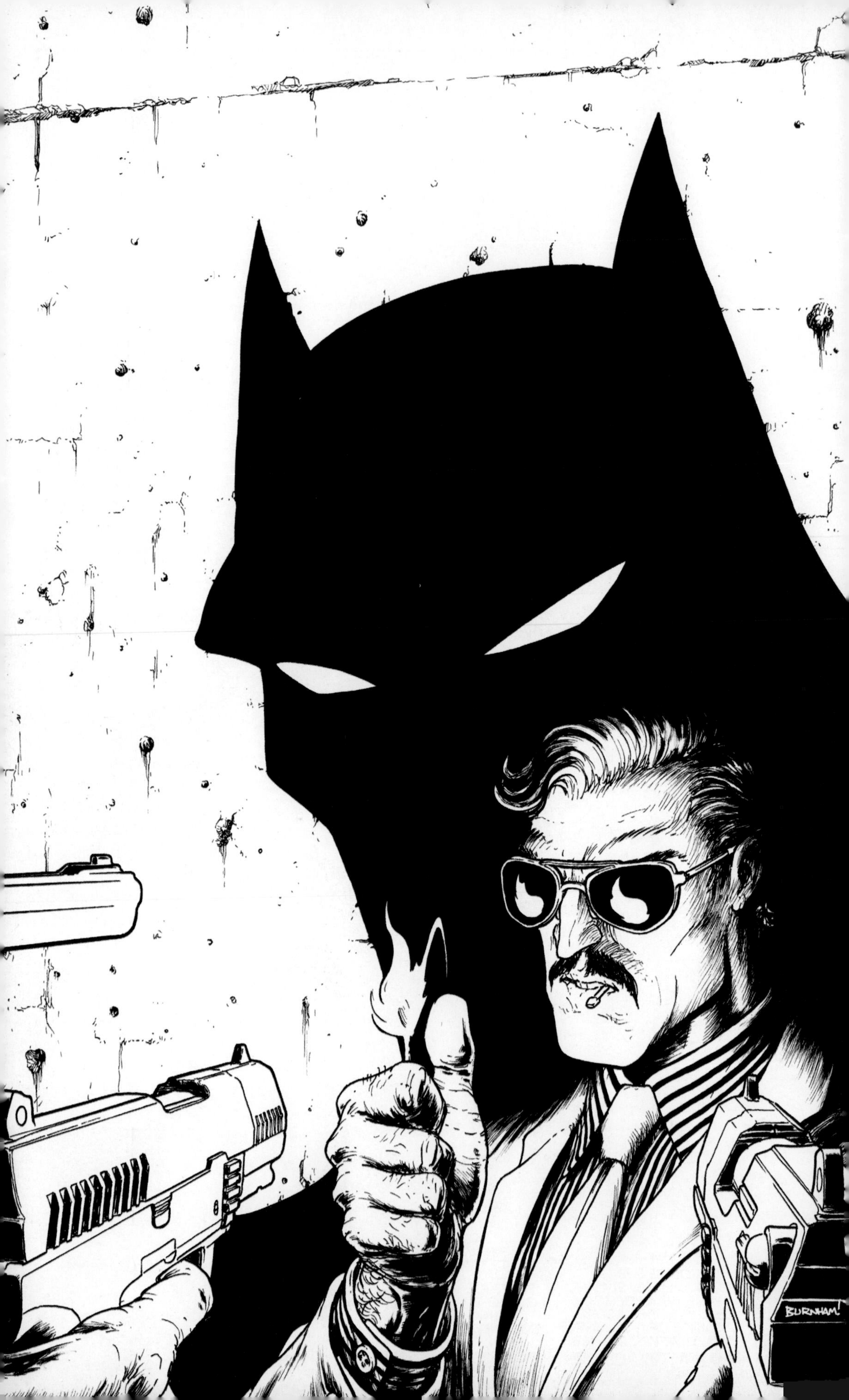
BURNHAM!

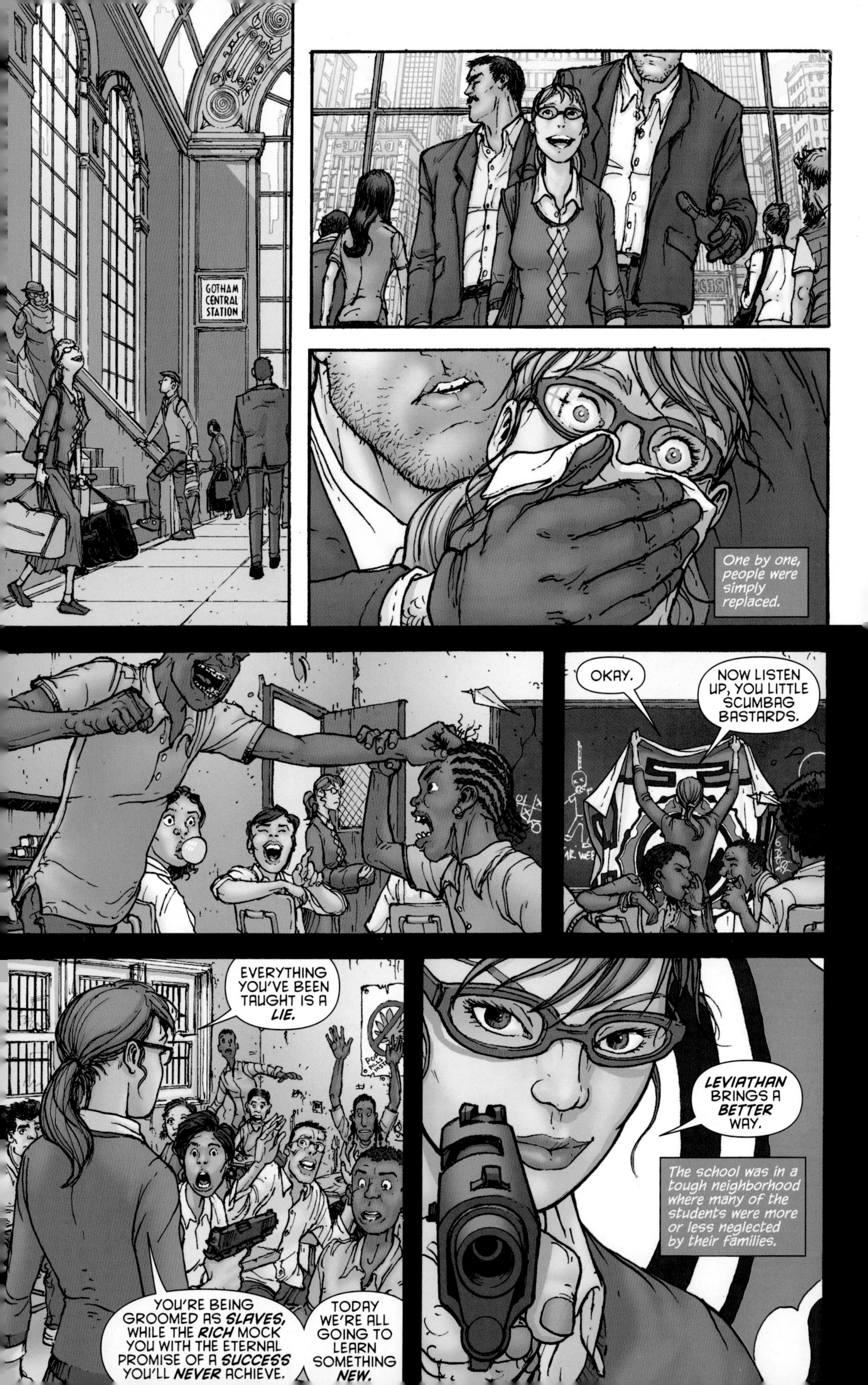
GOTHAM CENTRAL STATION
One by one, people were simply replaced.
OKAY.
NOW LISTEN UP, YOU LITTLE SCUMBAG BASTARDS.
EVERYTHING YOU'VE BEEN TAUGHT IS A LIE.
YOU'RE BEING GROOMED AS SLAVES, WHILE THE RICH MOCK YOU WITH THE ETERNAL PROMISE OF A SUCCESS YOU'LL NEVER ACHIEVE.
TODAY WE'RE ALL GOING TO LEARN SOMETHING NEW.
LEVIATHAN BRINGS A BETTER WAY.
The school was in a tough neighborhood where many of the students were more or less neglected by their families.

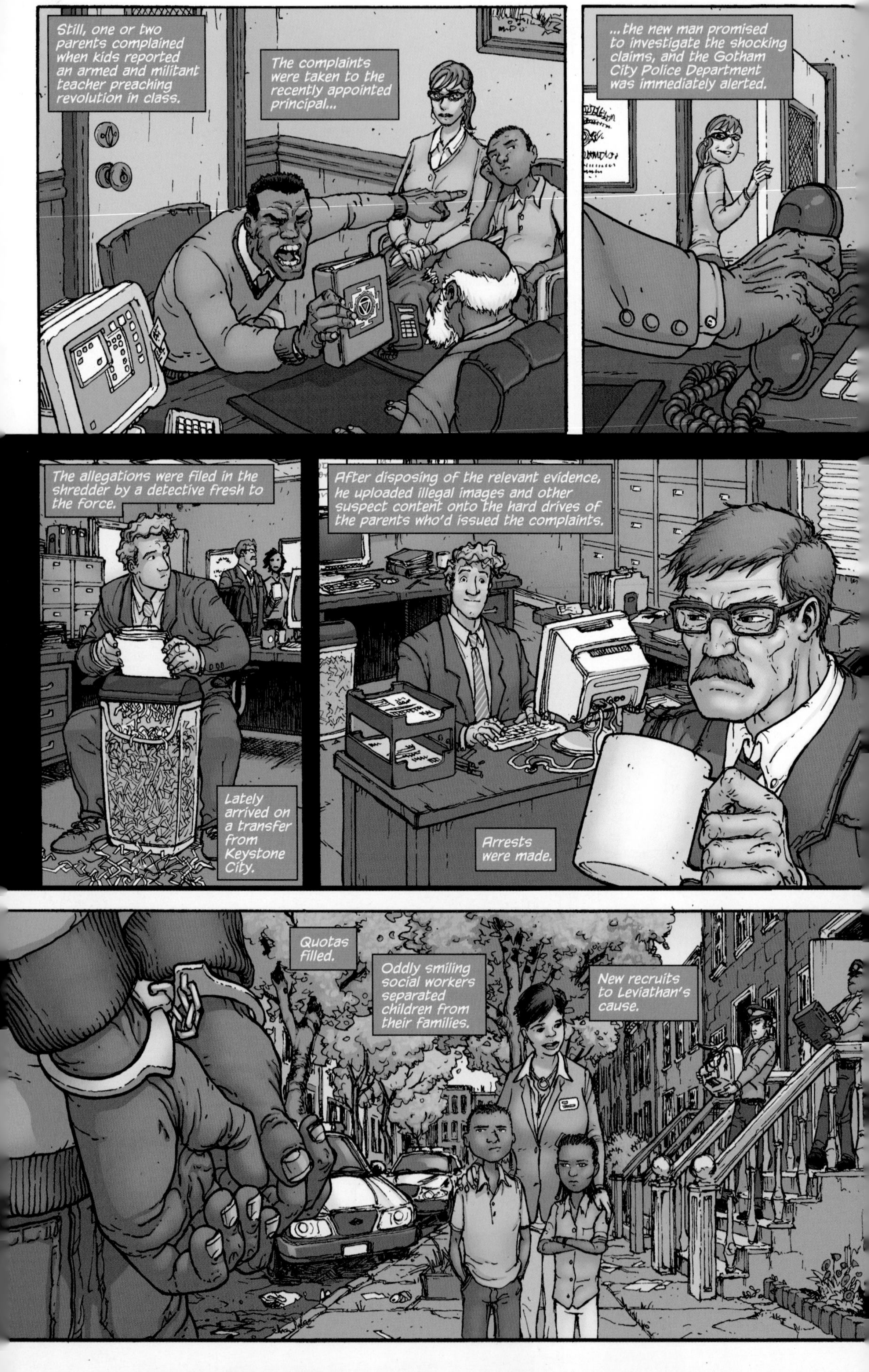
Still, one or two parents complained when kids reported an armed and militant teacher preaching revolution in class.
The complaints were taken to the recently appointed principal...
...the new man promised to investigate the shocking claims, and the Gotham City Police Department was immediately alerted.
The allegations were filed in the shredder by a detective fresh to the force.
Lately arrived on a transfer from Keystone City.
After disposing of the relevant evidence, he uploaded illegal images and other suspect content onto the hard drives of the parents who'd issued the complaints.
Arrests were made.
Quotas filled.
Oddly smiling social workers separated children from their families.
New recruits to Leviathan's cause.

Writer GRANT MORRISON   Artist CHRIS BURNHAM
Color NATHAN FAIRBAIRN   Lettering PATRICK BROSSEAU

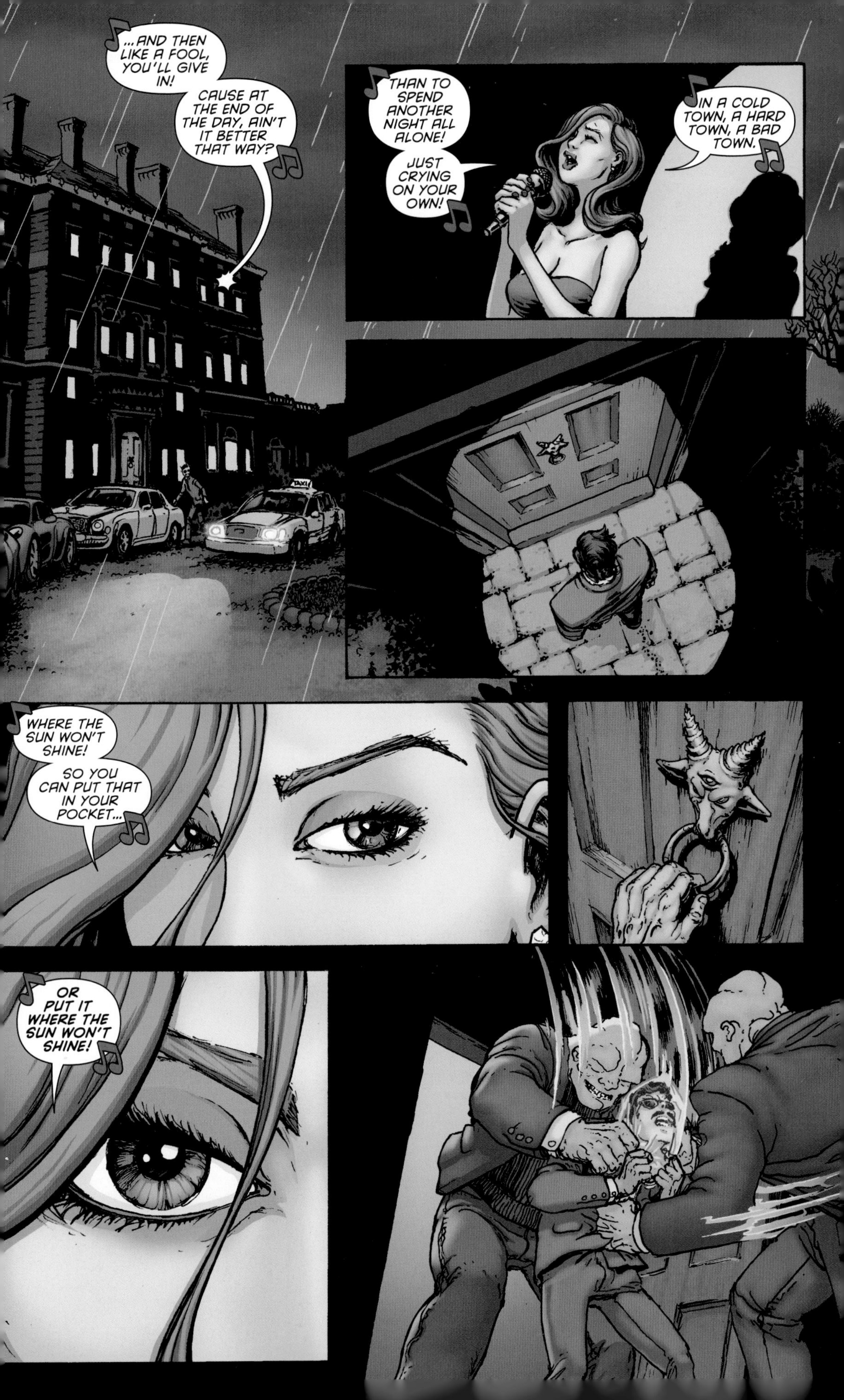
...AND THEN LIKE A FOOL, YOU'LL GIVE IN!
CAUSE AT THE END OF THE DAY, AIN'T IT BETTER THAT WAY?
THAN TO SPEND ANOTHER NIGHT ALL ALONE!
JUST CRYING ON YOUR OWN!
IN A COLD TOWN, A HARD TOWN, A BAD TOWN.
TAXI
WHERE THE SUN WON'T SHINE!
SO YOU CAN PUT THAT IN YOUR POCKET...
OR PUT IT WHERE THE SUN WON'T SHINE!

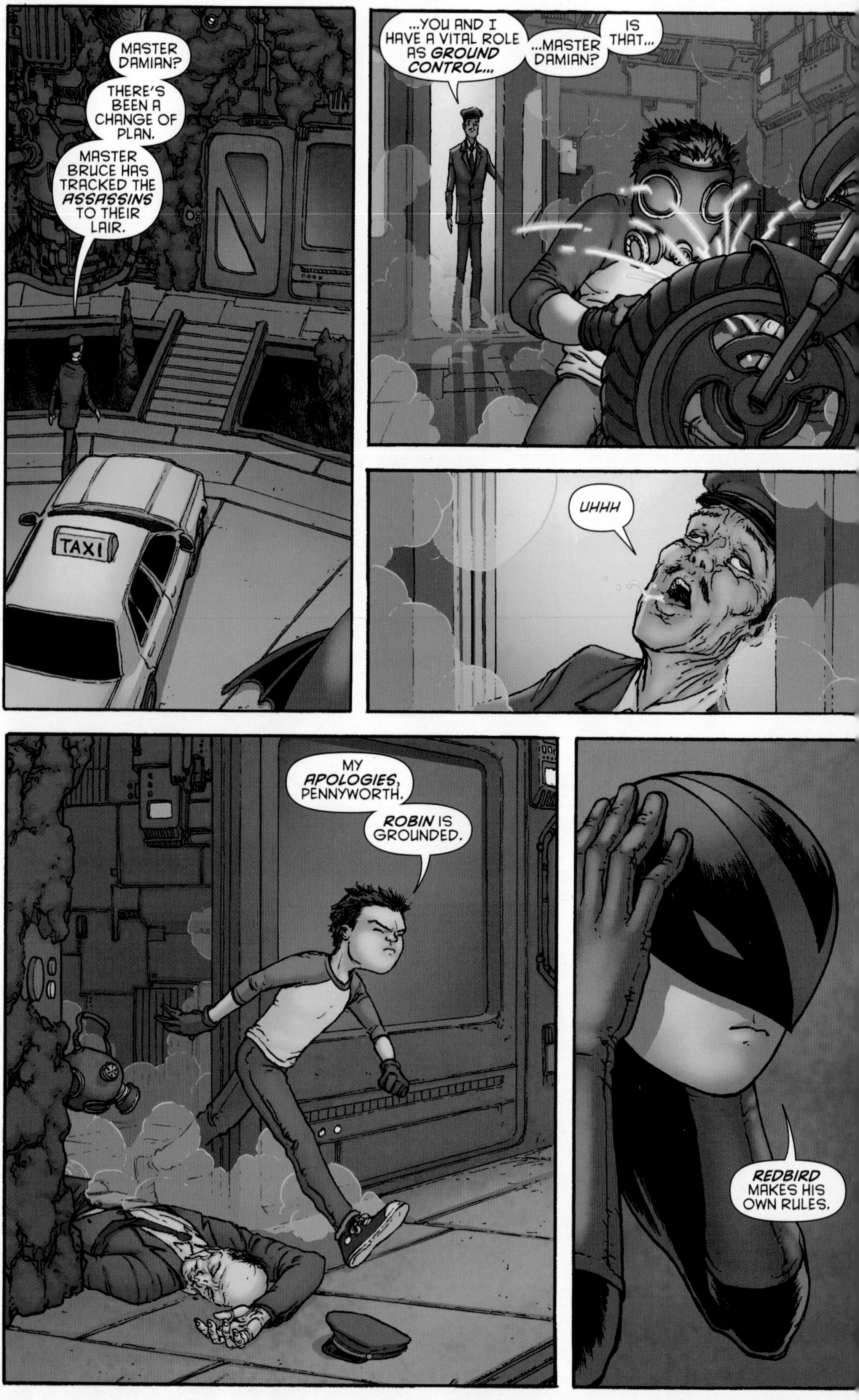
MASTER DAMIAN?
THERE'S BEEN A CHANGE OF PLAN.
MASTER BRUCE HAS TRACKED THE ASSASSINS TO THEIR LAIR.
TAXI
...YOU AND I HAVE A VITAL ROLE AS GROUND CONTROL...
...MASTER DAMIAN?
IS THAT...
UHHH
MY APOLOGIES, PENNYWORTH.
ROBIN IS GROUNDED.
REDBIRD MAKES HIS OWN RULES.

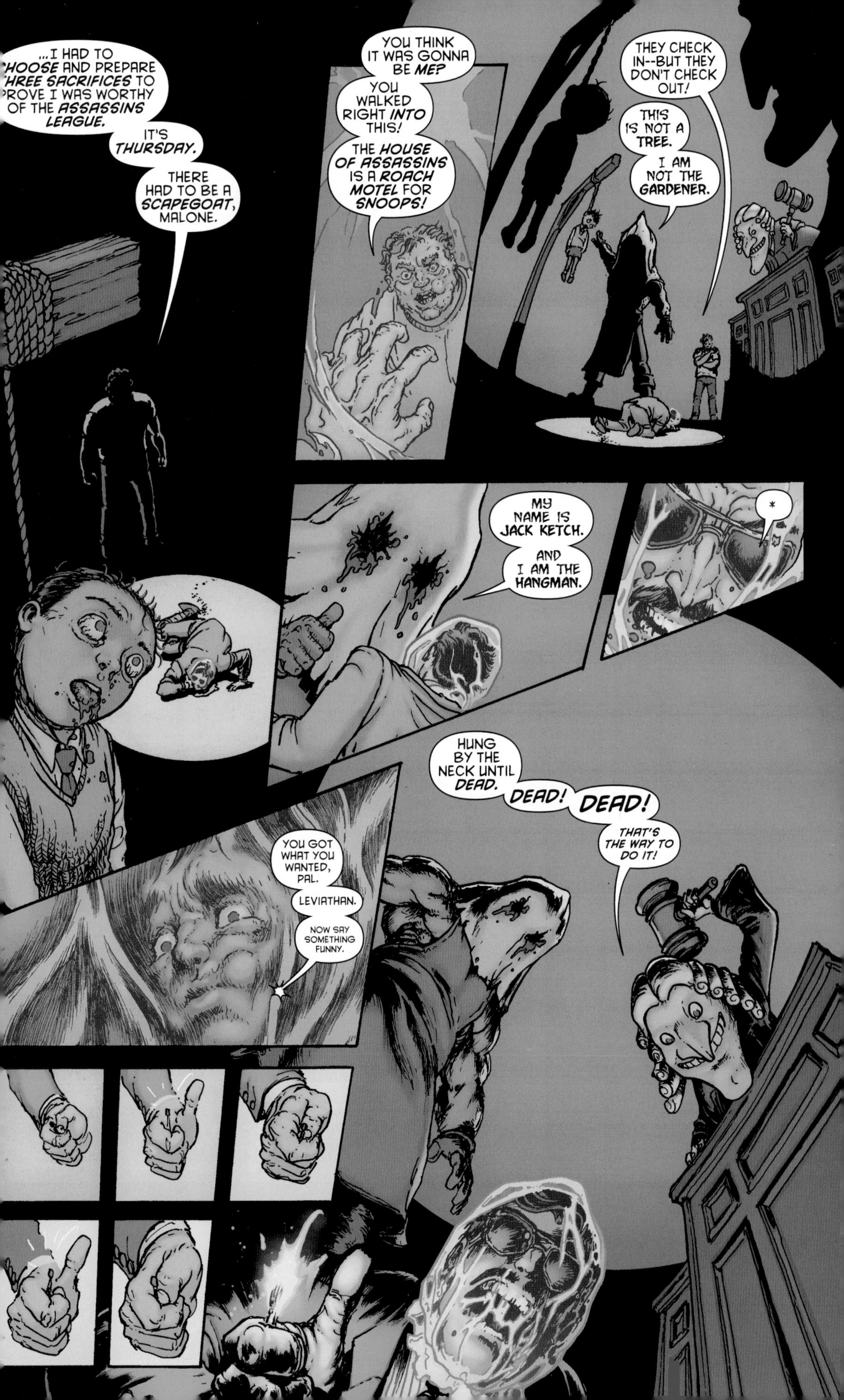
...I HAD TO CHOOSE AND PREPARE THREE SACRIFICES TO PROVE I WAS WORTHY OF THE ASSASSINS LEAGUE.
IT'S THURSDAY.
THERE HAD TO BE A SCAPEGOAT, MALONE.
YOU THINK IT WAS GONNA BE ME?
YOU WALKED RIGHT INTO THIS!
THE HOUSE OF ASSASSINS IS A ROACH MOTEL FOR SNOOPS!
THEY CHECK IN--BUT THEY DON'T CHECK OUT!
THIS IS NOT A TREE.
I AM NOT THE GARDENER.
MY NAME IS JACK KETCH.
AND I AM THE HANGMAN.
*
HUNG BY THE NECK UNTIL DEAD.
DEAD!
DEAD!
THAT'S THE WAY TO DO IT!
YOU GOT WHAT YOU WANTED, PAL.
LEVIATHAN.
NOW SAY SOMETHING FUNNY.

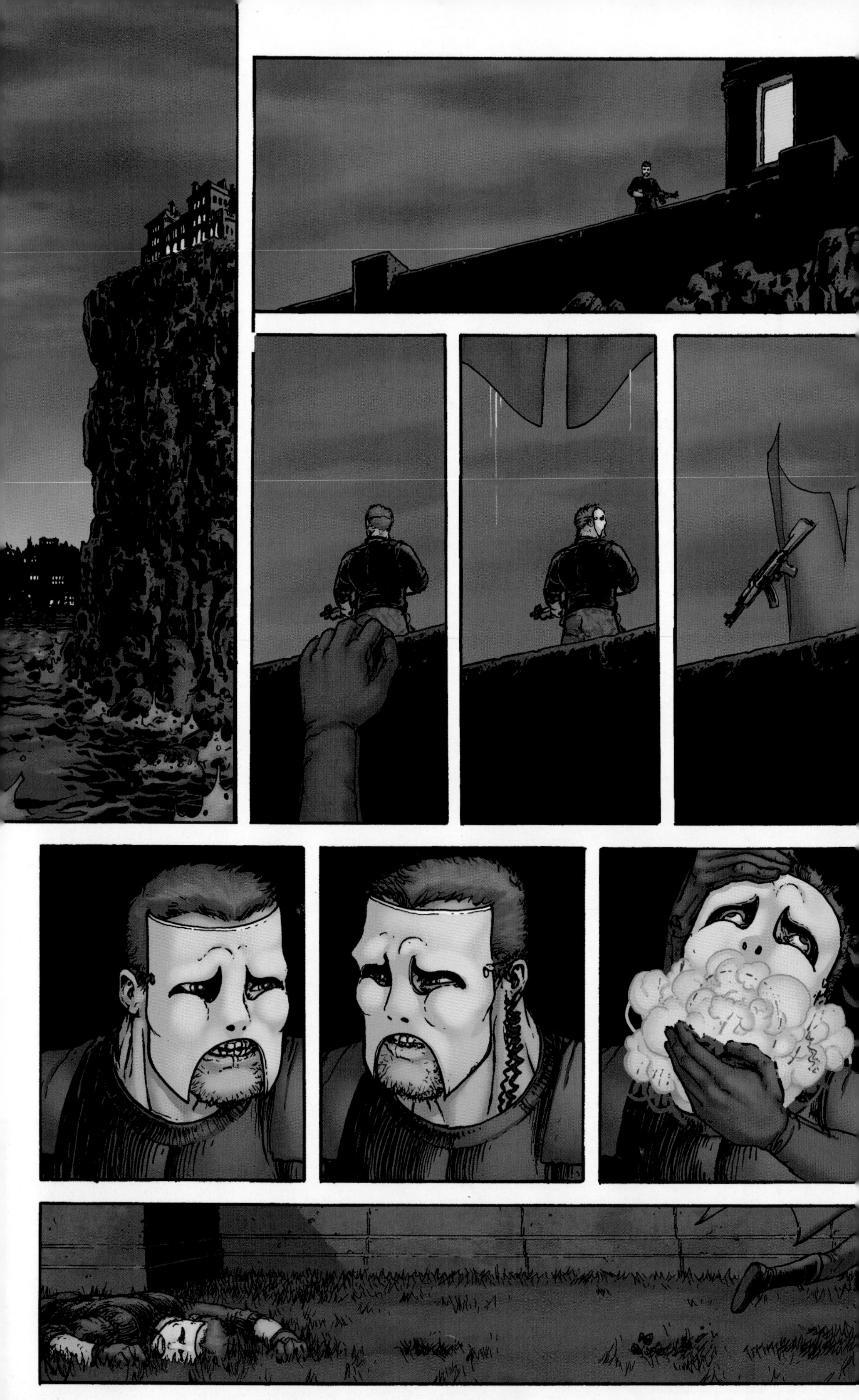

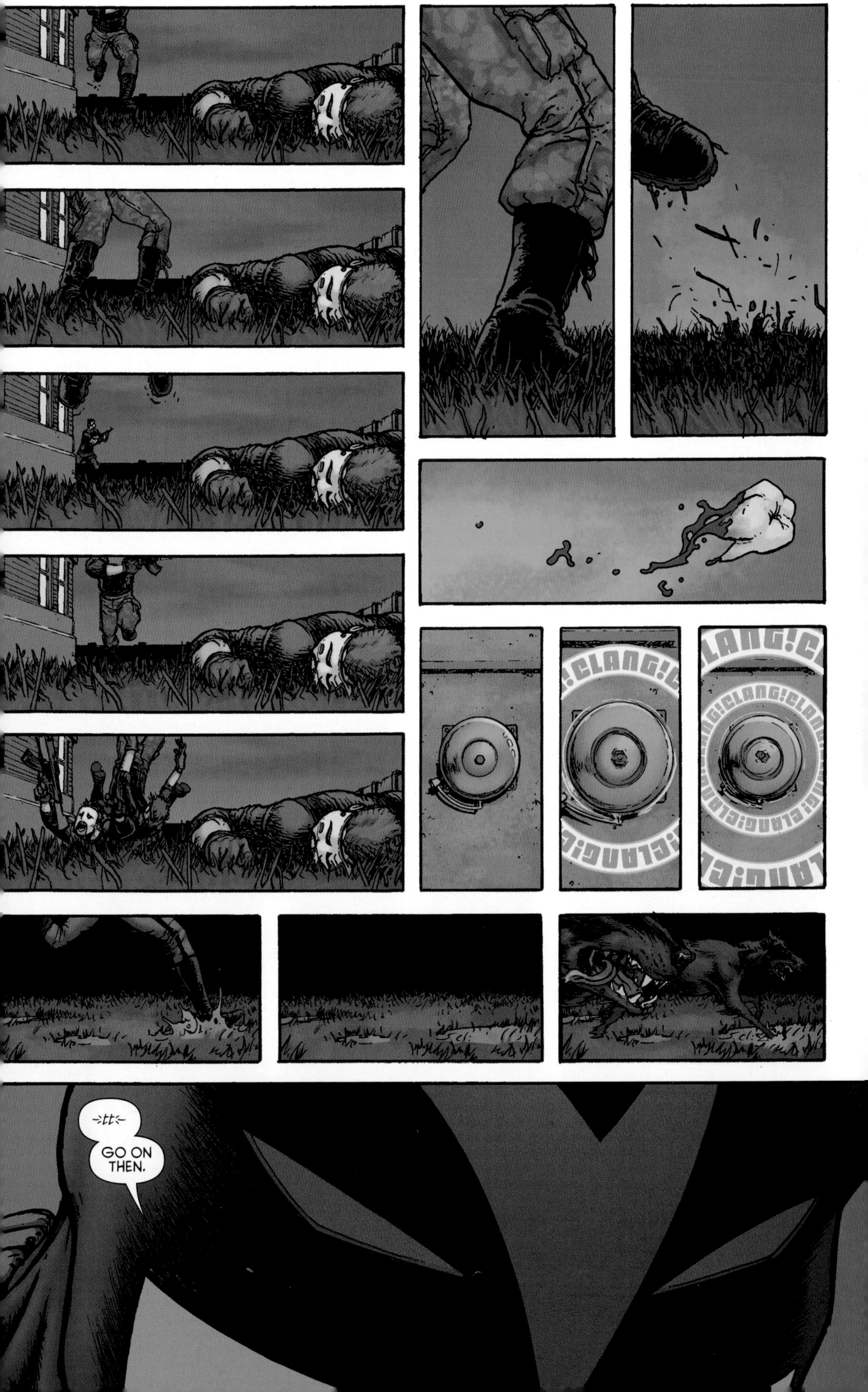

CLANG!CLANG!
CLANG!CLANG!CLANG!CLANG!
-tt-
GO ON THEN.

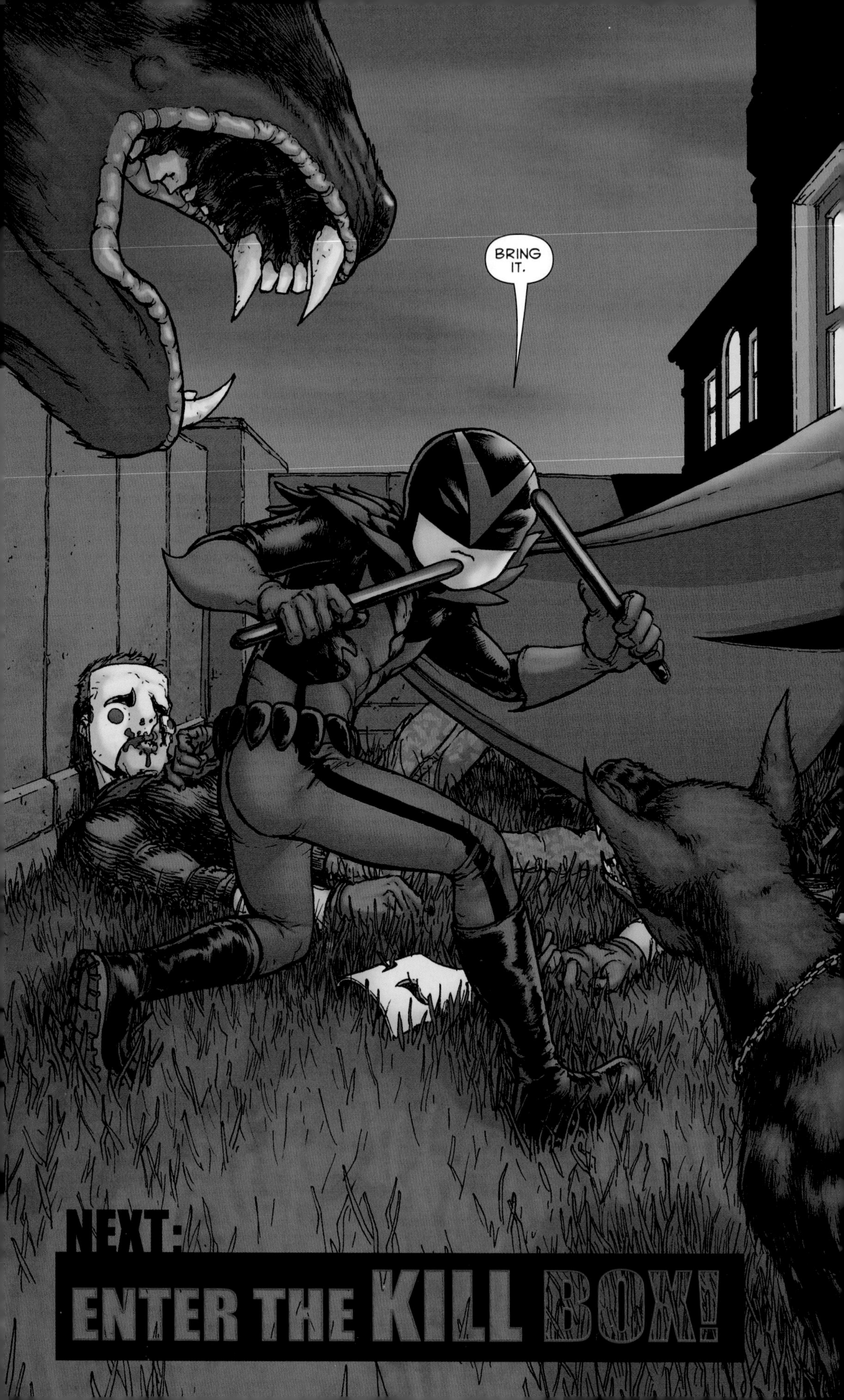
BRING IT.
NEXT:
ENTER THE KILL BOX!

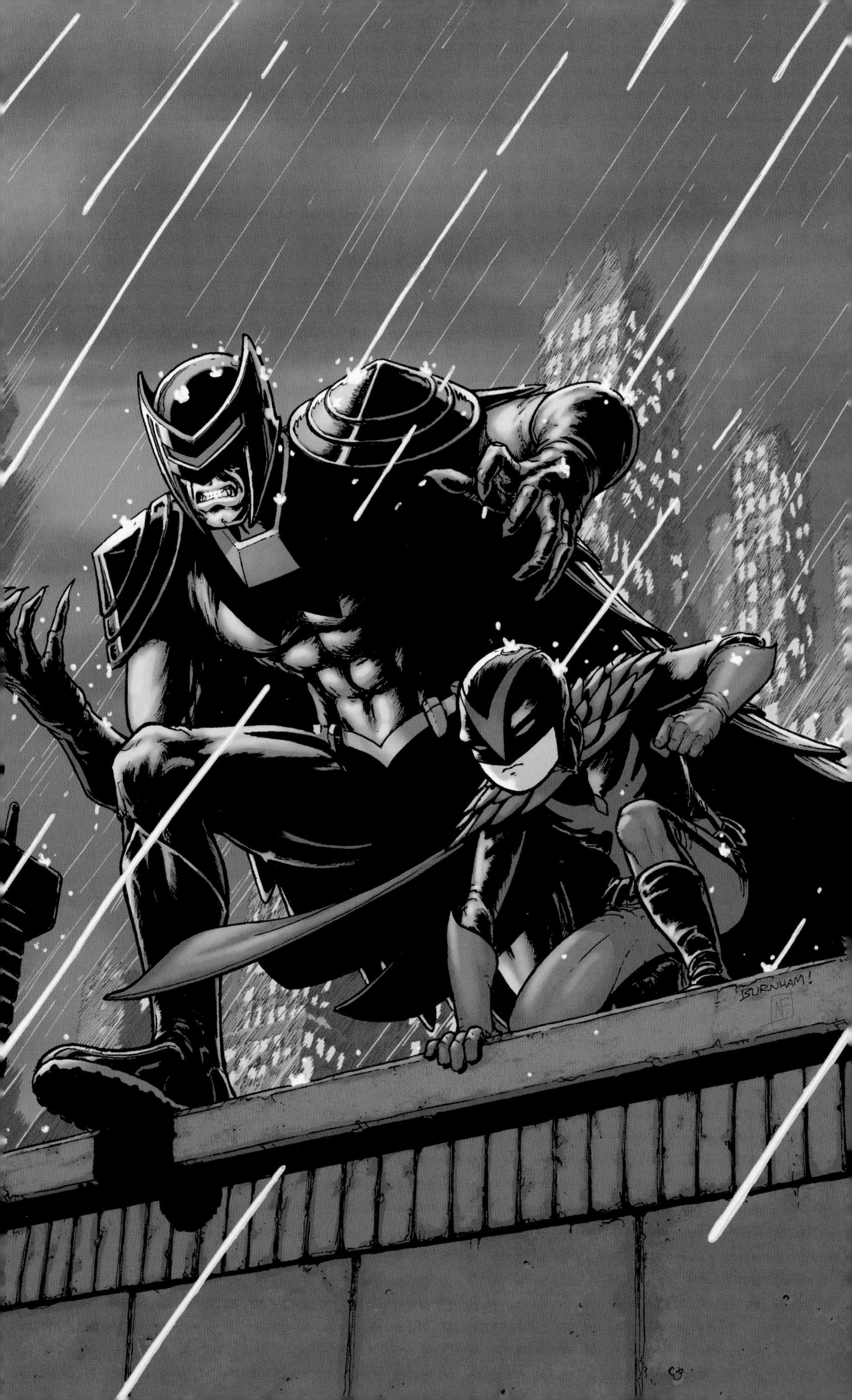
BURNHAM!

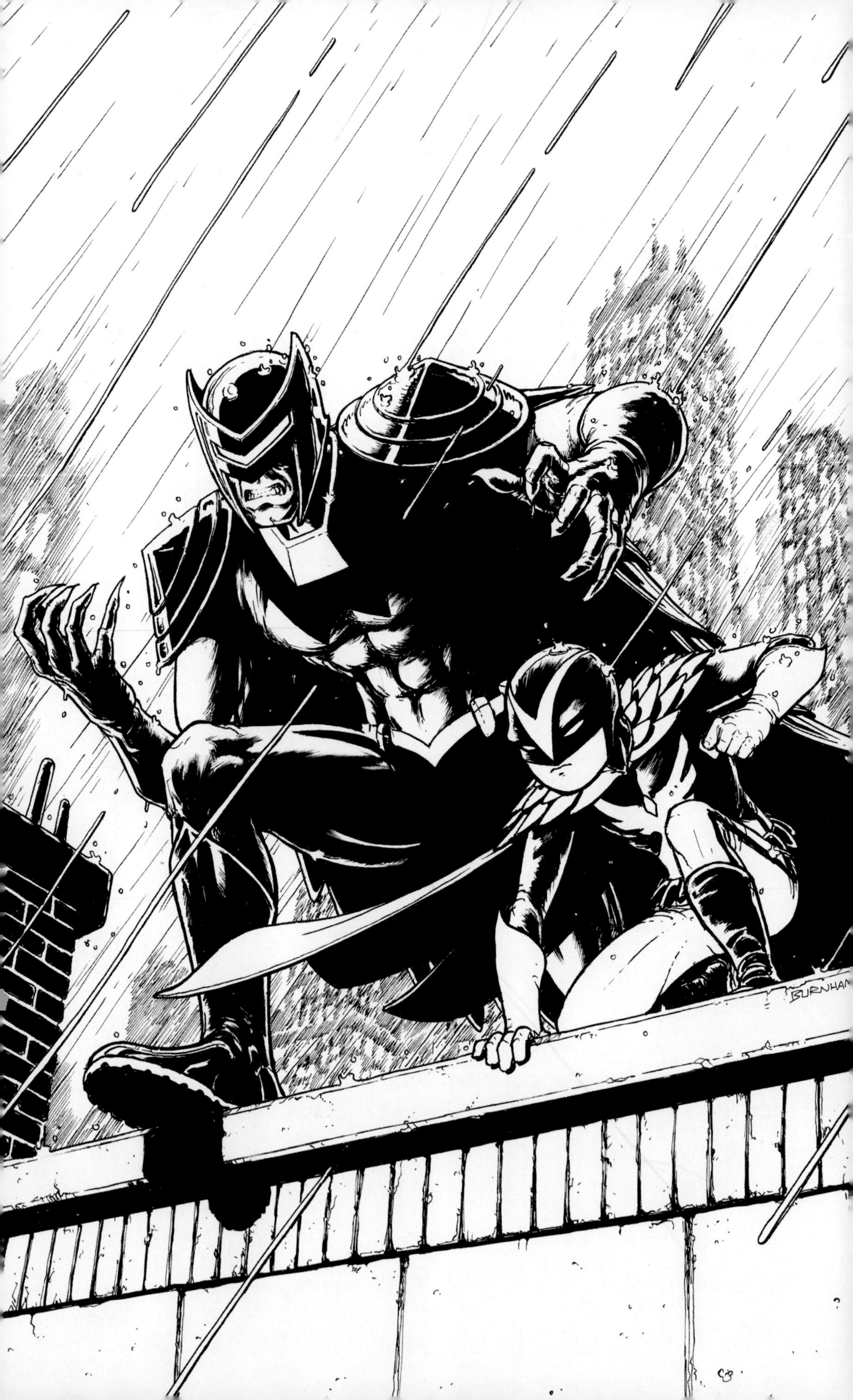
BURNHAM

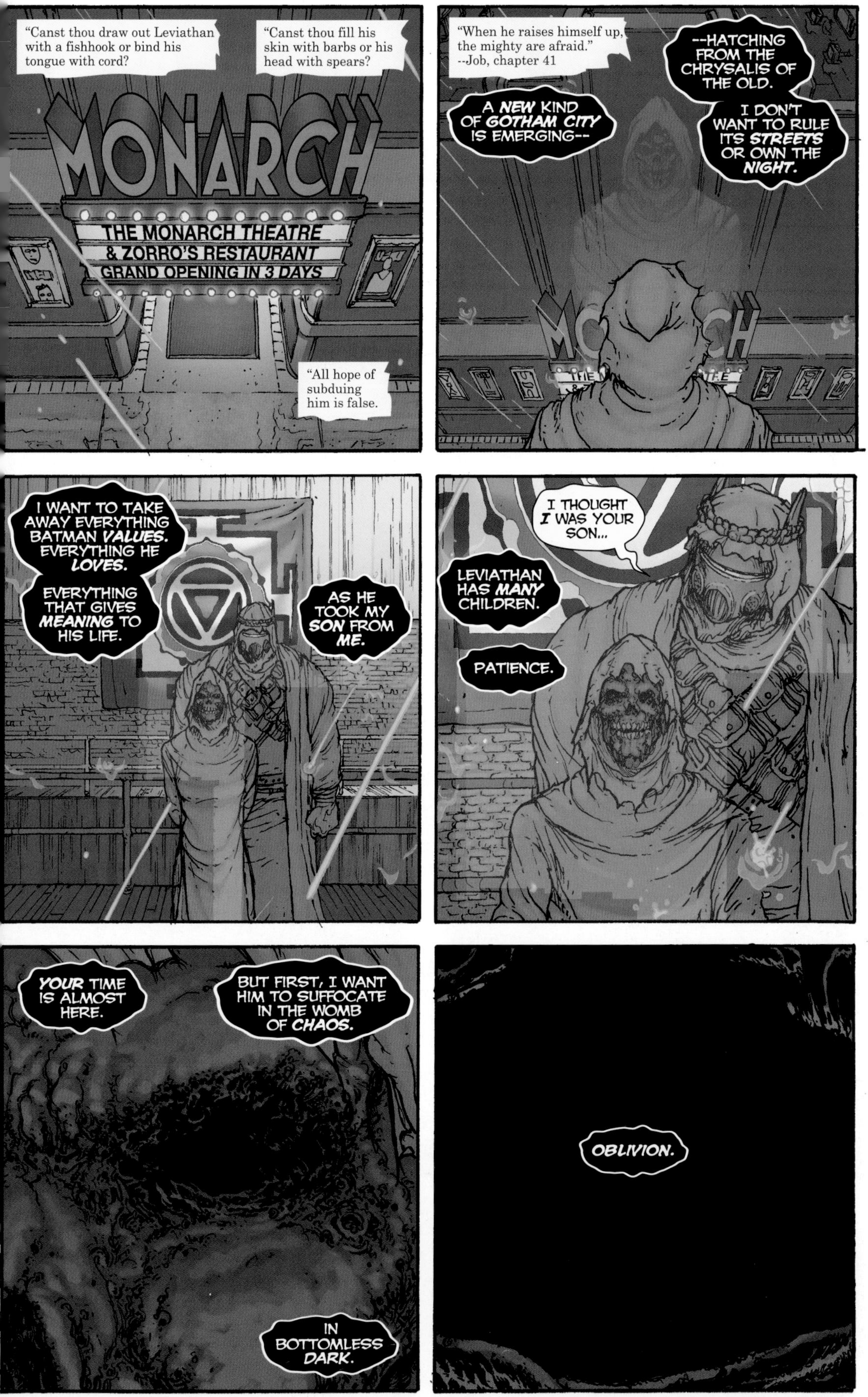
"Canst thou draw out Leviathan with a fishhook or bind his tongue with cord?
"Canst thou fill his skin with barbs or his head with spears?
MONARCH
THE MONARCH THEATRE
& ZORRO'S RESTAURANT
GRAND OPENING IN 3 DAYS
"All hope of subduing him is false.
"When he raises himself up, the mighty are afraid."
--Job, chapter 41
A NEW KIND OF GOTHAM CITY IS EMERGING--
--HATCHING FROM THE CHRYSALIS OF THE OLD.
I DON'T WANT TO RULE ITS STREETS OR OWN THE NIGHT.
I WANT TO TAKE AWAY EVERYTHING BATMAN VALUES. EVERYTHING HE LOVES.
EVERYTHING THAT GIVES MEANING TO HIS LIFE.
AS HE TOOK MY SON FROM ME.
I THOUGHT I WAS YOUR SON...
LEVIATHAN HAS MANY CHILDREN.
PATIENCE.
YOUR TIME IS ALMOST HERE.
BUT FIRST, I WANT HIM TO SUFFOCATE IN THE WOMB OF CHAOS.
IN BOTTOMLESS DARK.
OBLIVION.

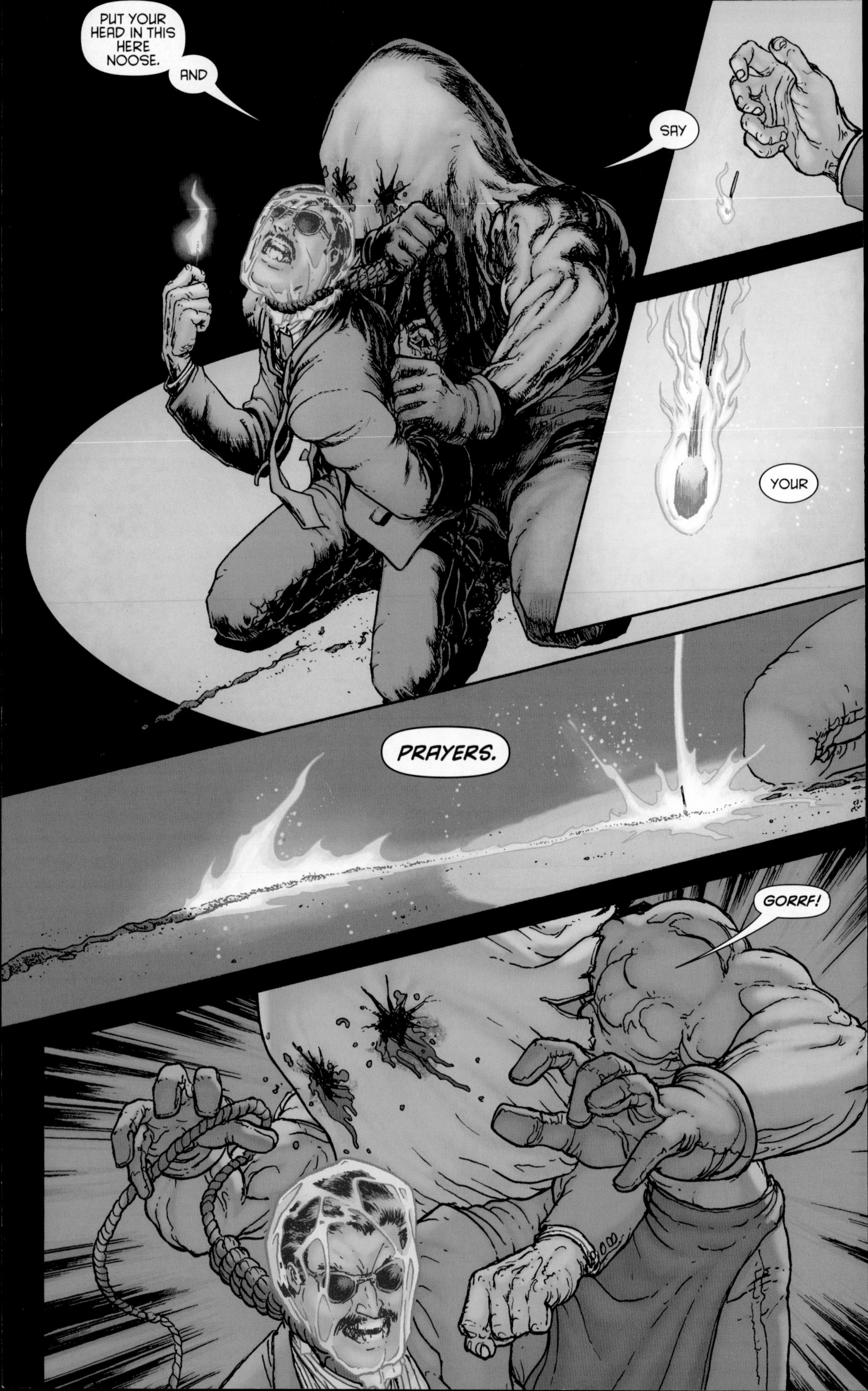
PUT YOUR HEAD IN THIS HERE NOOSE.
AND
SAY
YOUR
PRAYERS.
GORRF!

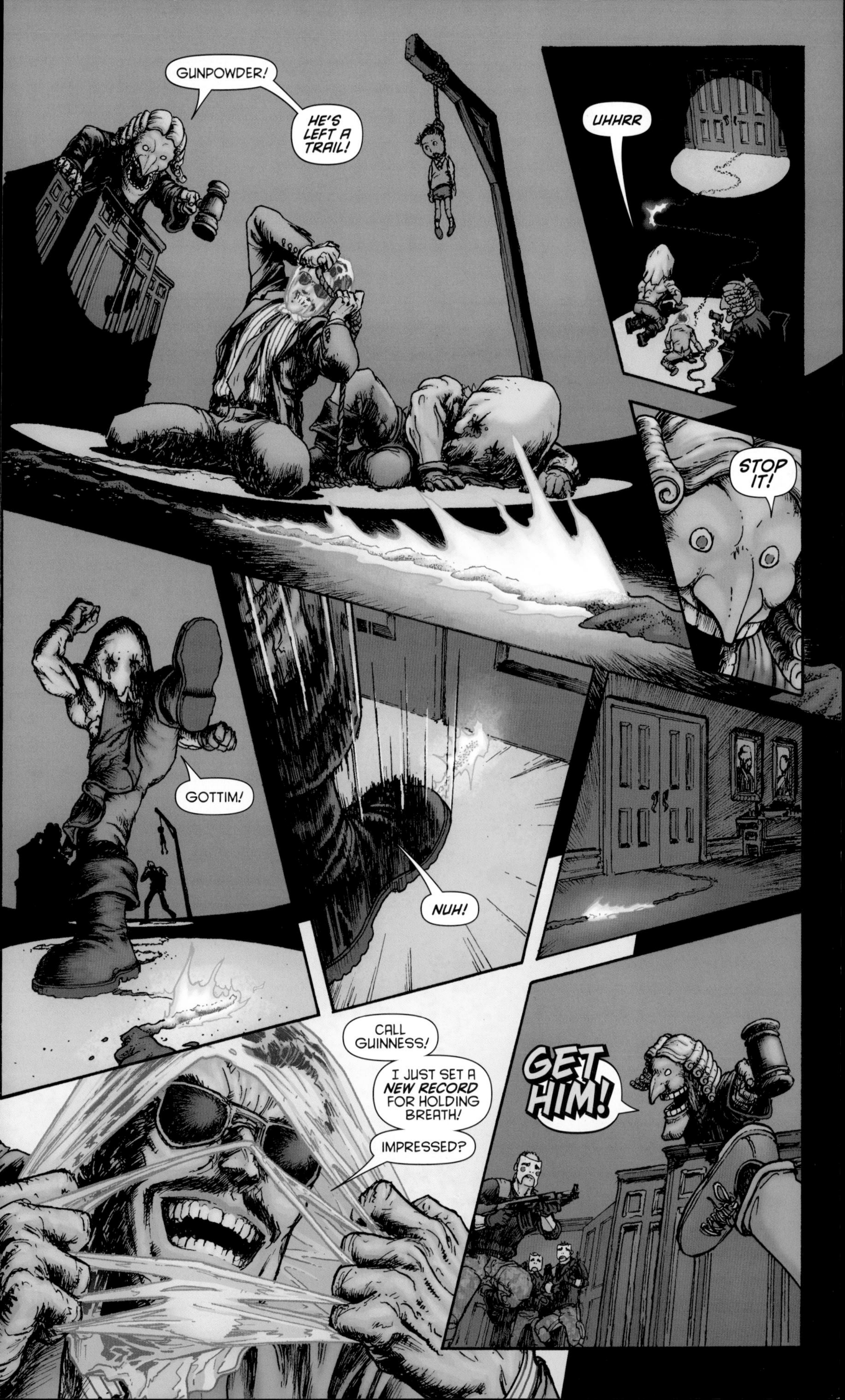
GUNPOWDER!
HE'S LEFT A TRAIL!
UHHRR
STOP IT!
GOTTIM!
NUH!
CALL GUINNESS!
I JUST SET A NEW RECORD FOR HOLDING BREATH!
IMPRESSED?
GET HIM!

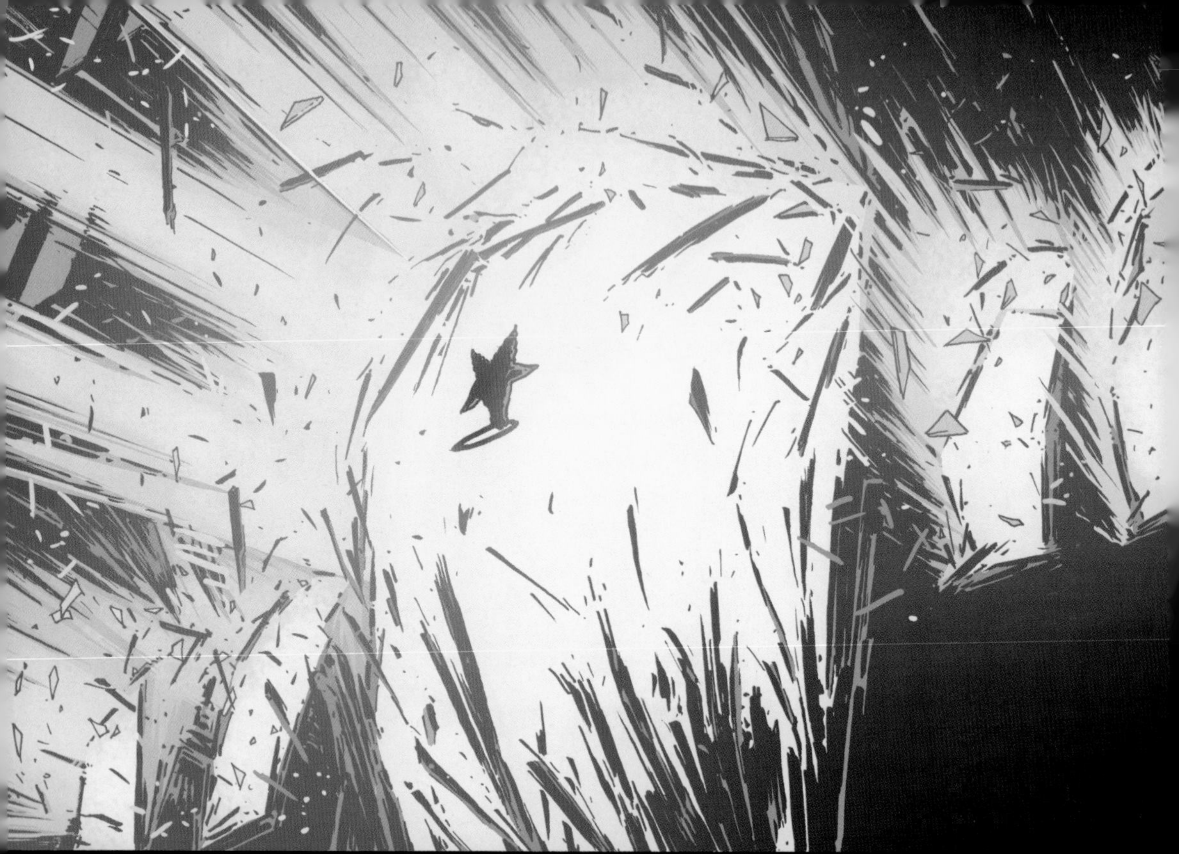

writer GRANT MORRISON artist CHRIS BURNHAM
color NATHAN FAIRBAIRN lettering DAVE SHARPE
cover BURNHAM and FAIRBAIRN

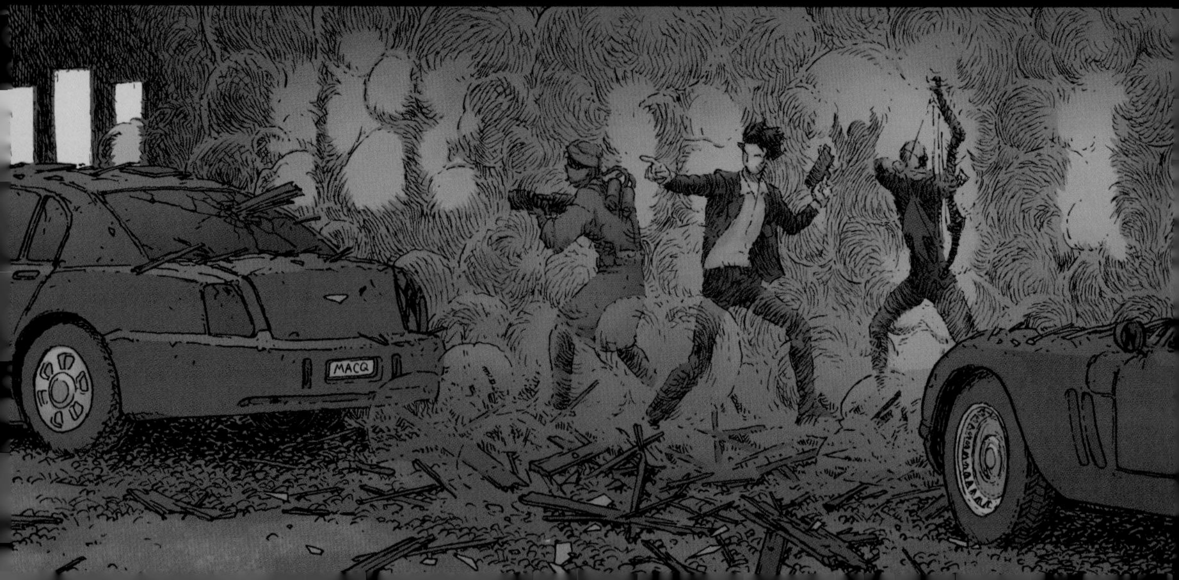
MACQ

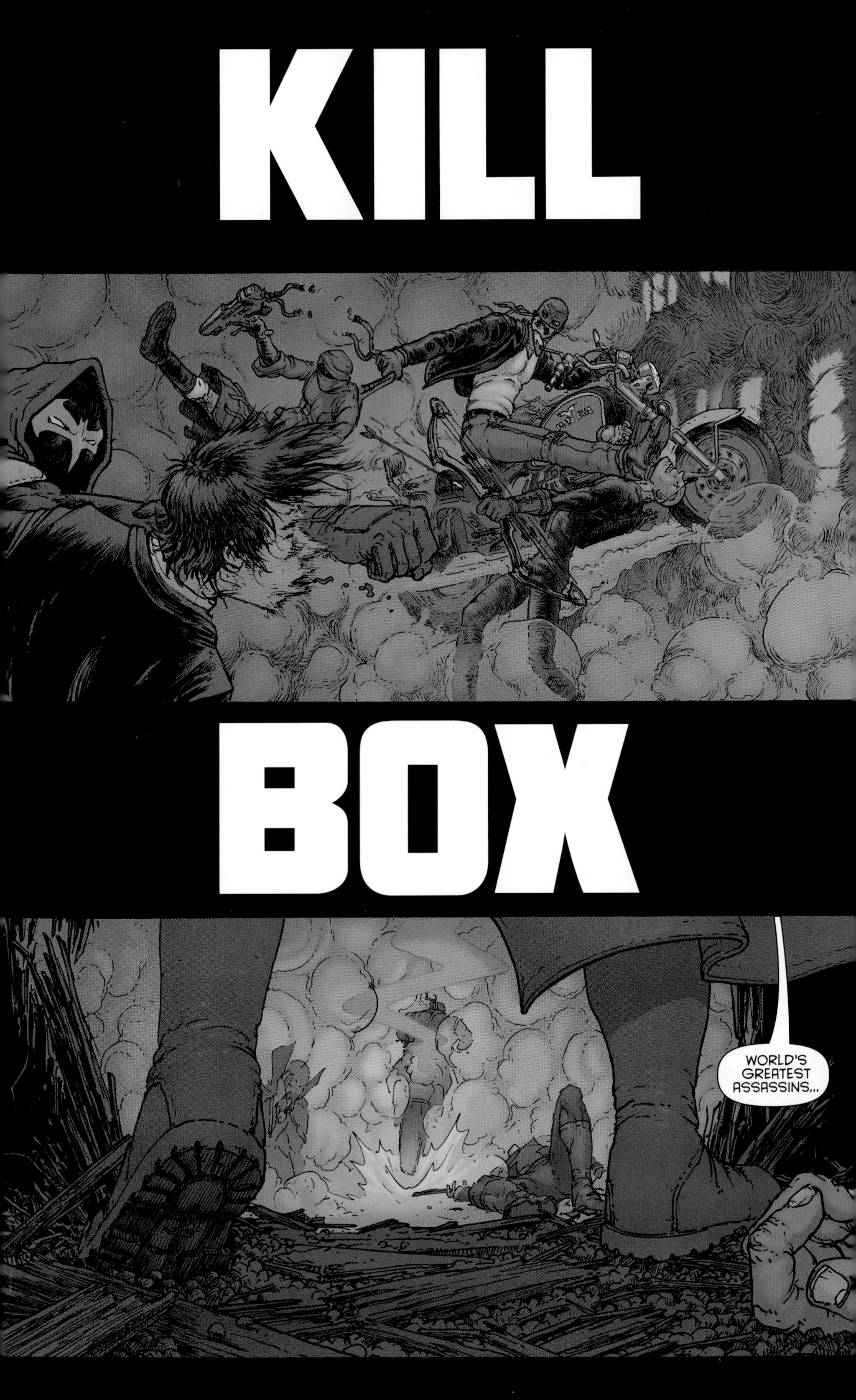
KILL
BOX
WORLD'S GREATEST ASSASSINS...

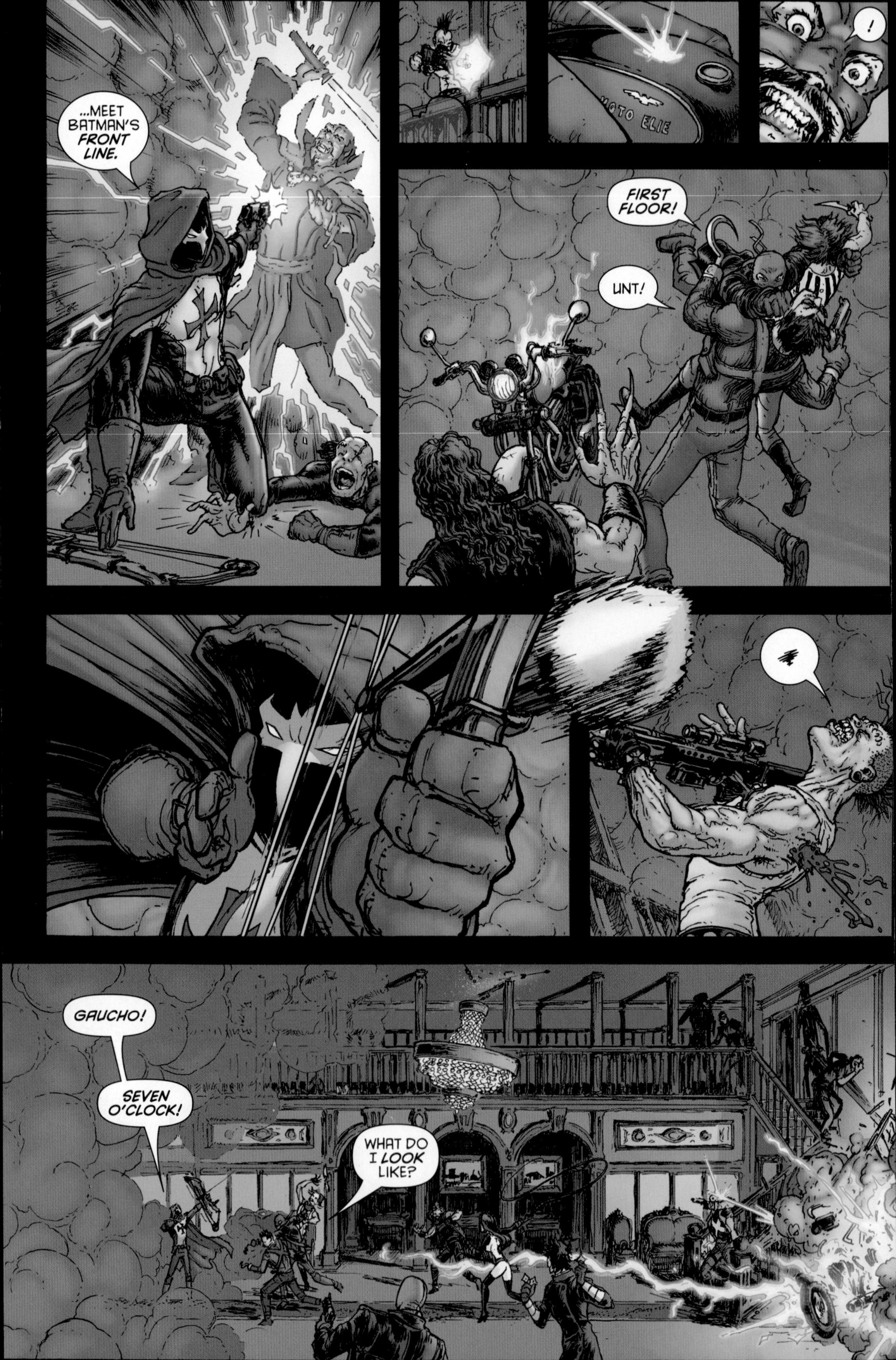
...MEET BATMAN'S FRONT LINE.
!
FIRST FLOOR!
UNT!
GAUCHO!
SEVEN O'CLOCK!
WHAT DO I LOOK LIKE?

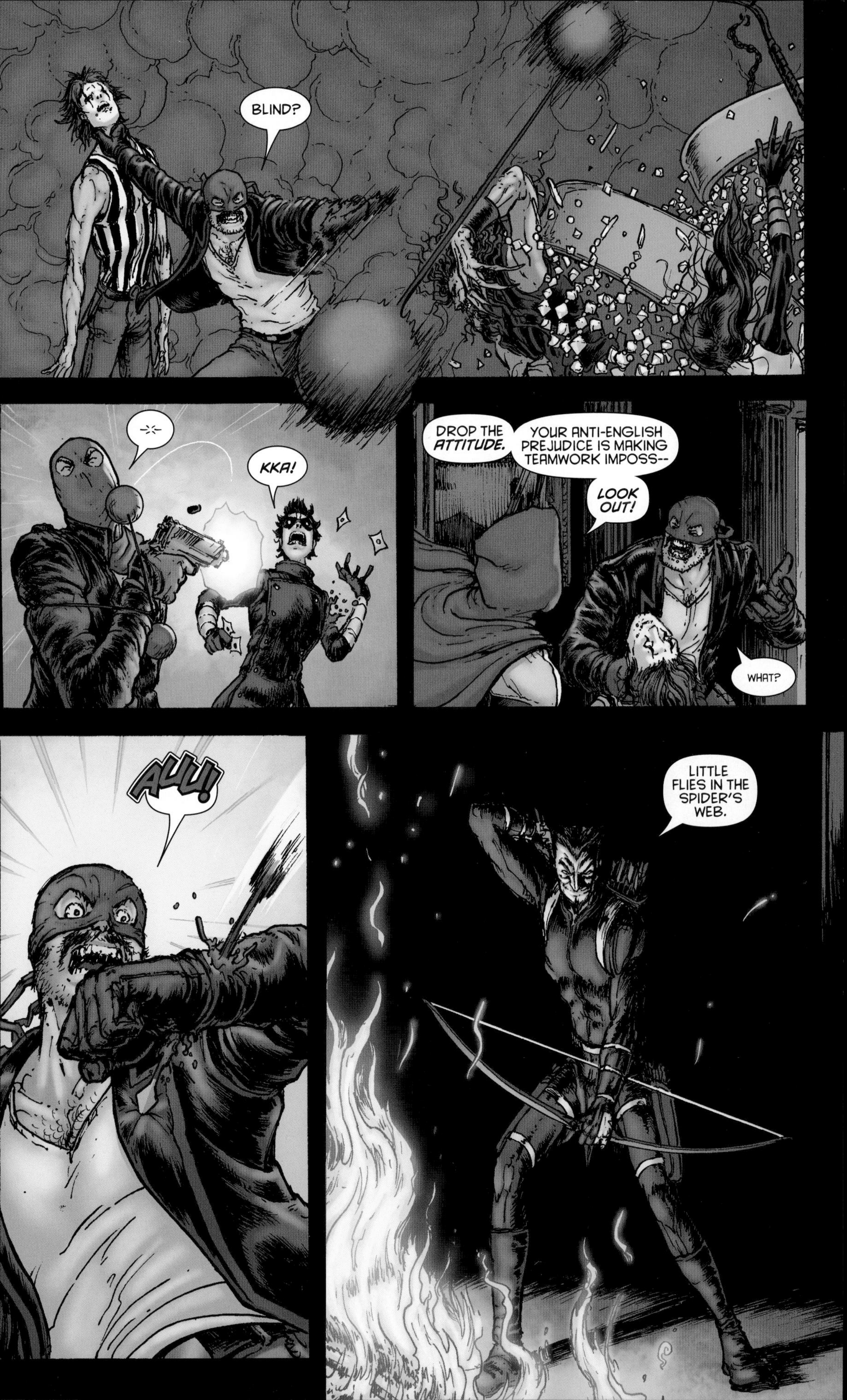
BLIND?
-:-
KKA!
DROP THE *ATTITUDE.*
YOUR ANTI-ENGLISH PREJUDICE IS MAKING TEAMWORK IMPOSS--
LOOK OUT!
WHAT?
AUU!
LITTLE FLIES IN THE SPIDER'S WEB.

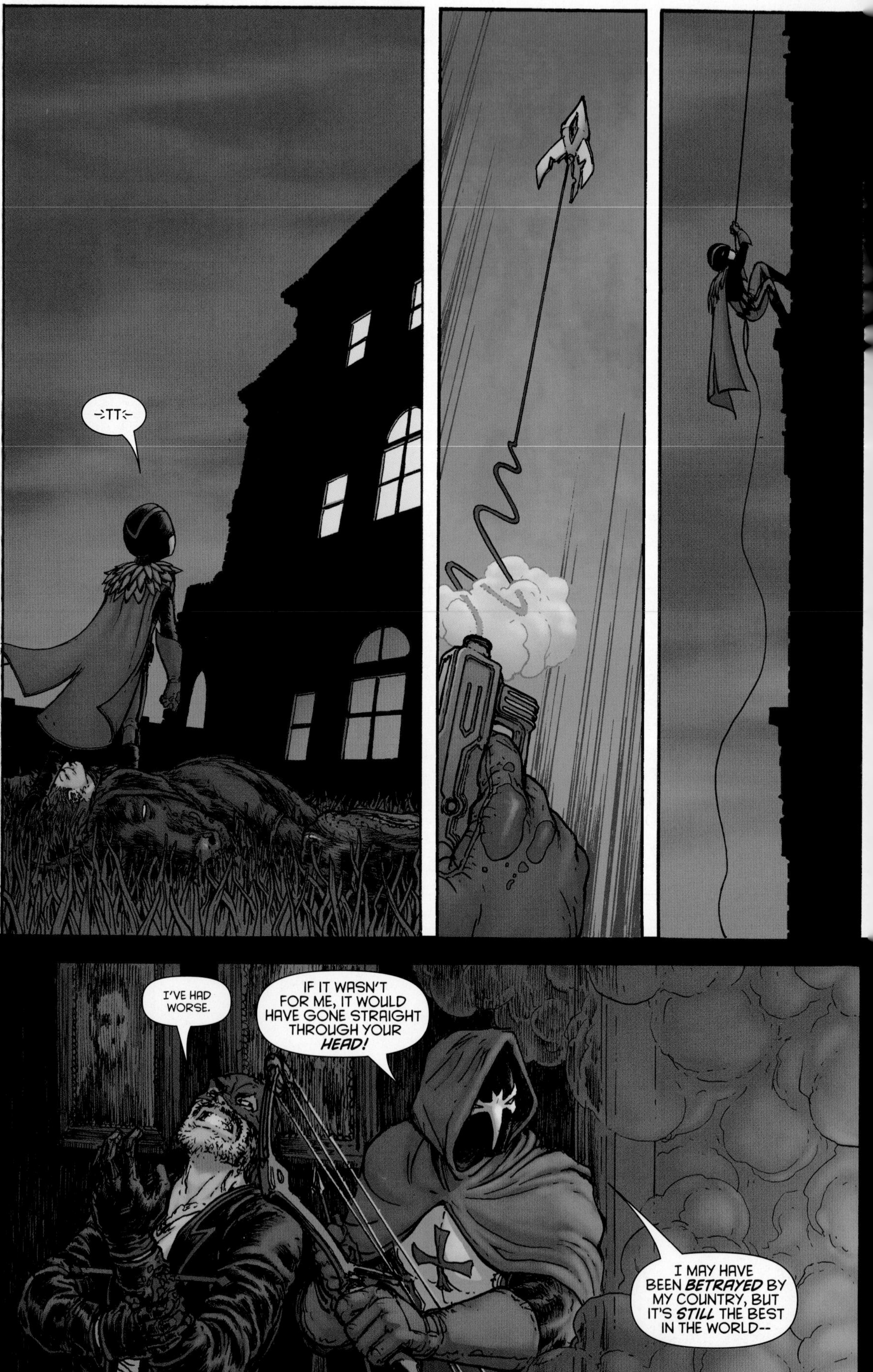
-TT-
I'VE HAD WORSE.
IF IT WASN'T FOR ME, IT WOULD HAVE GONE STRAIGHT THROUGH YOUR HEAD!
I MAY HAVE BEEN BETRAYED BY MY COUNTRY, BUT IT'S STILL THE BEST IN THE WORLD--

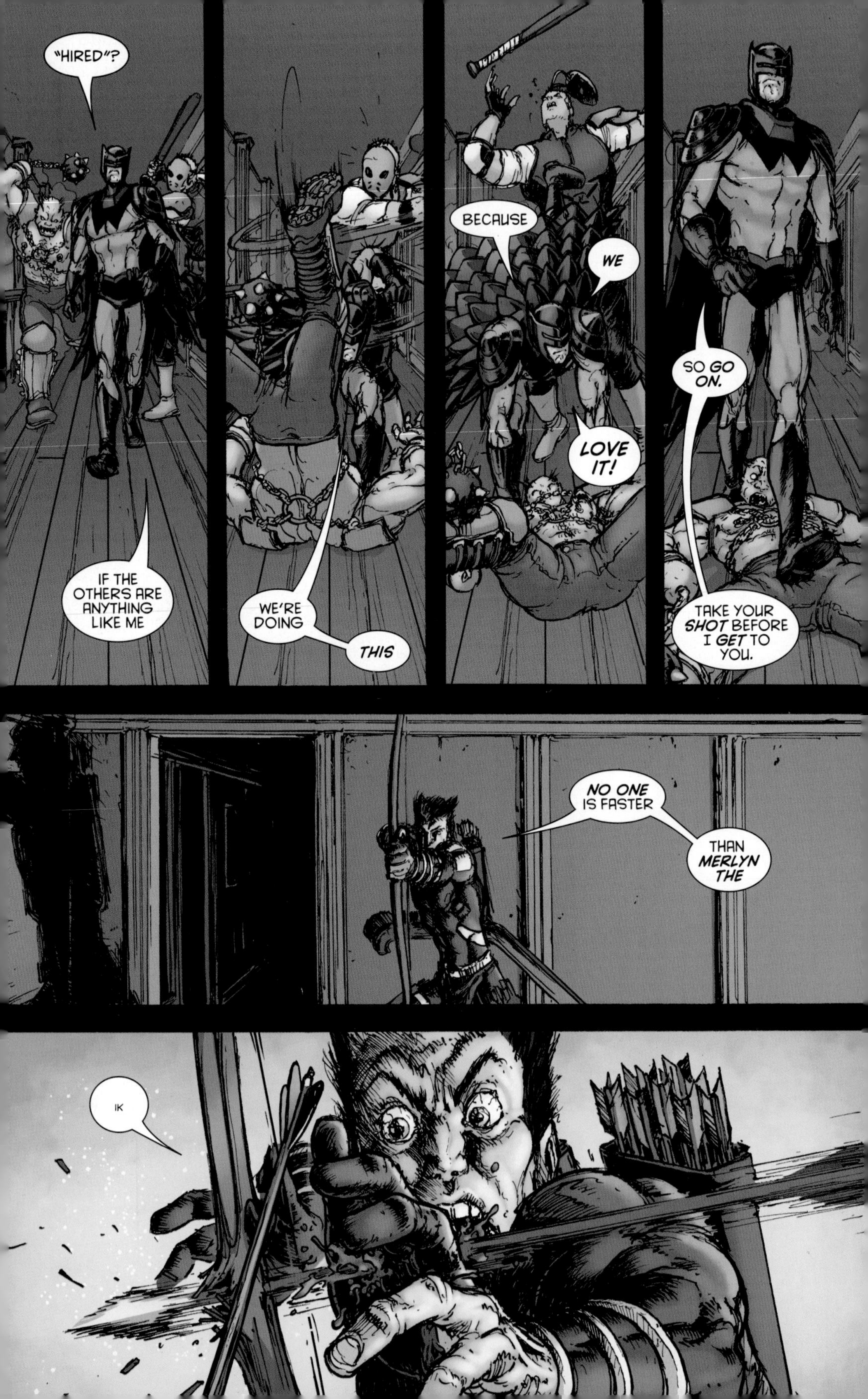
"HIRED"?
IF THE OTHERS ARE ANYTHING LIKE ME
WE'RE DOING
THIS
BECAUSE
WE
LOVE IT!
SO GO ON.
TAKE YOUR SHOT BEFORE I GET TO YOU.
NO ONE IS FASTER
THAN MERLYN THE
IK

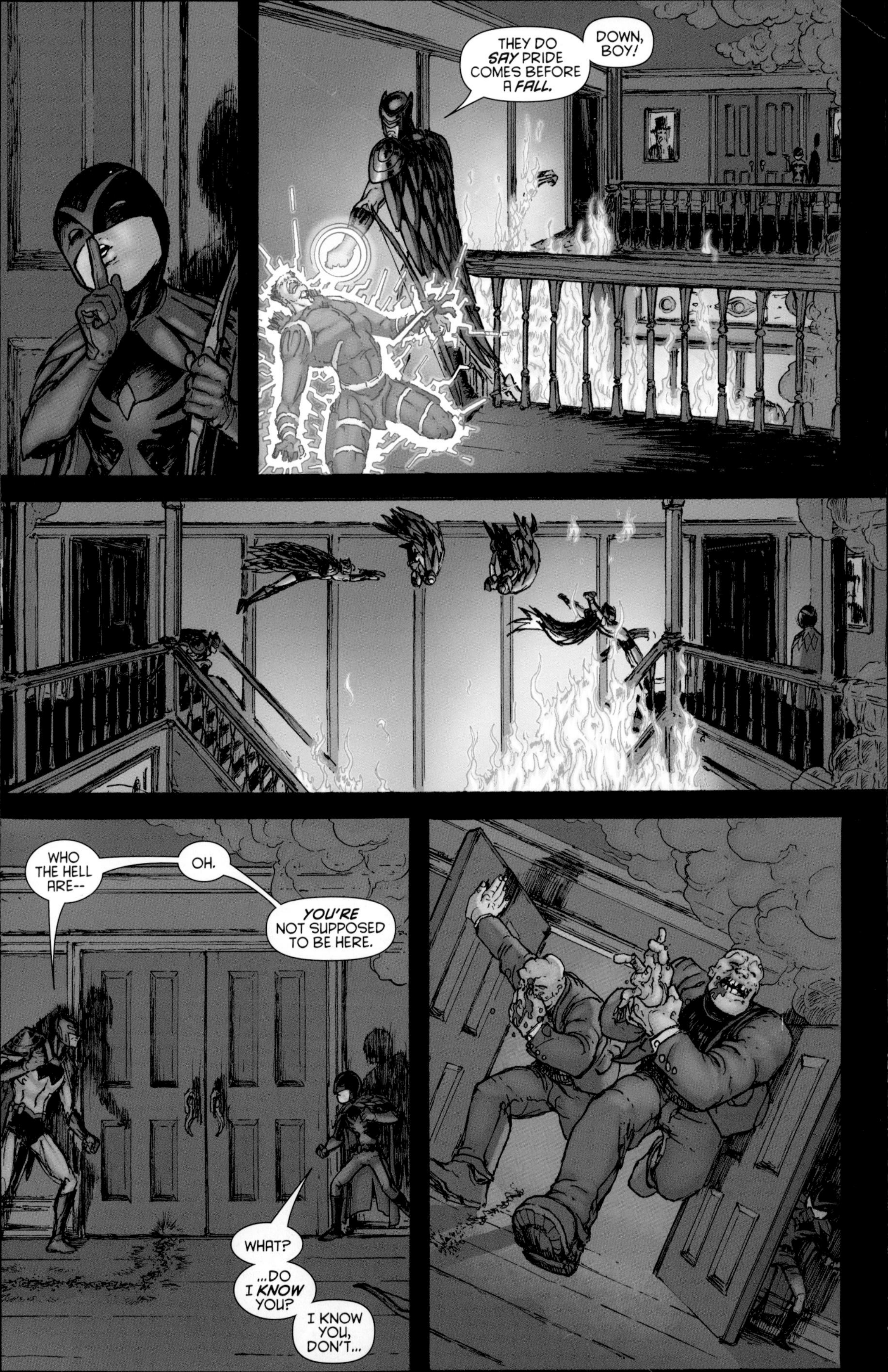
THEY DO SAY PRIDE COMES BEFORE A FALL.
DOWN, BOY!
WHO THE HELL ARE--
OH.
YOU'RE NOT SUPPOSED TO BE HERE.
WHAT?
...DO I KNOW YOU?
I KNOW YOU, DON'T...

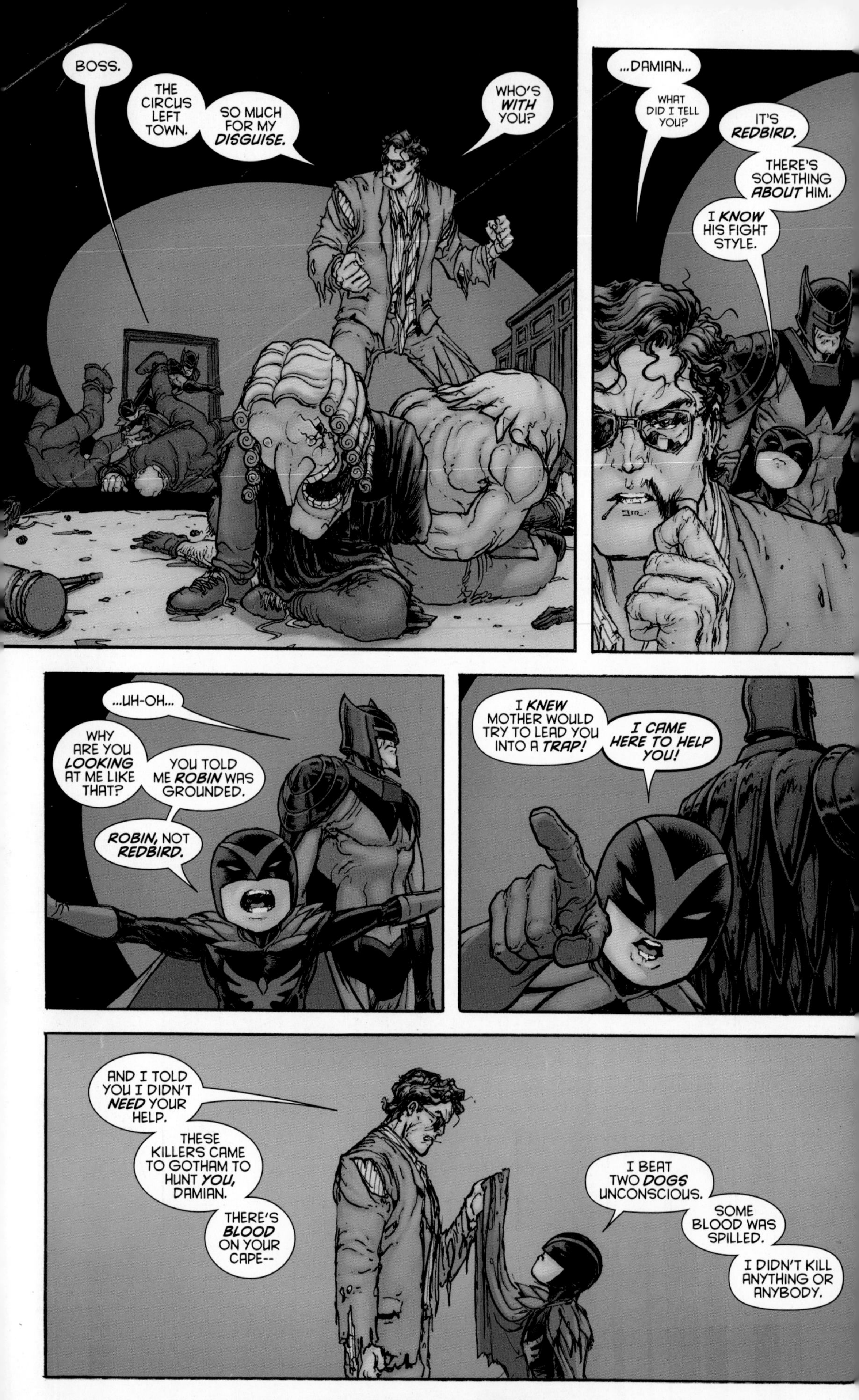
BOSS.
THE CIRCUS LEFT TOWN.
SO MUCH FOR MY DISGUISE.
WHO'S WITH YOU?
...DAMIAN...
WHAT DID I TELL YOU?
IT'S REDBIRD.
THERE'S SOMETHING ABOUT HIM.
I KNOW HIS FIGHT STYLE.
...UH-OH...
WHY ARE YOU LOOKING AT ME LIKE THAT?
YOU TOLD ME ROBIN WAS GROUNDED.
ROBIN, NOT REDBIRD.
I KNEW MOTHER WOULD TRY TO LEAD YOU INTO A TRAP!
I CAME HERE TO HELP YOU!
AND I TOLD YOU I DIDN'T NEED YOUR HELP.
THESE KILLERS CAME TO GOTHAM TO HUNT YOU, DAMIAN.
THERE'S BLOOD ON YOUR CAPE--
I BEAT TWO DOGS UNCONSCIOUS.
SOME BLOOD WAS SPILLED.
I DIDN'T KILL ANYTHING OR ANYBODY.

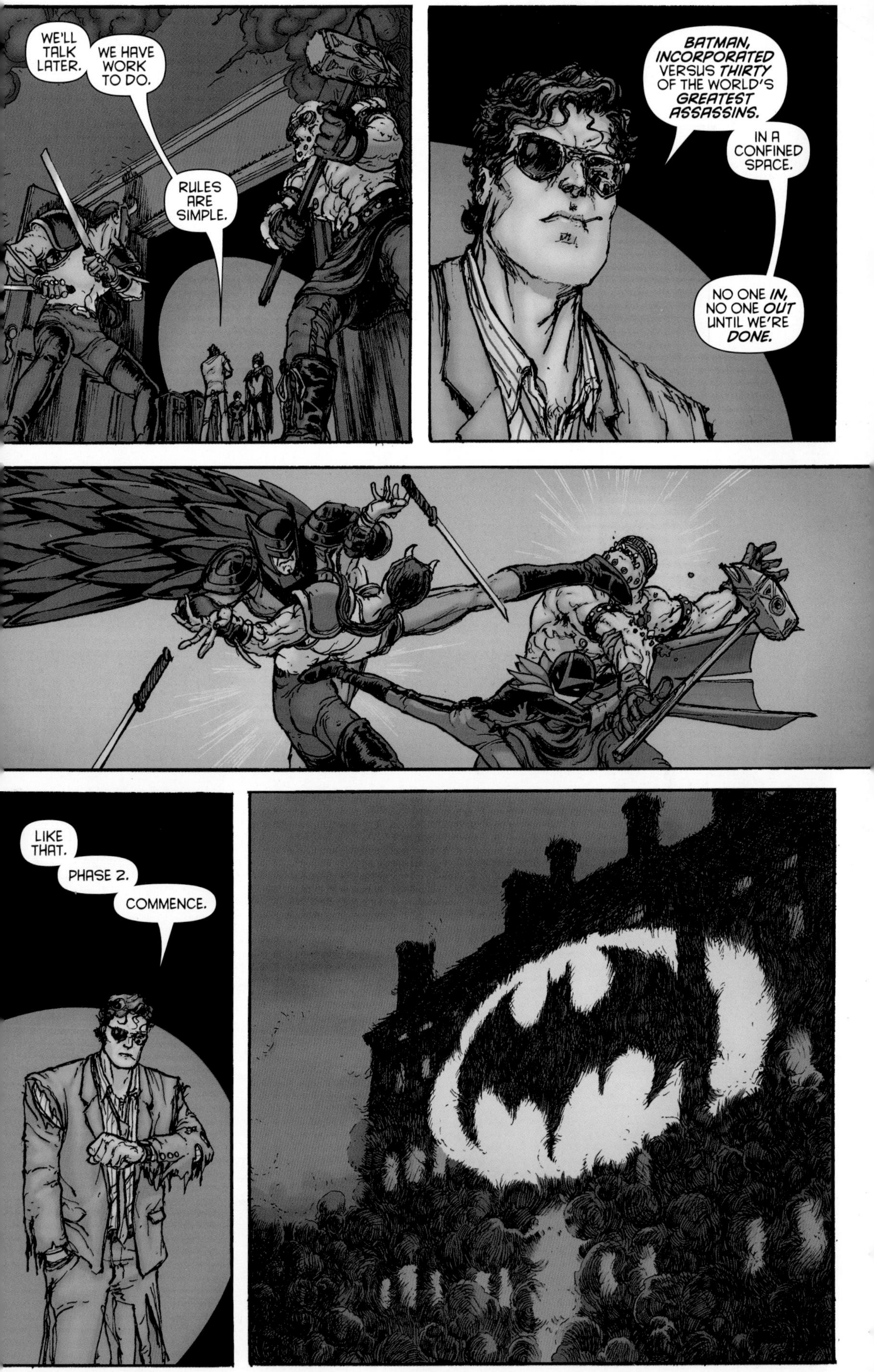
WE'LL TALK LATER.
WE HAVE WORK TO DO.
RULES ARE SIMPLE.
BATMAN, INCORPORATED VERSUS THIRTY OF THE WORLD'S GREATEST ASSASSINS.
IN A CONFINED SPACE.
NO ONE IN, NO ONE OUT UNTIL WE'RE DONE.
LIKE THAT.
PHASE 2.
COMMENCE.

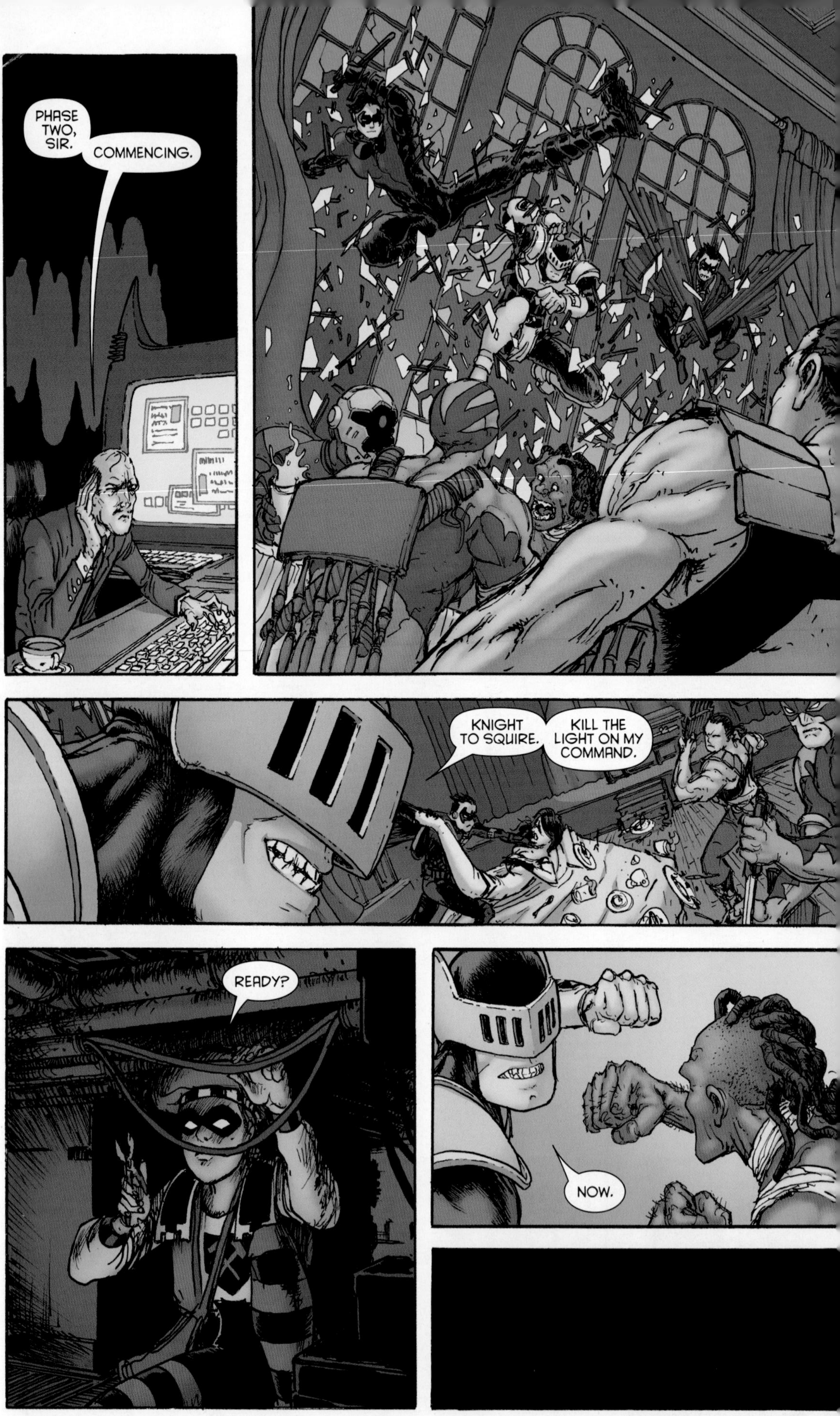
PHASE TWO, SIR.
COMMENCING.
KNIGHT TO SQUIRE.
KILL THE LIGHT ON MY COMMAND.
READY?
NOW.

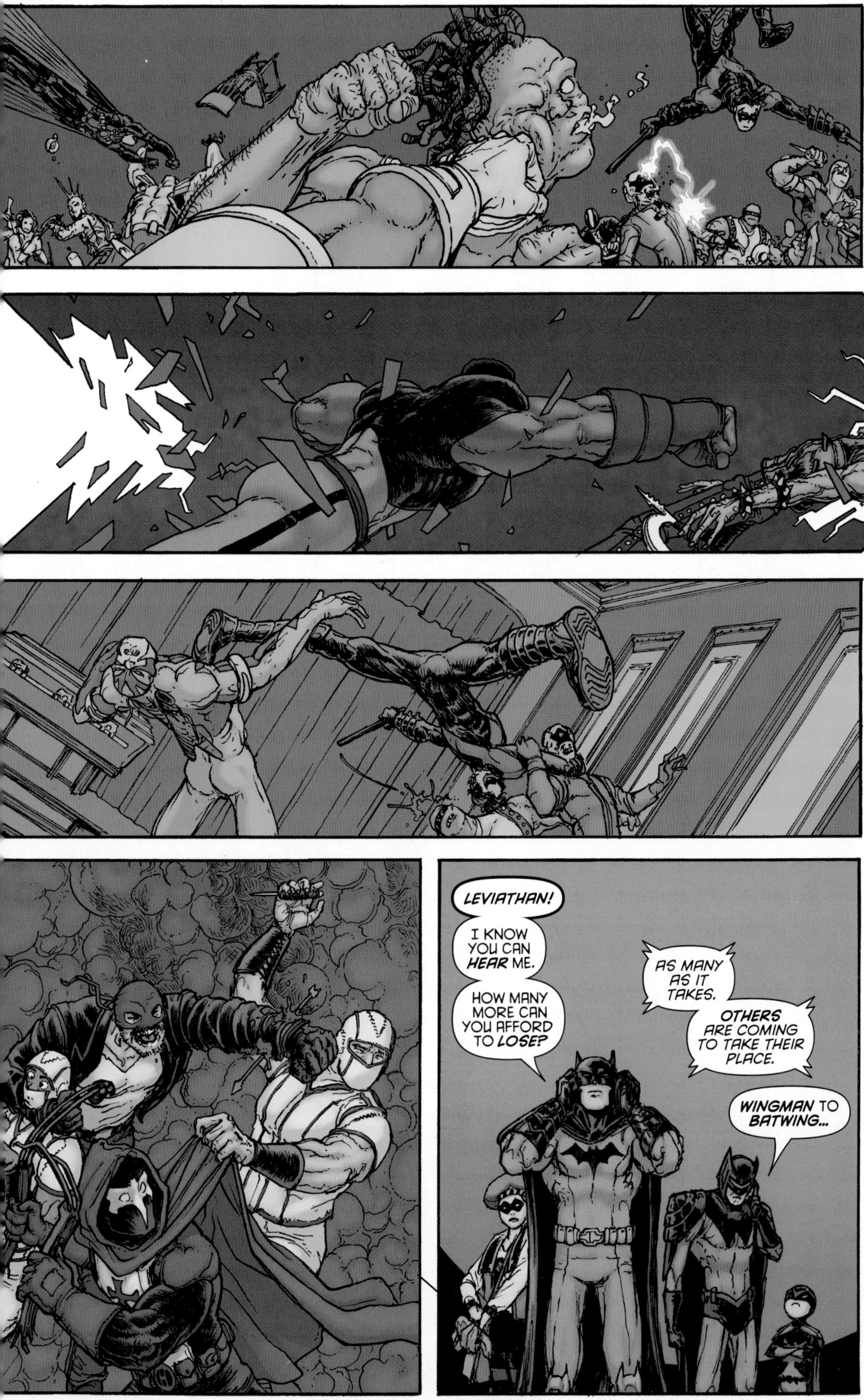
LEVIATHAN!
I KNOW YOU CAN HEAR ME.
HOW MANY MORE CAN YOU AFFORD TO LOSE?
AS MANY AS IT TAKES.
OTHERS ARE COMING TO TAKE THEIR PLACE.
WINGMAN TO BATWING...

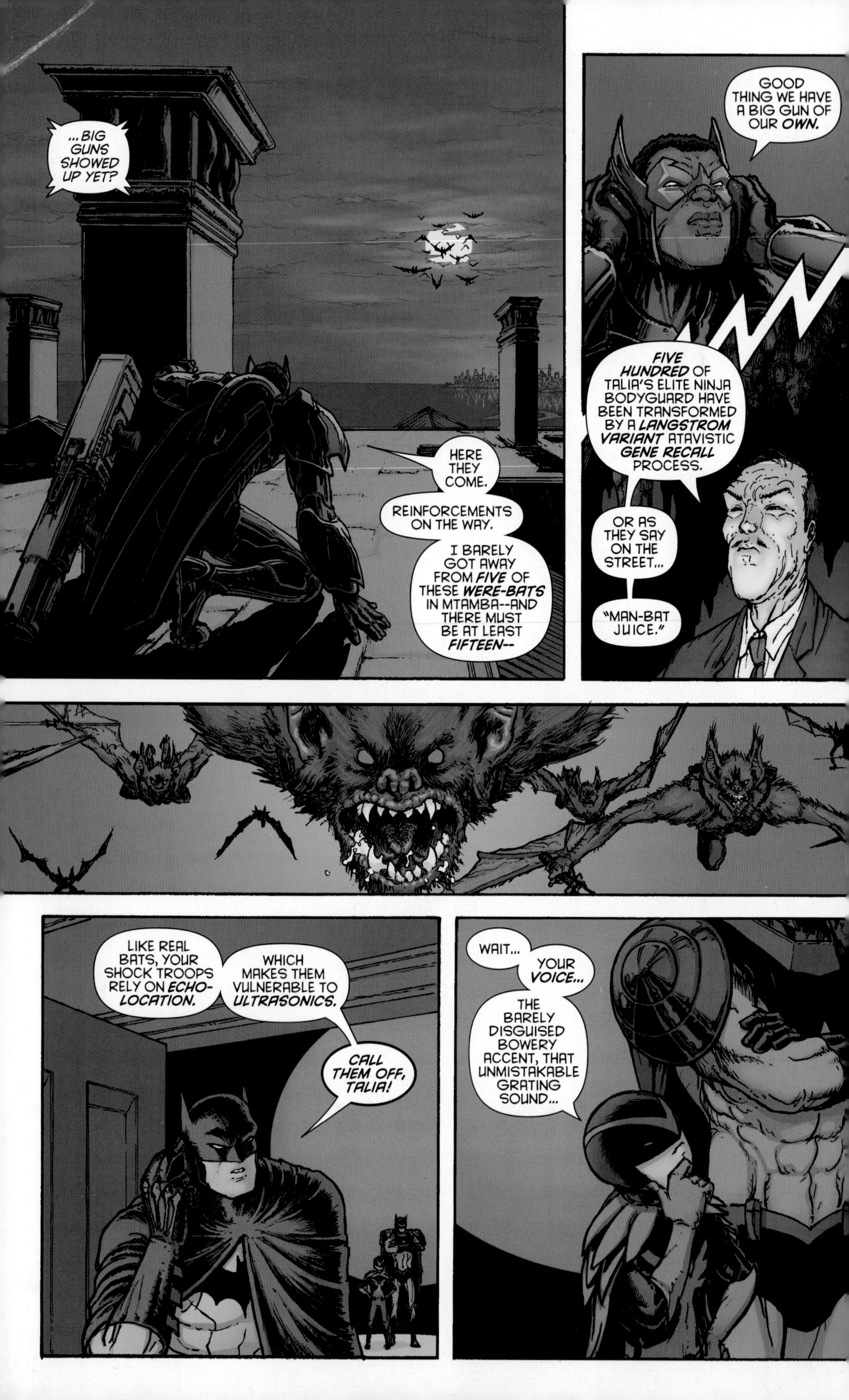
...BIG GUNS SHOWED UP YET?
GOOD THING WE HAVE A BIG GUN OF OUR OWN.
HERE THEY COME.
REINFORCEMENTS ON THE WAY.
I BARELY GOT AWAY FROM FIVE OF THESE WERE-BATS IN MTAMBA--AND THERE MUST BE AT LEAST FIFTEEN--
FIVE HUNDRED OF TALIA'S ELITE NINJA BODYGUARD HAVE BEEN TRANSFORMED BY A LANGSTROM VARIANT ATAVISTIC GENE RECALL PROCESS.
OR AS THEY SAY ON THE STREET...
"MAN-BAT JUICE."
LIKE REAL BATS, YOUR SHOCK TROOPS RELY ON ECHO-LOCATION.
WHICH MAKES THEM VULNERABLE TO ULTRASONICS.
CALL THEM OFF, TALIA!
WAIT...
YOUR VOICE...
THE BARELY DISGUISED BOWERY ACCENT, THAT UNMISTAKABLE GRATING SOUND...

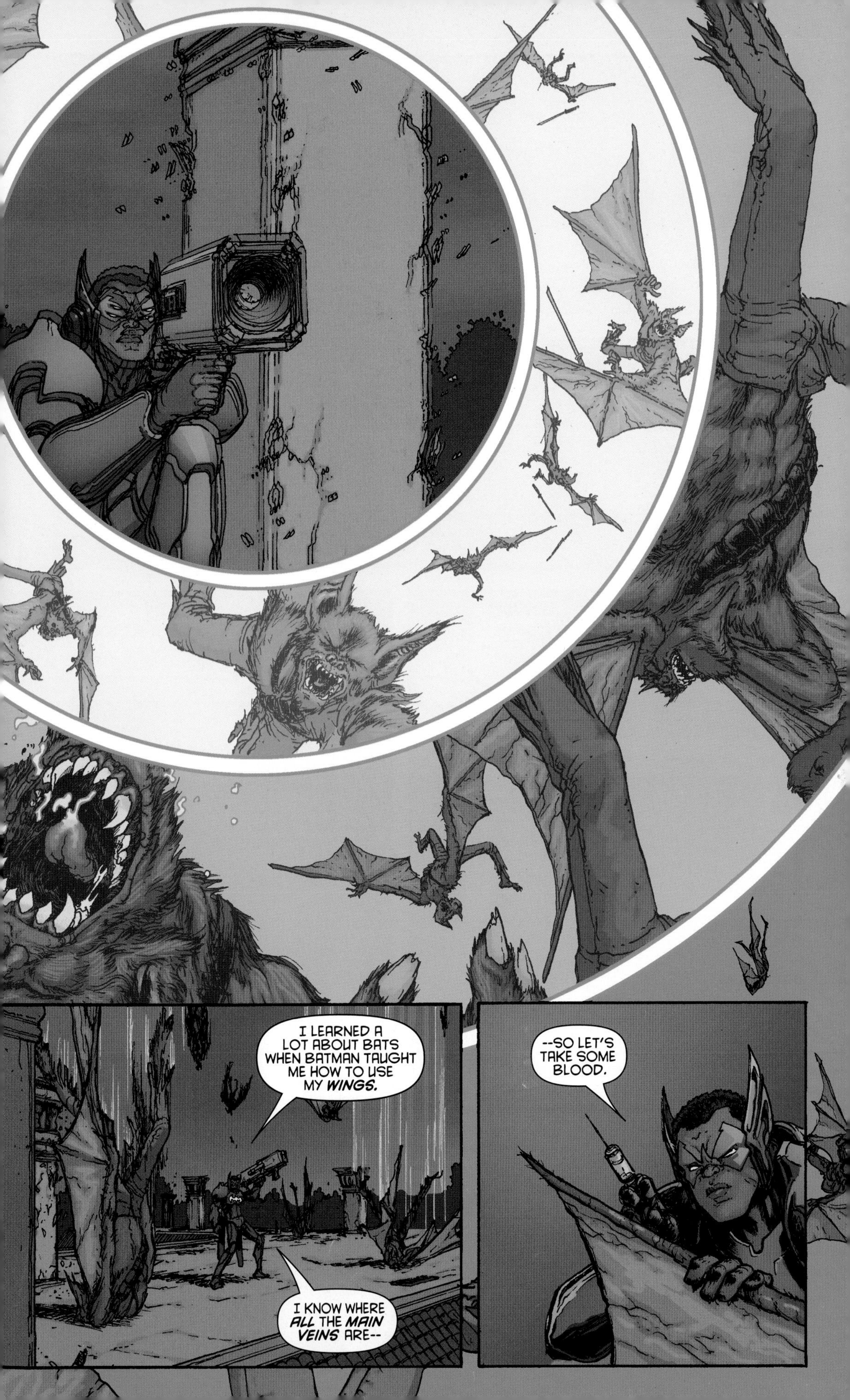

I LEARNED A LOT ABOUT BATS WHEN BATMAN TAUGHT ME HOW TO USE MY *WINGS.*
I KNOW WHERE *ALL* THE *MAIN VEINS* ARE--
--SO LET'S TAKE SOME BLOOD.

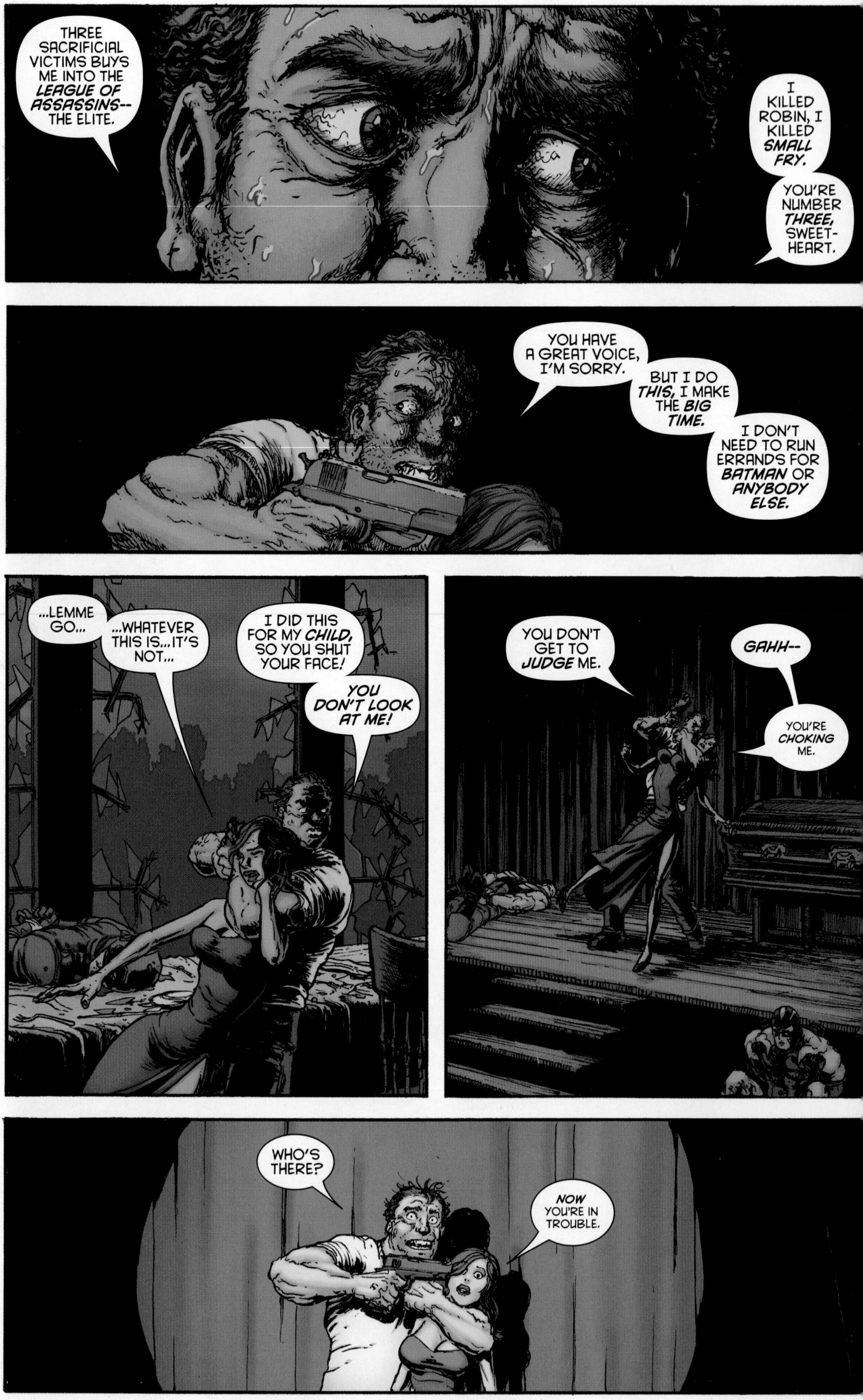
THREE SACRIFICIAL VICTIMS BUYS ME INTO THE LEAGUE OF ASSASSINS-- THE ELITE.
I KILLED ROBIN, I KILLED SMALL FRY.
YOU'RE NUMBER THREE, SWEET-HEART.
YOU HAVE A GREAT VOICE, I'M SORRY.
BUT I DO THIS, I MAKE THE BIG TIME.
I DON'T NEED TO RUN ERRANDS FOR BATMAN OR ANYBODY ELSE.
...LEMME GO...
...WHATEVER THIS IS...IT'S NOT...
I DID THIS FOR MY CHILD, SO YOU SHUT YOUR FACE!
YOU DON'T LOOK AT ME!
YOU DON'T GET TO JUDGE ME.
GAHH--
YOU'RE CHOKING ME.
WHO'S THERE?
NOW YOU'RE IN TROUBLE.

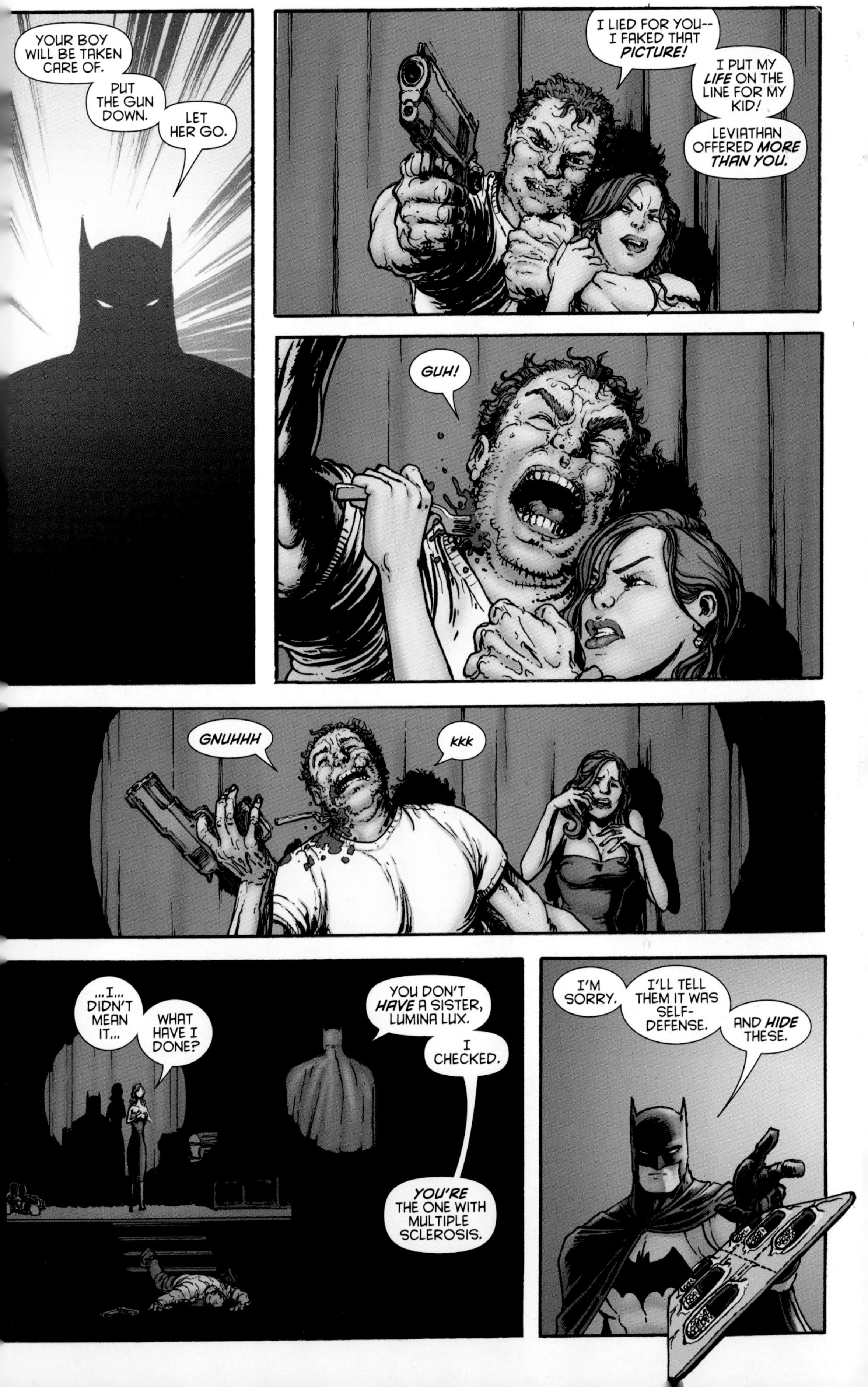
YOUR BOY WILL BE TAKEN CARE OF.
PUT THE GUN DOWN.
LET HER GO.
I LIED FOR YOU-- I FAKED THAT PICTURE!
I PUT MY LIFE ON THE LINE FOR MY KID!
LEVIATHAN OFFERED MORE THAN YOU.
GUH!
GNUHHH
kkk
...I... DIDN'T MEAN IT...
WHAT HAVE I DONE?
YOU DON'T HAVE A SISTER, LUMINA LUX.
I CHECKED.
YOU'RE THE ONE WITH MULTIPLE SCLEROSIS.
I'M SORRY.
I'LL TELL THEM IT WAS SELF-DEFENSE.
AND HIDE THESE.

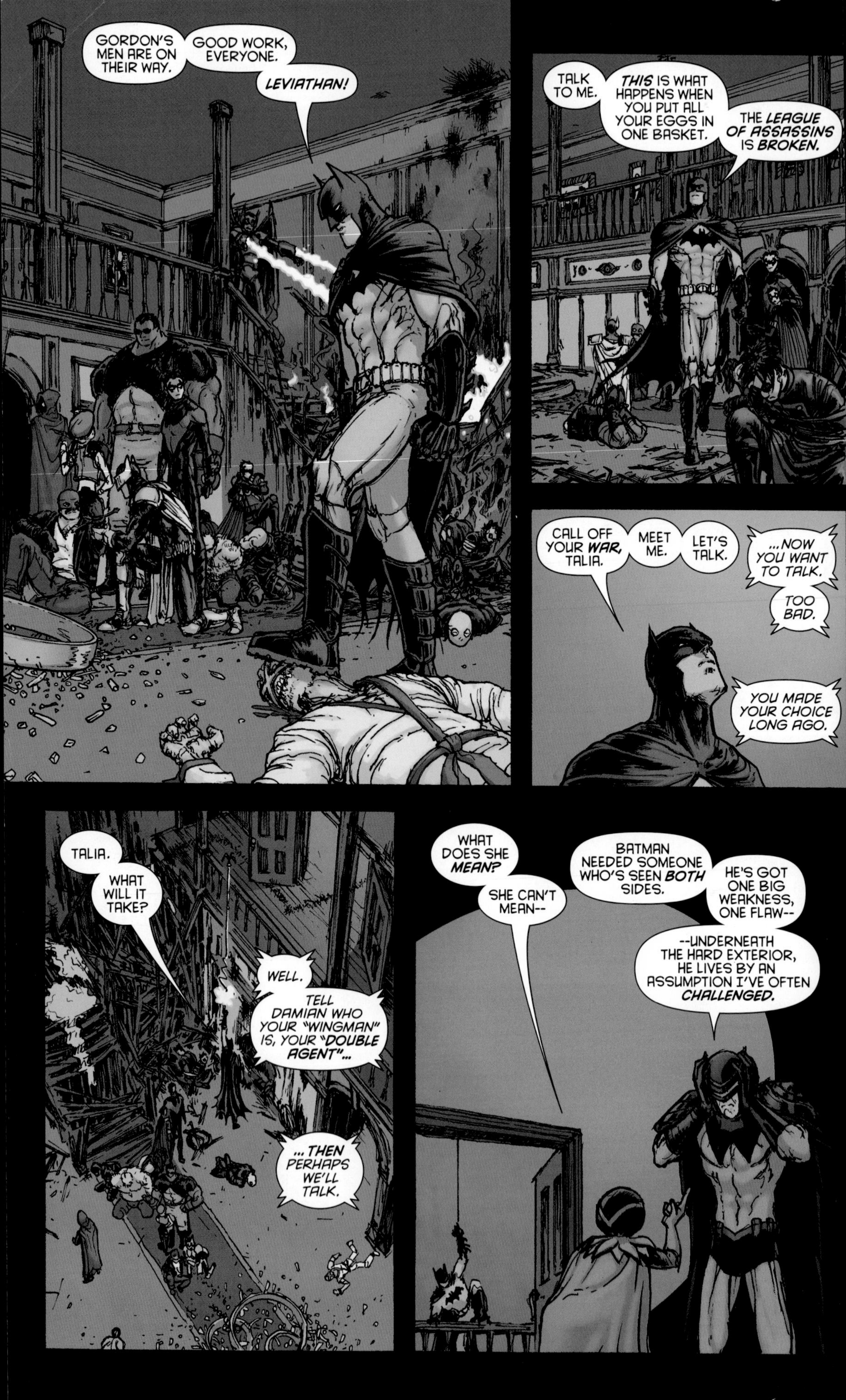
GORDON'S MEN ARE ON THEIR WAY.
GOOD WORK, EVERYONE.
LEVIATHAN!
TALK TO ME.
THIS IS WHAT HAPPENS WHEN YOU PUT ALL YOUR EGGS IN ONE BASKET.
THE LEAGUE OF ASSASSINS IS BROKEN.
CALL OFF YOUR WAR, TALIA.
MEET ME.
LET'S TALK.
...NOW YOU WANT TO TALK.
TOO BAD.
YOU MADE YOUR CHOICE LONG AGO.
TALIA.
WHAT WILL IT TAKE?
WELL.
TELL DAMIAN WHO YOUR "WINGMAN" IS, YOUR "DOUBLE AGENT"...
...THEN PERHAPS WE'LL TALK.
WHAT DOES SHE MEAN?
SHE CAN'T MEAN--
BATMAN NEEDED SOMEONE WHO'S SEEN BOTH SIDES.
HE'S GOT ONE BIG WEAKNESS, ONE FLAW--
--UNDERNEATH THE HARD EXTERIOR, HE LIVES BY AN ASSUMPTION I'VE OFTEN CHALLENGED.

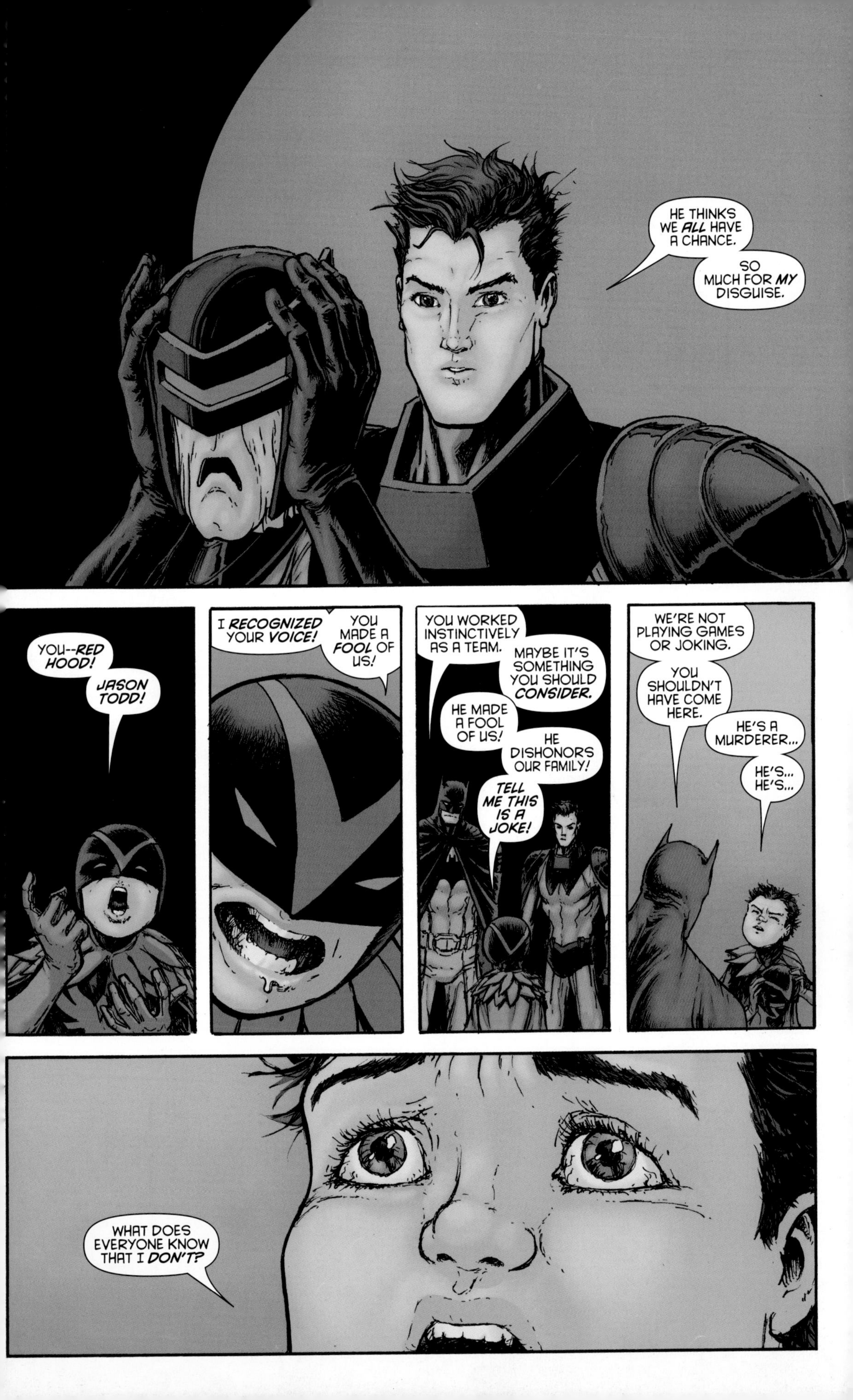
HE THINKS WE *ALL* HAVE A CHANCE.
SO MUCH FOR *MY* DISGUISE.
YOU--*RED HOOD!*
JASON TODD!
I *RECOGNIZED* YOUR *VOICE!*
YOU MADE A *FOOL* OF US!
YOU WORKED INSTINCTIVELY AS A TEAM.
MAYBE IT'S SOMETHING YOU SHOULD *CONSIDER.*
HE MADE A FOOL OF US!
HE DISHONORS OUR FAMILY!
TELL ME THIS IS A JOKE!
WE'RE NOT PLAYING GAMES OR JOKING.
YOU SHOULDN'T HAVE COME HERE.
HE'S A MURDERER...
HE'S... HE'S...
WHAT DOES EVERYONE KNOW THAT I *DON'T?*

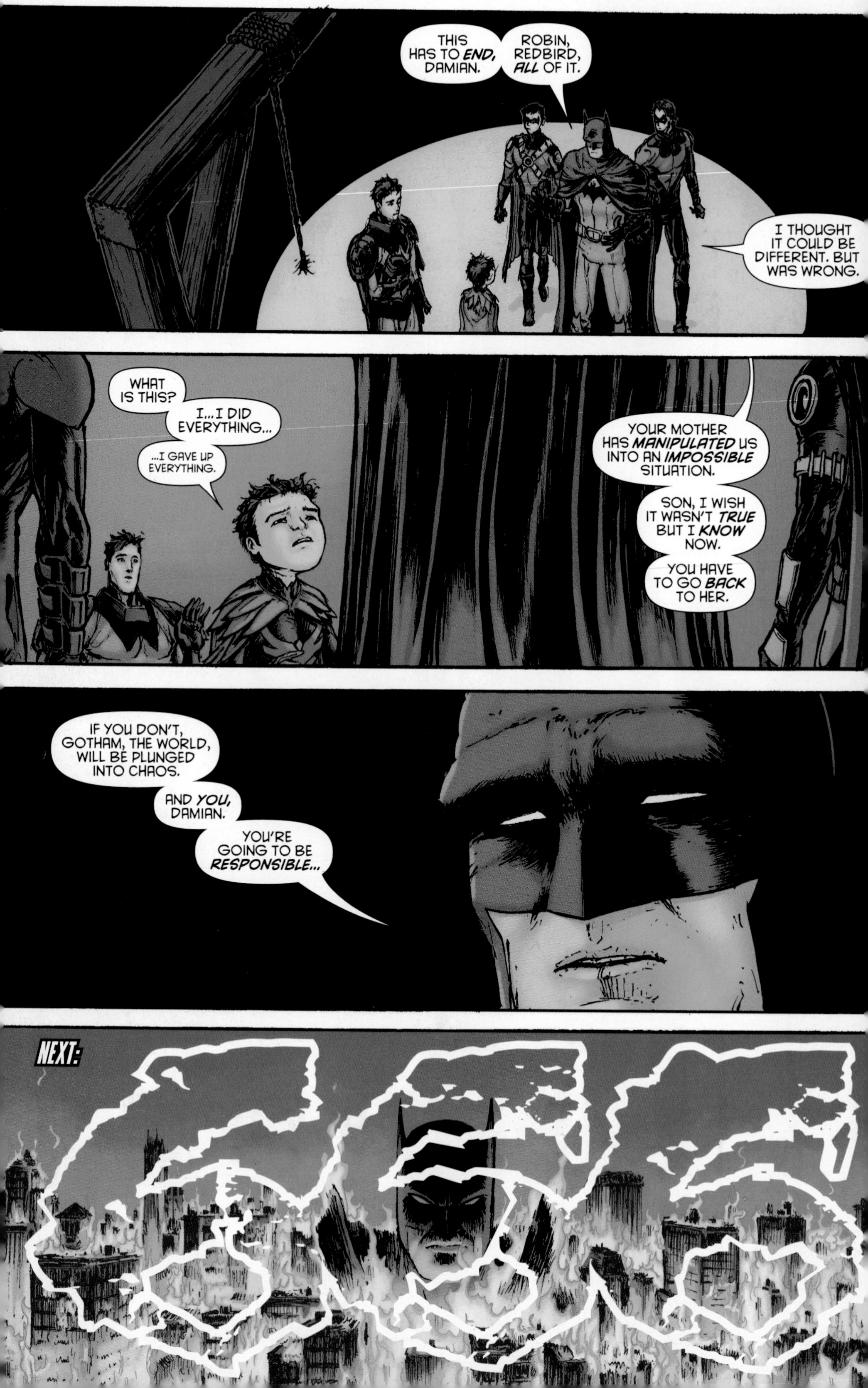
THIS HAS TO END, DAMIAN.
ROBIN, REDBIRD, ALL OF IT.
I THOUGHT IT COULD BE DIFFERENT. BUT WAS WRONG.
WHAT IS THIS?
I...I DID EVERYTHING...
...I GAVE UP EVERYTHING.
YOUR MOTHER HAS MANIPULATED US INTO AN IMPOSSIBLE SITUATION.
SON, I WISH IT WASN'T TRUE BUT I KNOW NOW.
YOU HAVE TO GO BACK TO HER.
IF YOU DON'T, GOTHAM, THE WORLD, WILL BE PLUNGED INTO CHAOS.
AND YOU, DAMIAN.
YOU'RE GOING TO BE RESPONSIBLE...
NEXT:

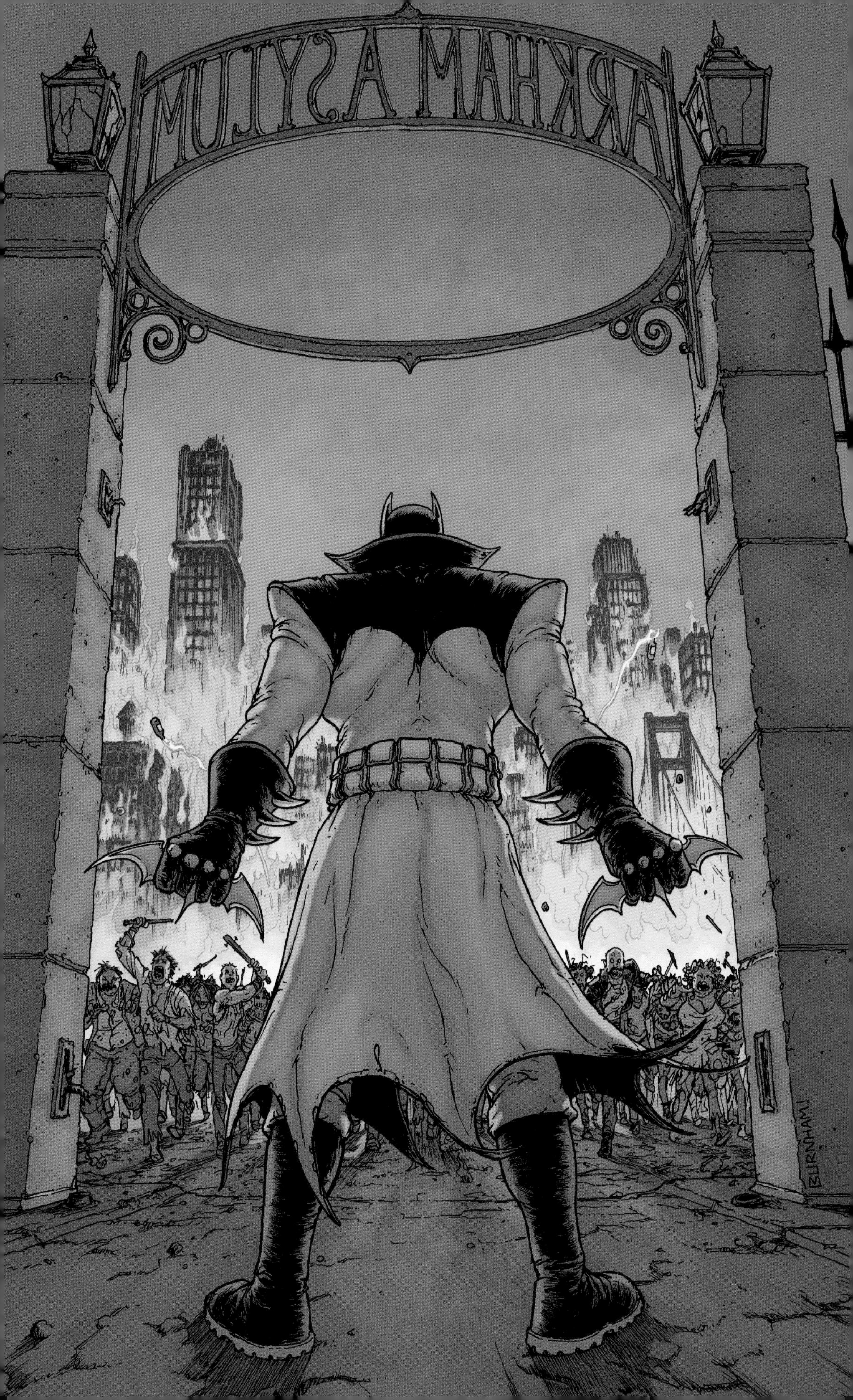
ARKHAM ASYLUM
BURNHAM!

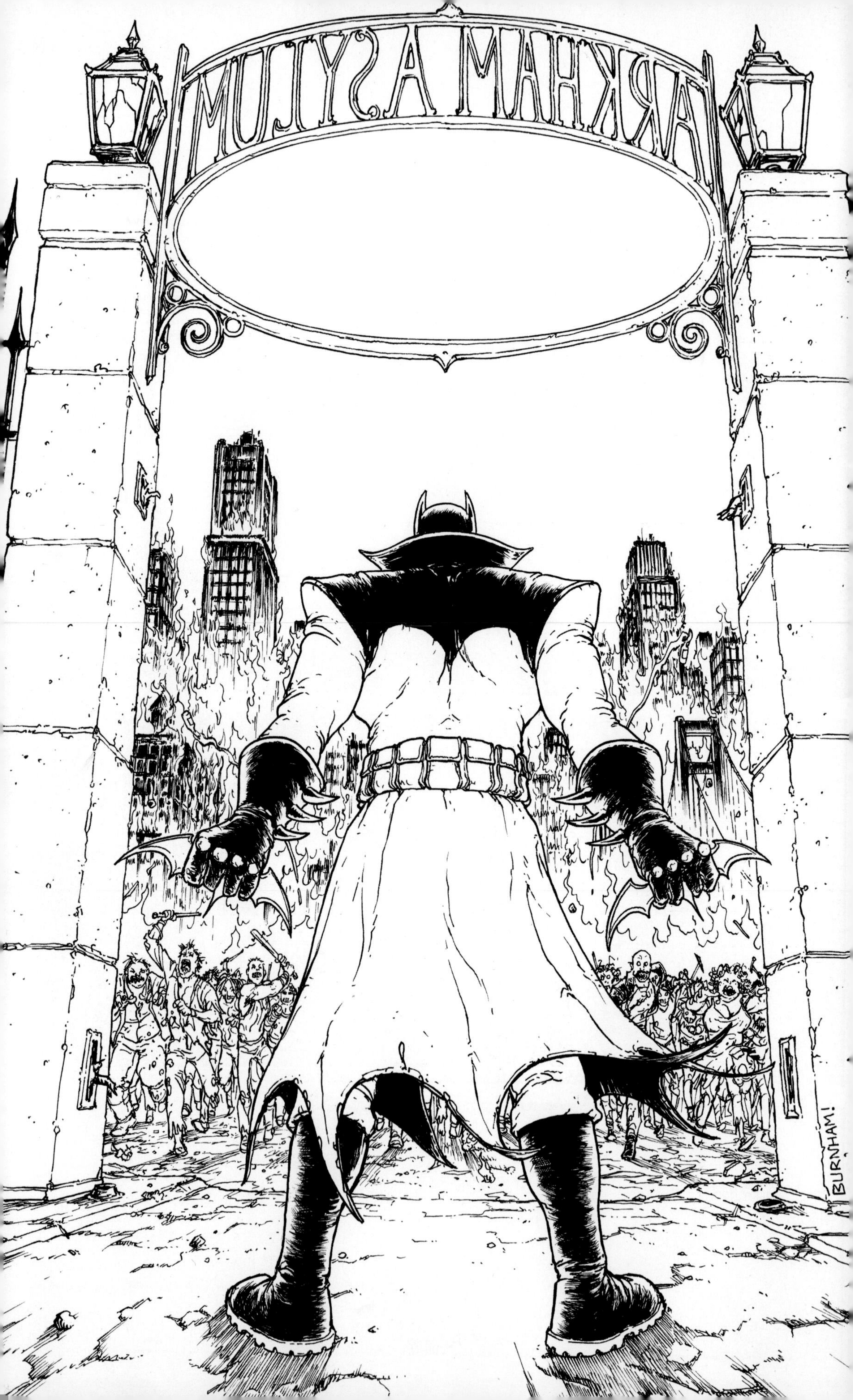
ARKHAM ASYLUM
BURNHAM!

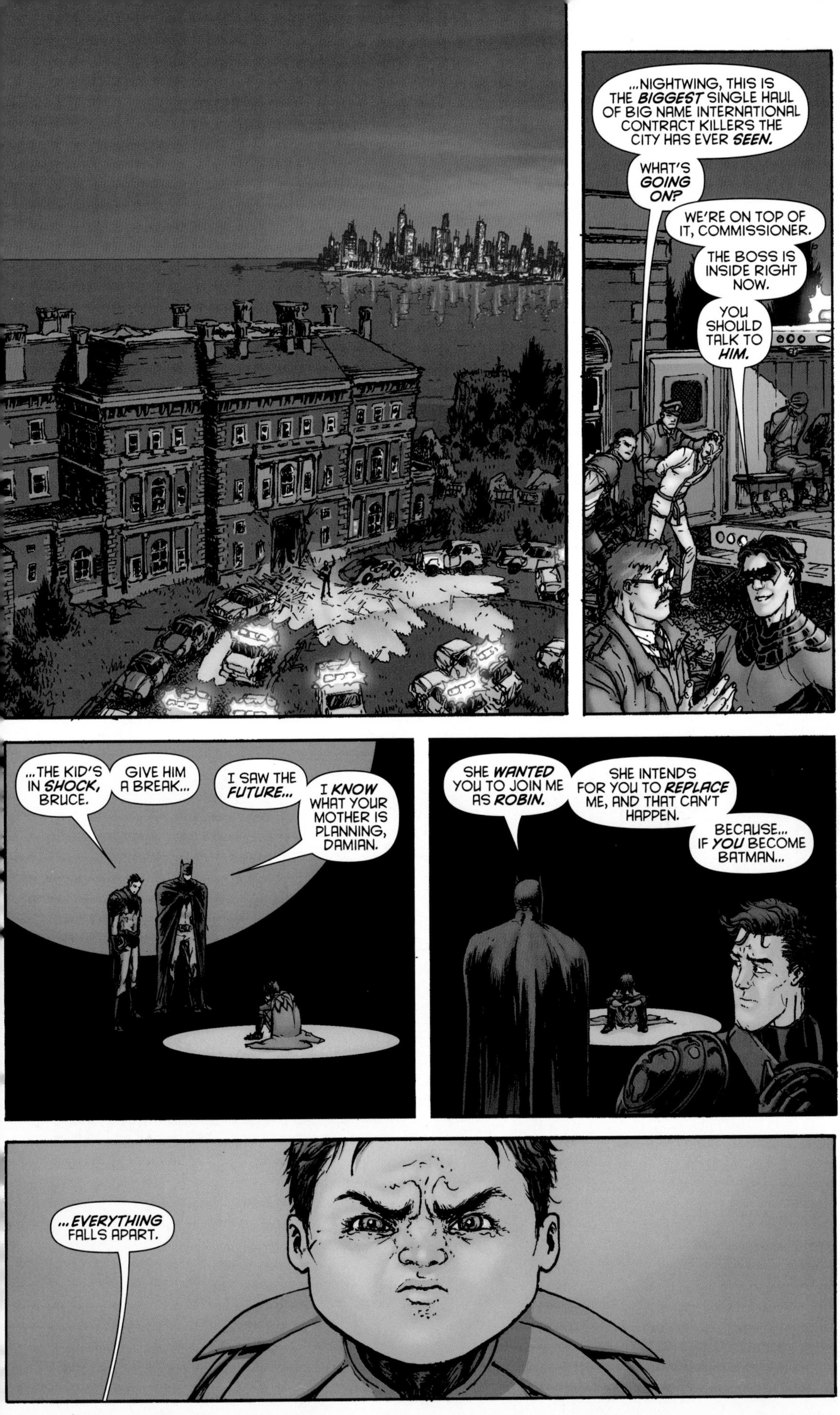
...NIGHTWING, THIS IS THE BIGGEST SINGLE HAUL OF BIG NAME INTERNATIONAL CONTRACT KILLERS THE CITY HAS EVER SEEN.
WHAT'S GOING ON?
WE'RE ON TOP OF IT, COMMISSIONER.
THE BOSS IS INSIDE RIGHT NOW.
YOU SHOULD TALK TO HIM.
...THE KID'S IN SHOCK, BRUCE.
GIVE HIM A BREAK...
I SAW THE FUTURE...
I KNOW WHAT YOUR MOTHER IS PLANNING, DAMIAN.
SHE WANTED YOU TO JOIN ME AS ROBIN.
SHE INTENDS FOR YOU TO REPLACE ME, AND THAT CAN'T HAPPEN.
BECAUSE... IF YOU BECOME BATMAN...
...EVERYTHING FALLS APART.

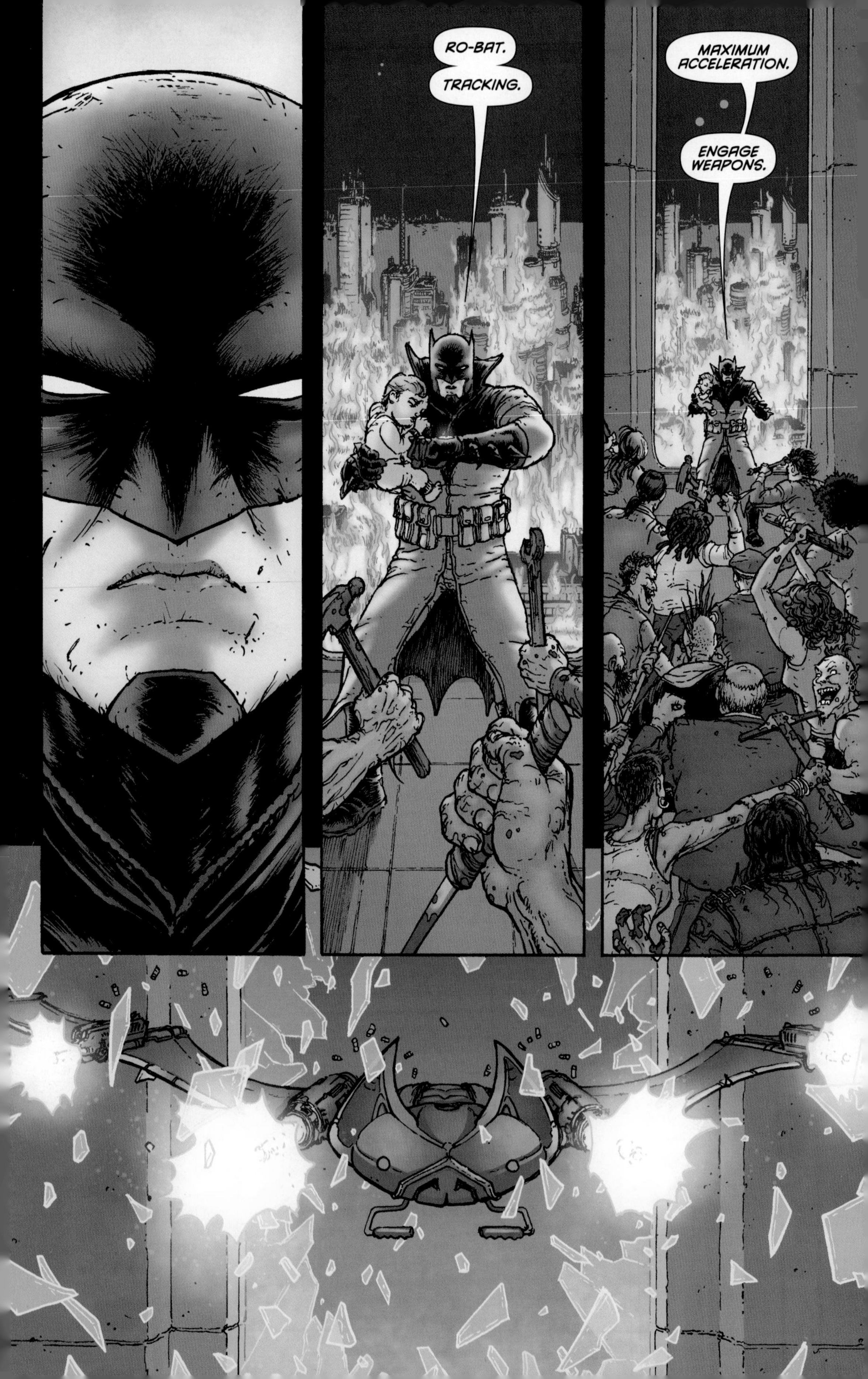
RO-BAT.
TRACKING.
MAXIMUM ACCELERATION.
ENGAGE WEAPONS.

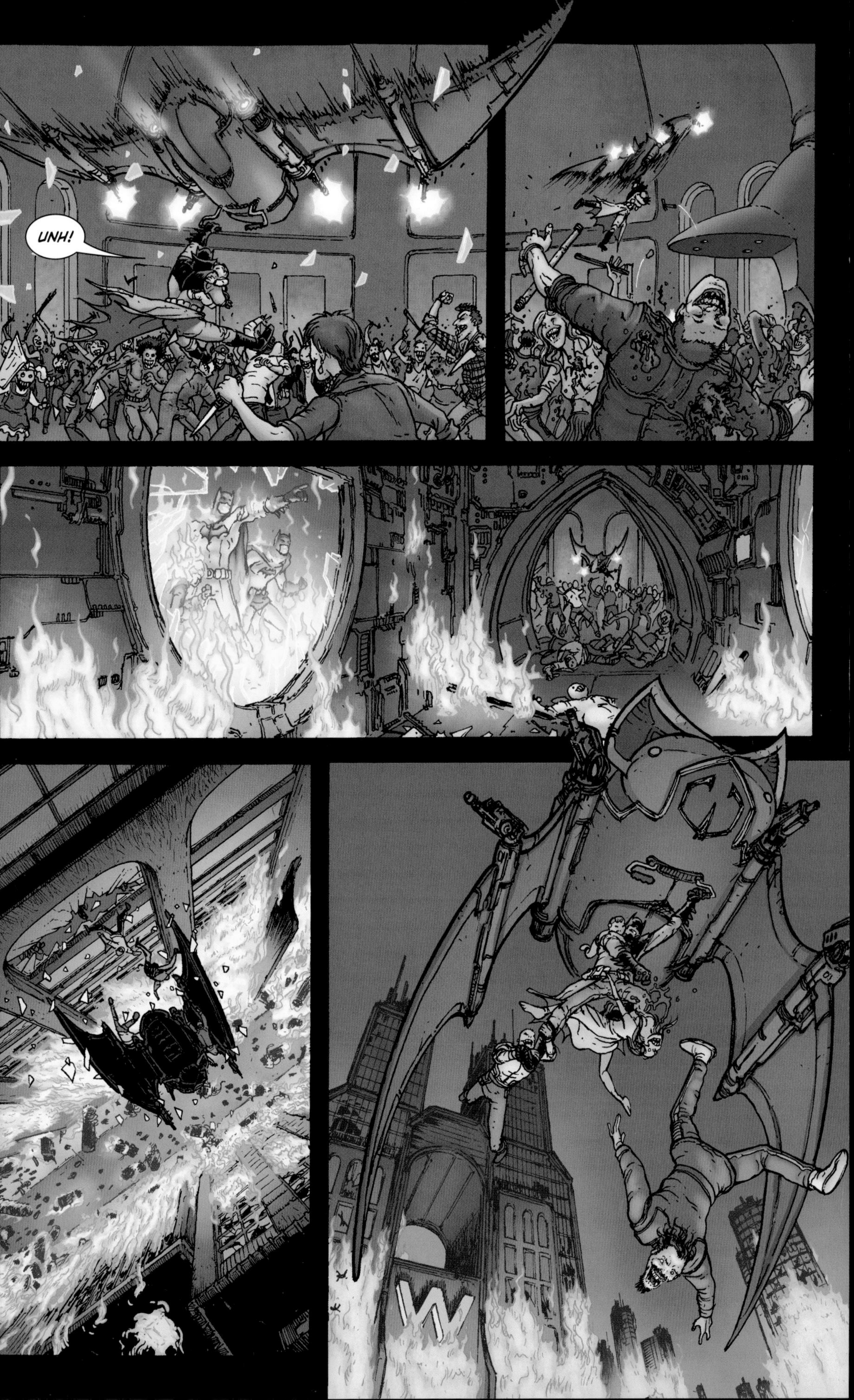
UNH!

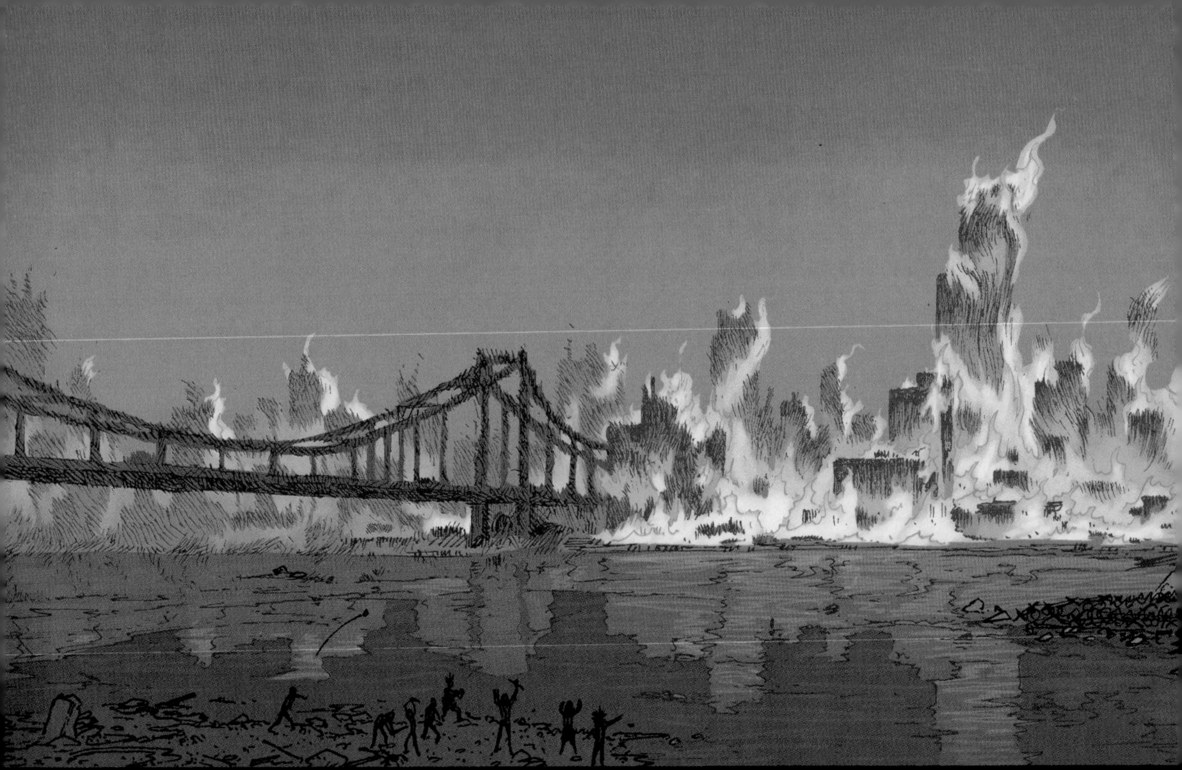

ASYLUM

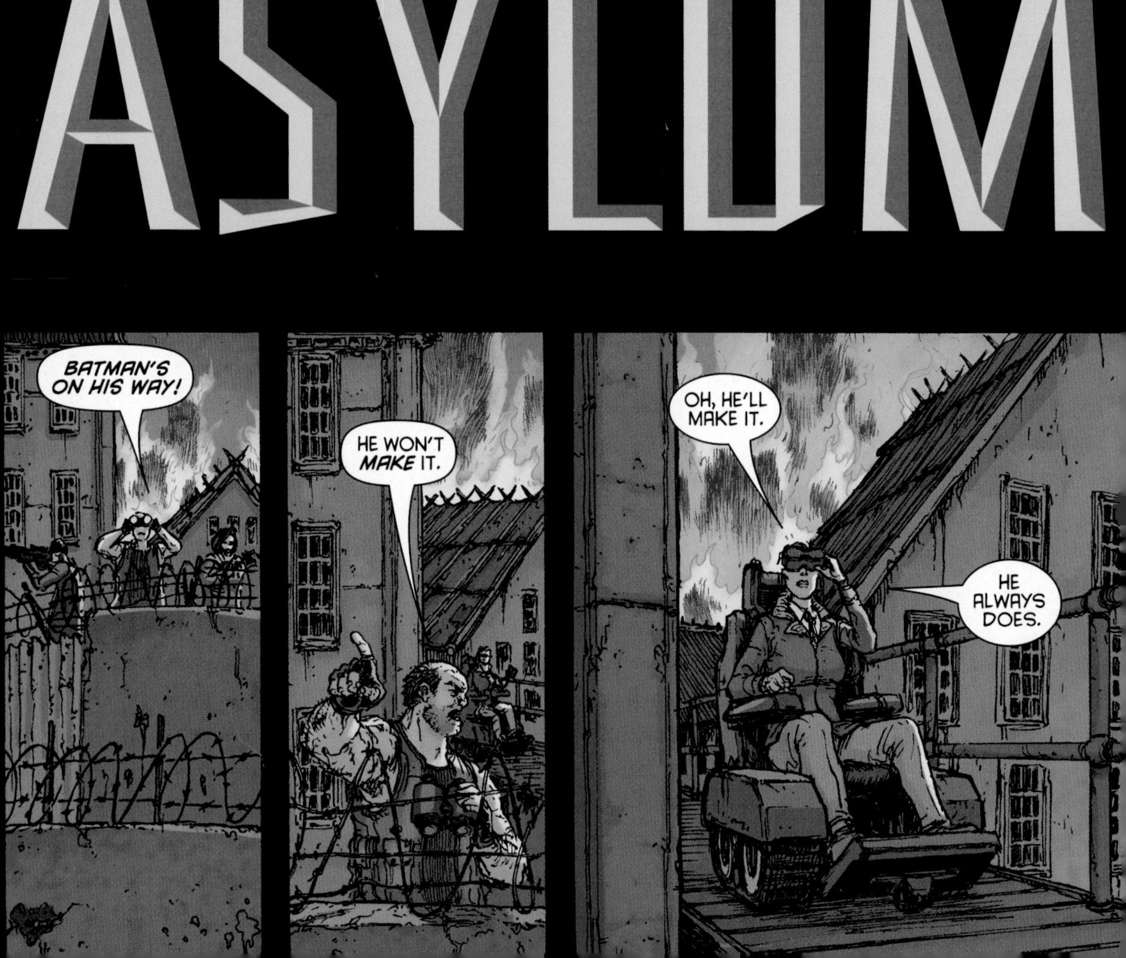
BATMAN'S ON HIS WAY!
HE WON'T *MAKE* IT.
OH, HE'LL MAKE IT.
HE ALWAYS DOES.

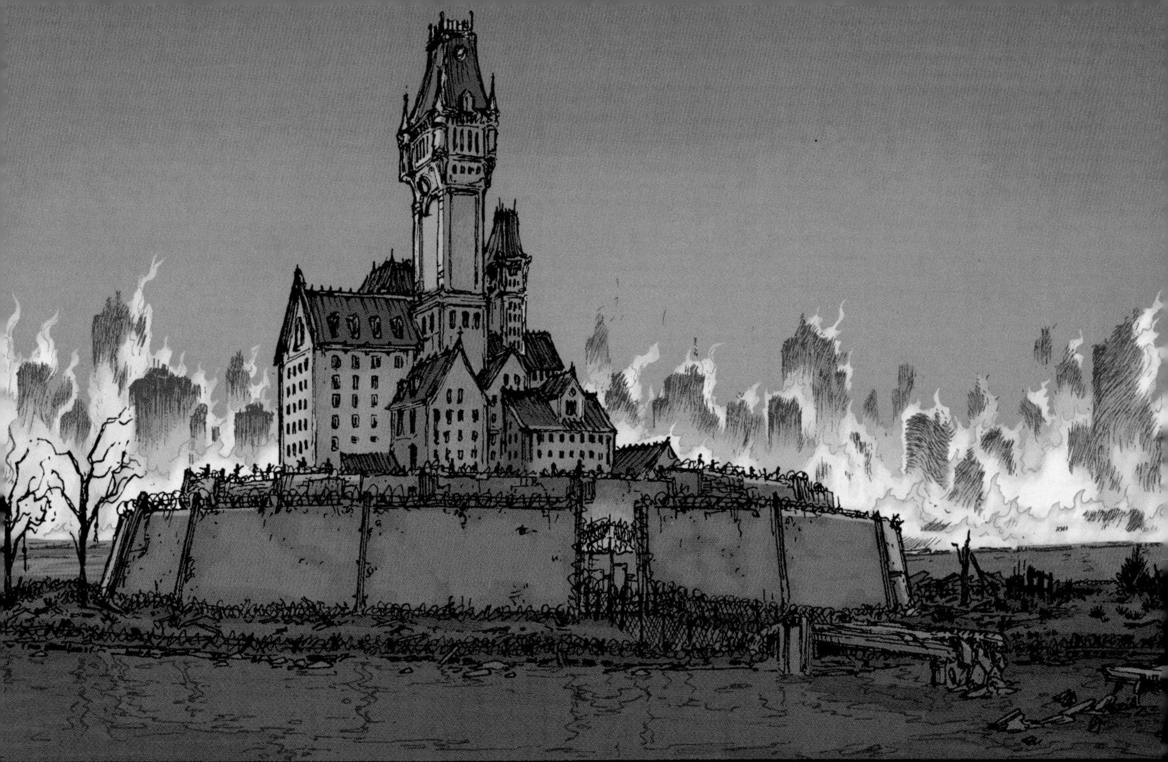

WRITER GRANT MORRISON ARTIST CHRIS BURNHAM
COLOR NATHAN FAIRBAIRN LETTERING DAVE SHARPE
COVER BY BURNHAM WITH FAIRBAIRN

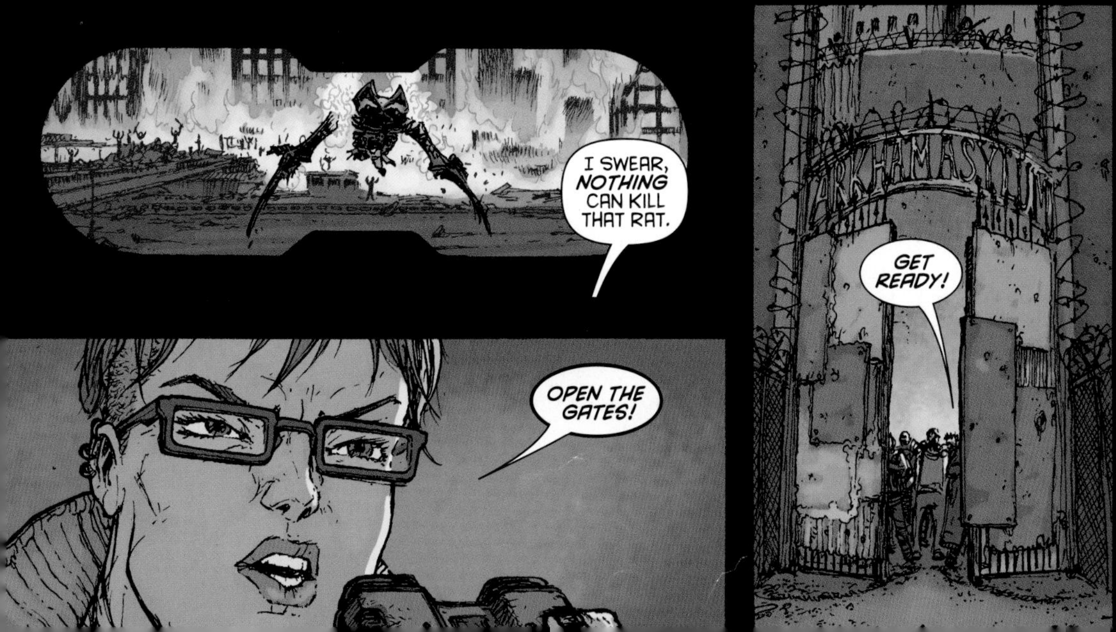
I SWEAR, *NOTHING* CAN KILL THAT RAT.
OPEN THE GATES!
ARKHAM ASYLUM
GET READY!

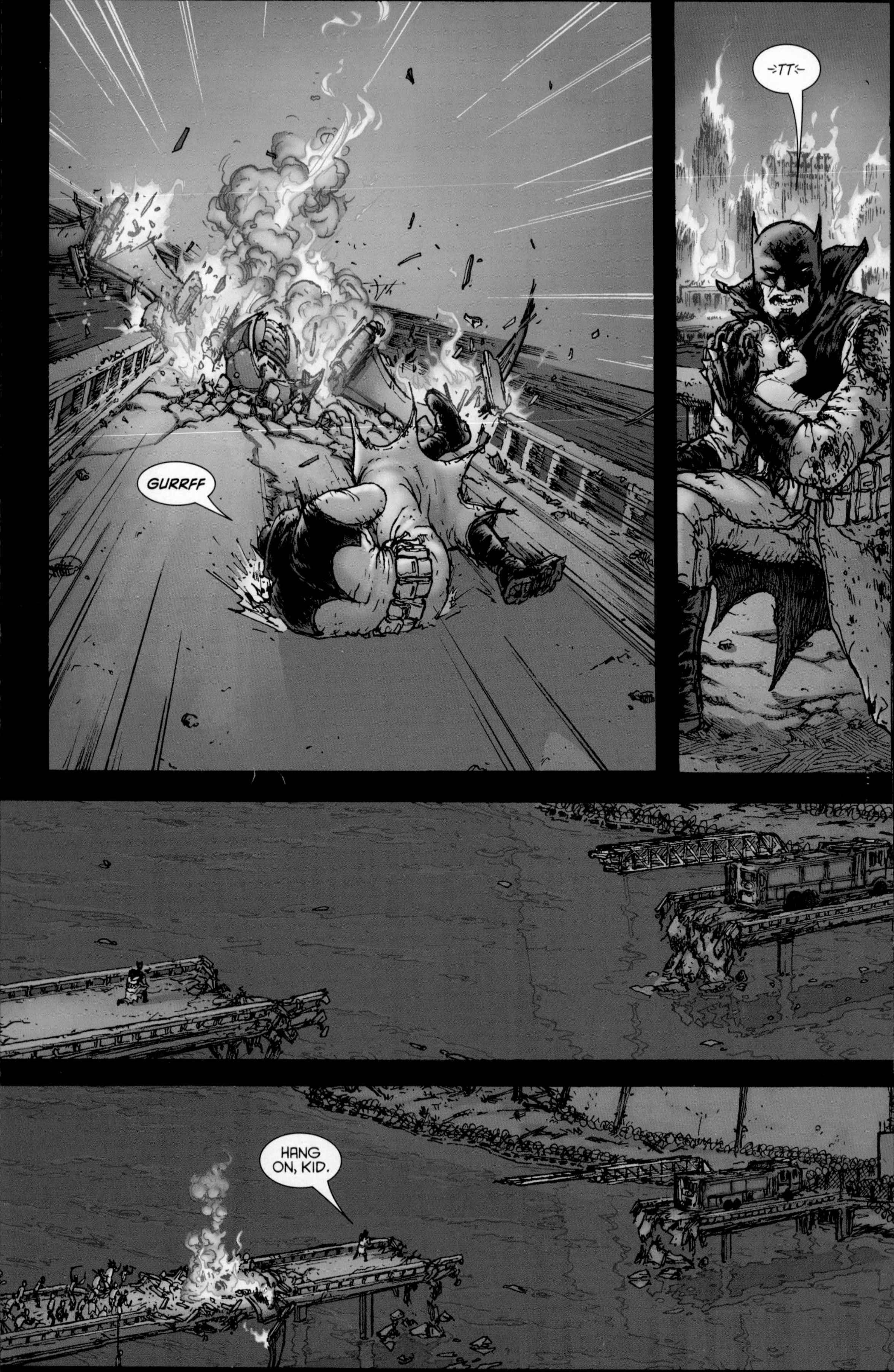
GURRFF
-TT-
HANG ON, KID.

RRRAAAAAAAAAAAAAAAAAAAAA
BDEEP
*
DRIVE!

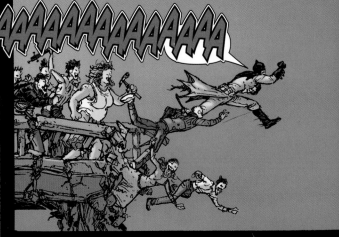

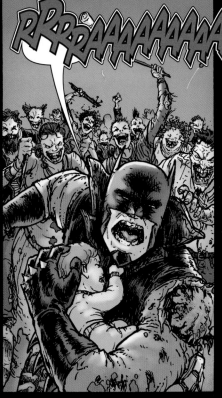

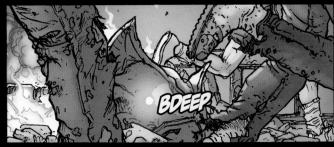

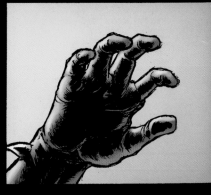

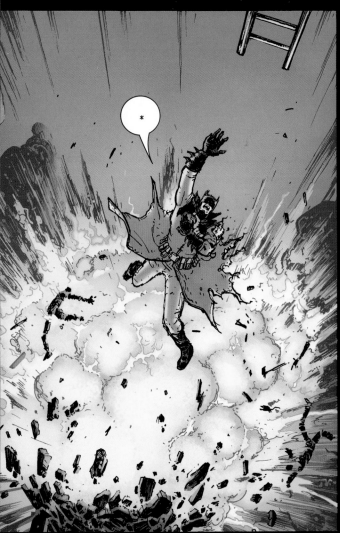

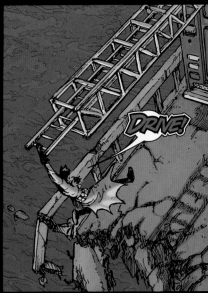

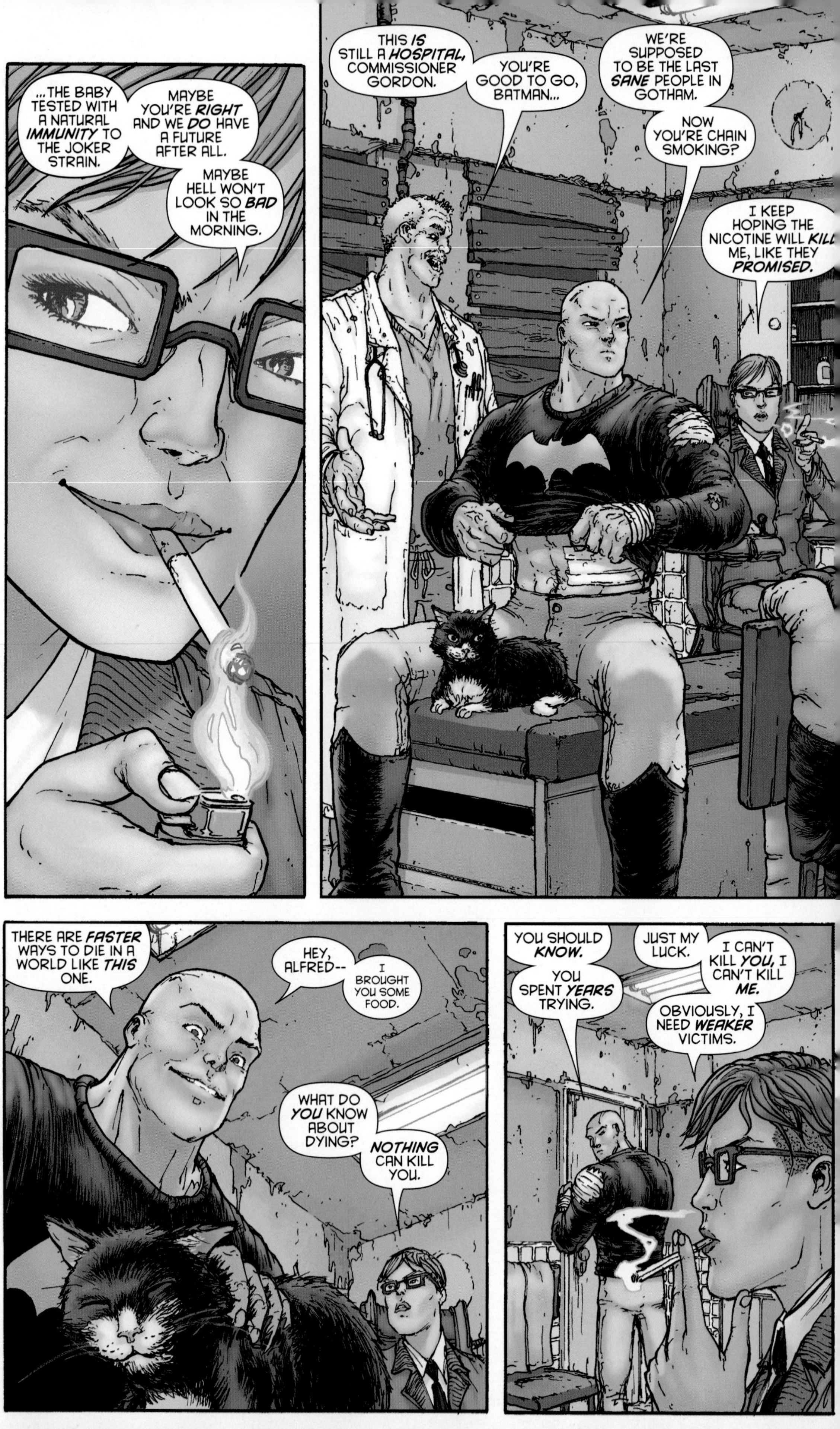
...THE BABY TESTED WITH A NATURAL IMMUNITY TO THE JOKER STRAIN.
MAYBE YOU'RE RIGHT AND WE DO HAVE A FUTURE AFTER ALL.
MAYBE HELL WON'T LOOK SO BAD IN THE MORNING.
THIS IS STILL A HOSPITAL, COMMISSIONER GORDON.
YOU'RE GOOD TO GO, BATMAN...
WE'RE SUPPOSED TO BE THE LAST SANE PEOPLE IN GOTHAM.
NOW YOU'RE CHAIN SMOKING?
I KEEP HOPING THE NICOTINE WILL KILL ME, LIKE THEY PROMISED.
THERE ARE FASTER WAYS TO DIE IN A WORLD LIKE THIS ONE.
HEY, ALFRED--
I BROUGHT YOU SOME FOOD.
WHAT DO YOU KNOW ABOUT DYING?
NOTHING CAN KILL YOU.
YOU SHOULD KNOW.
YOU SPENT YEARS TRYING.
JUST MY LUCK.
I CAN'T KILL YOU, I CAN'T KILL ME.
OBVIOUSLY, I NEED WEAKER VICTIMS.

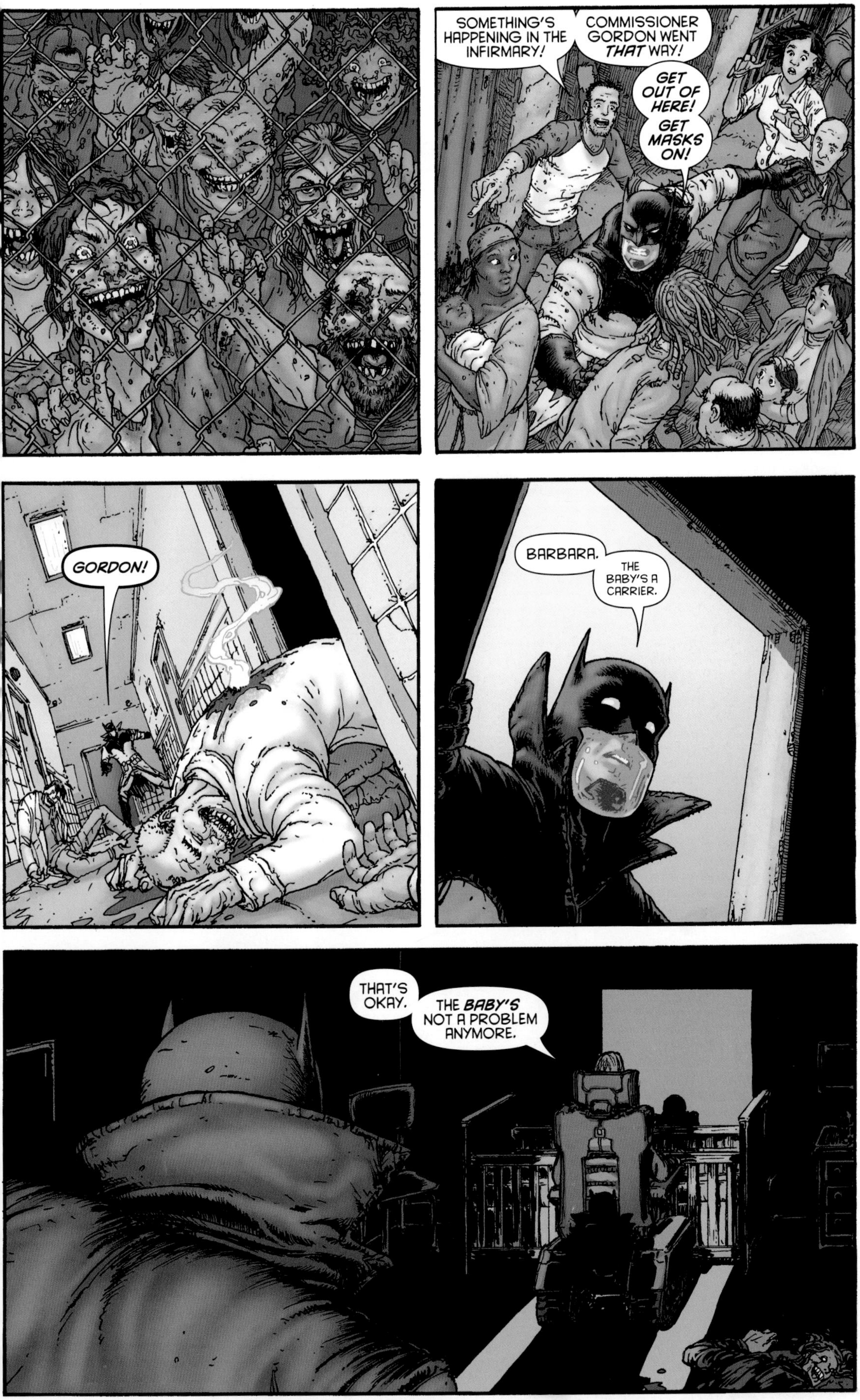
SOMETHING'S HAPPENING IN THE INFIRMARY!
COMMISSIONER GORDON WENT *THAT* WAY!
GET OUT OF HERE!
GET MASKS ON!
GORDON!
BARBARA.
THE BABY'S A CARRIER.
THAT'S OKAY.
THE *BABY'S* NOT A PROBLEM ANYMORE.

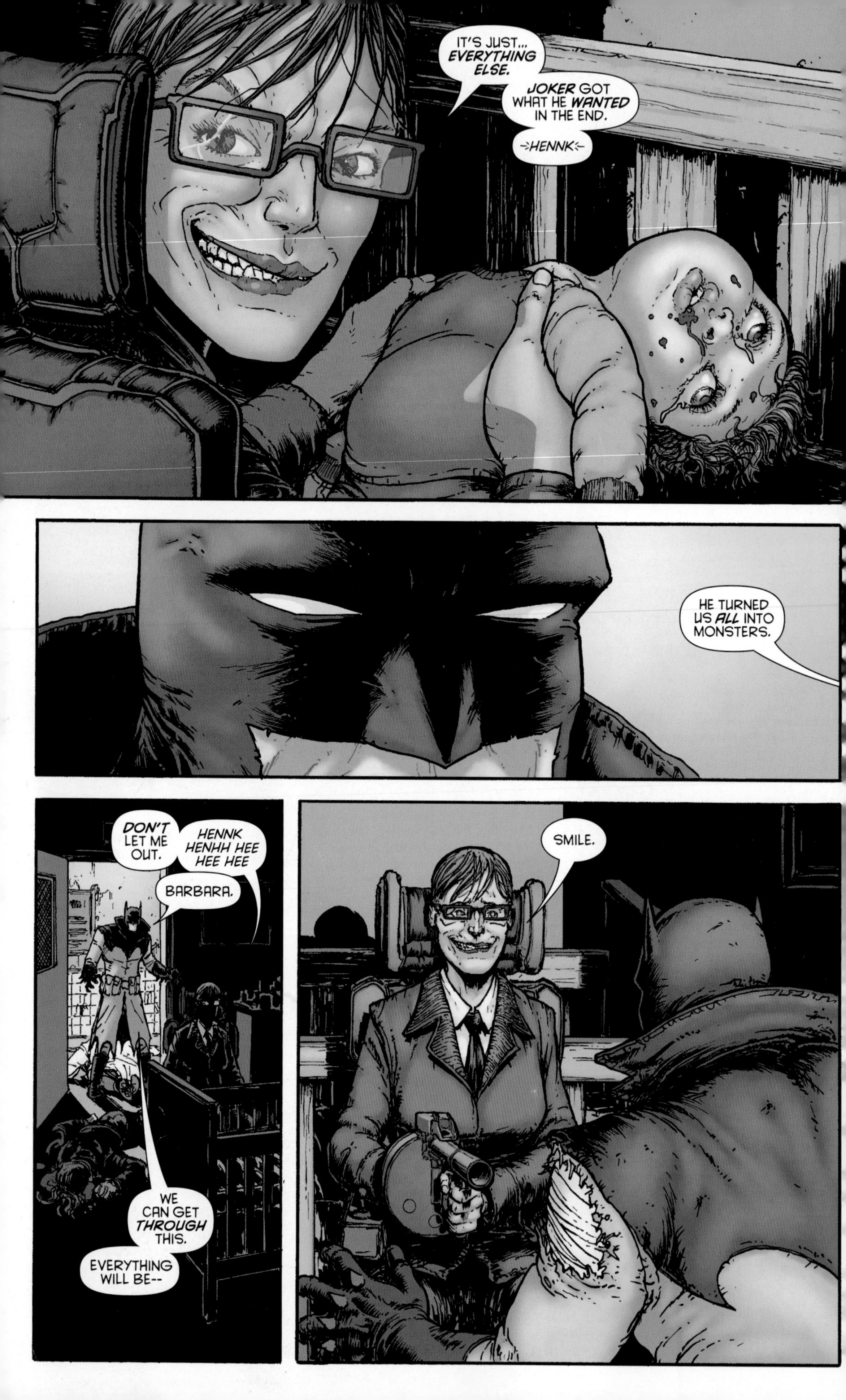
IT'S JUST... EVERYTHING ELSE.
JOKER GOT WHAT HE WANTED IN THE END.
-HENNK-
HE TURNED US ALL INTO MONSTERS.
DON'T LET ME OUT.
HENNK HENHH HEE HEE HEE
BARBARA.
WE CAN GET THROUGH THIS.
EVERYTHING WILL BE--
SMILE.

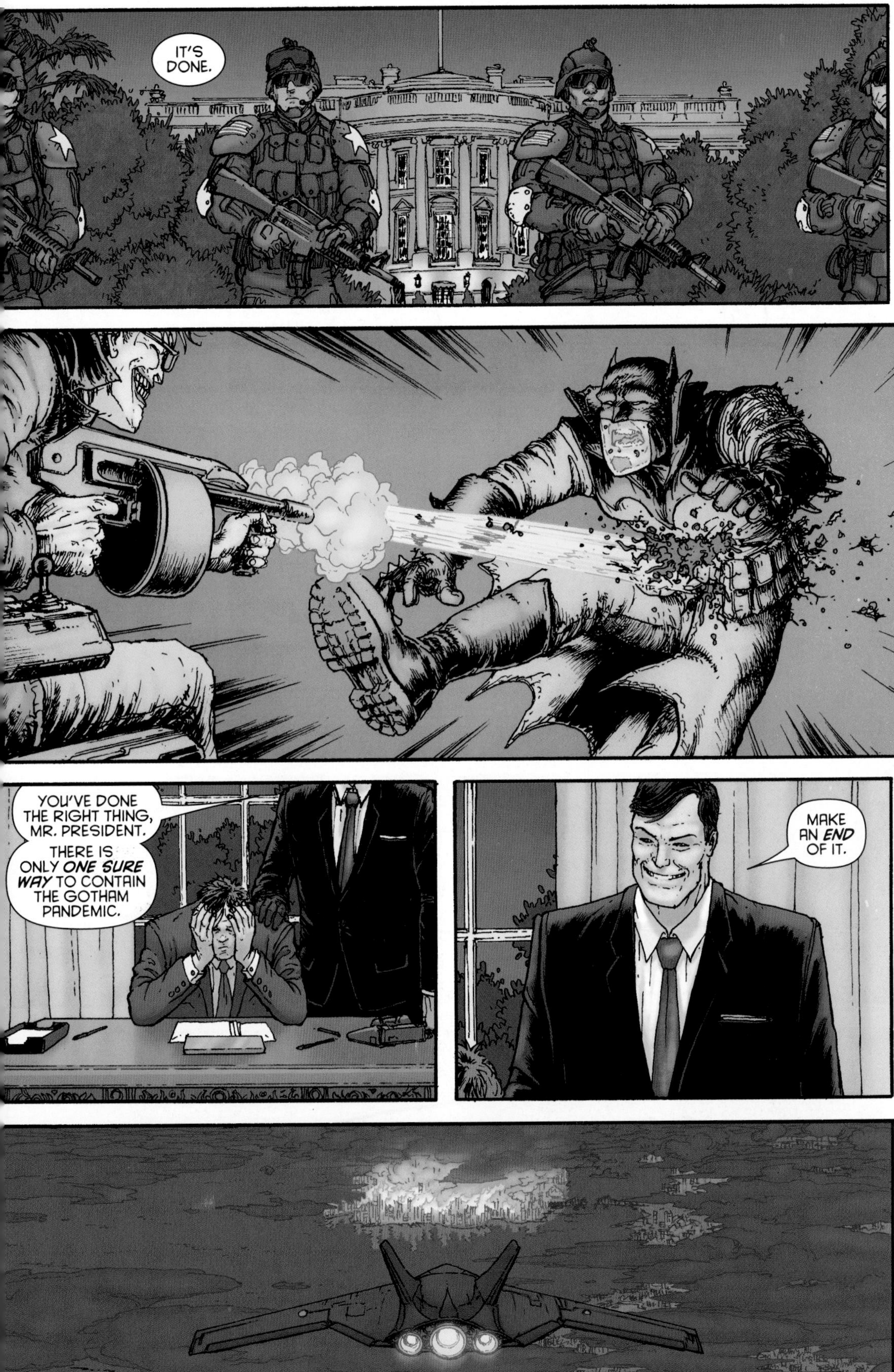
IT'S DONE.
YOU'VE DONE THE RIGHT THING, MR. PRESIDENT.
THERE IS ONLY ONE SURE WAY TO CONTAIN THE GOTHAM PANDEMIC.
MAKE AN END OF IT.

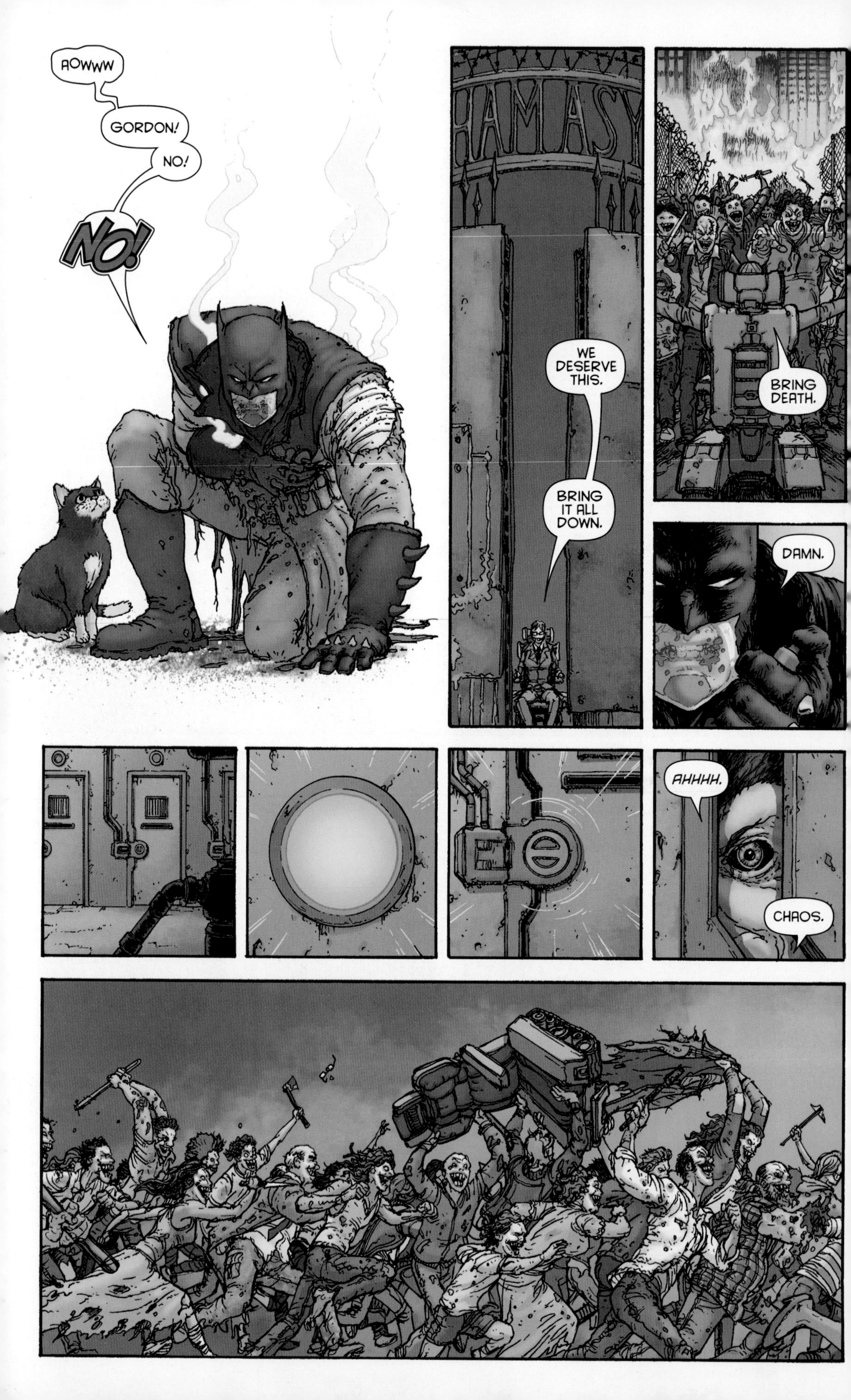
AOWWW
GORDON!
NO!
NO!
WE DESERVE THIS.
BRING IT ALL DOWN.
BRING DEATH.
DAMN.
AHHHH.
CHAOS.

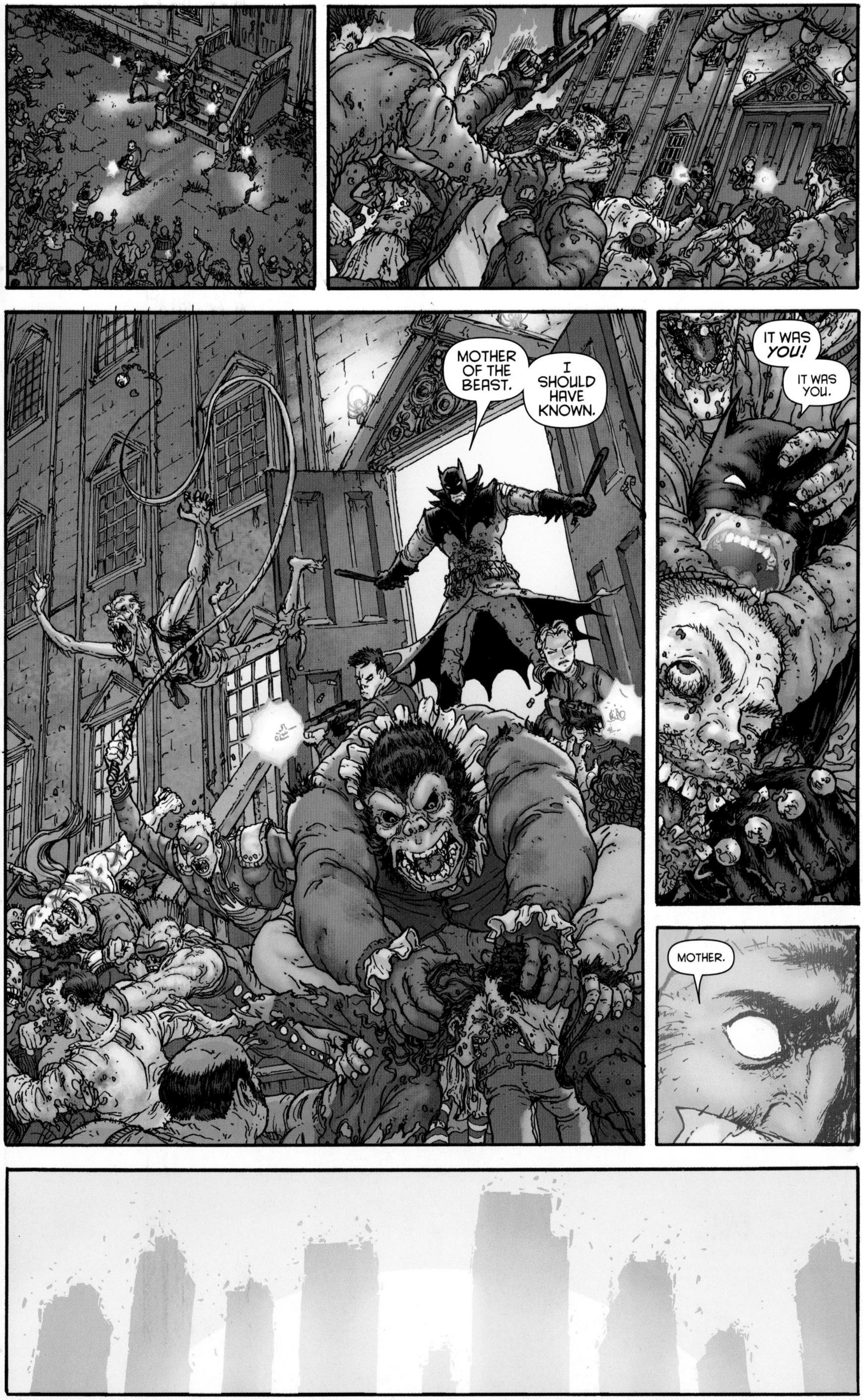
MOTHER OF THE BEAST.
I SHOULD HAVE KNOWN.
IT WAS YOU!
IT WAS YOU.
MOTHER.

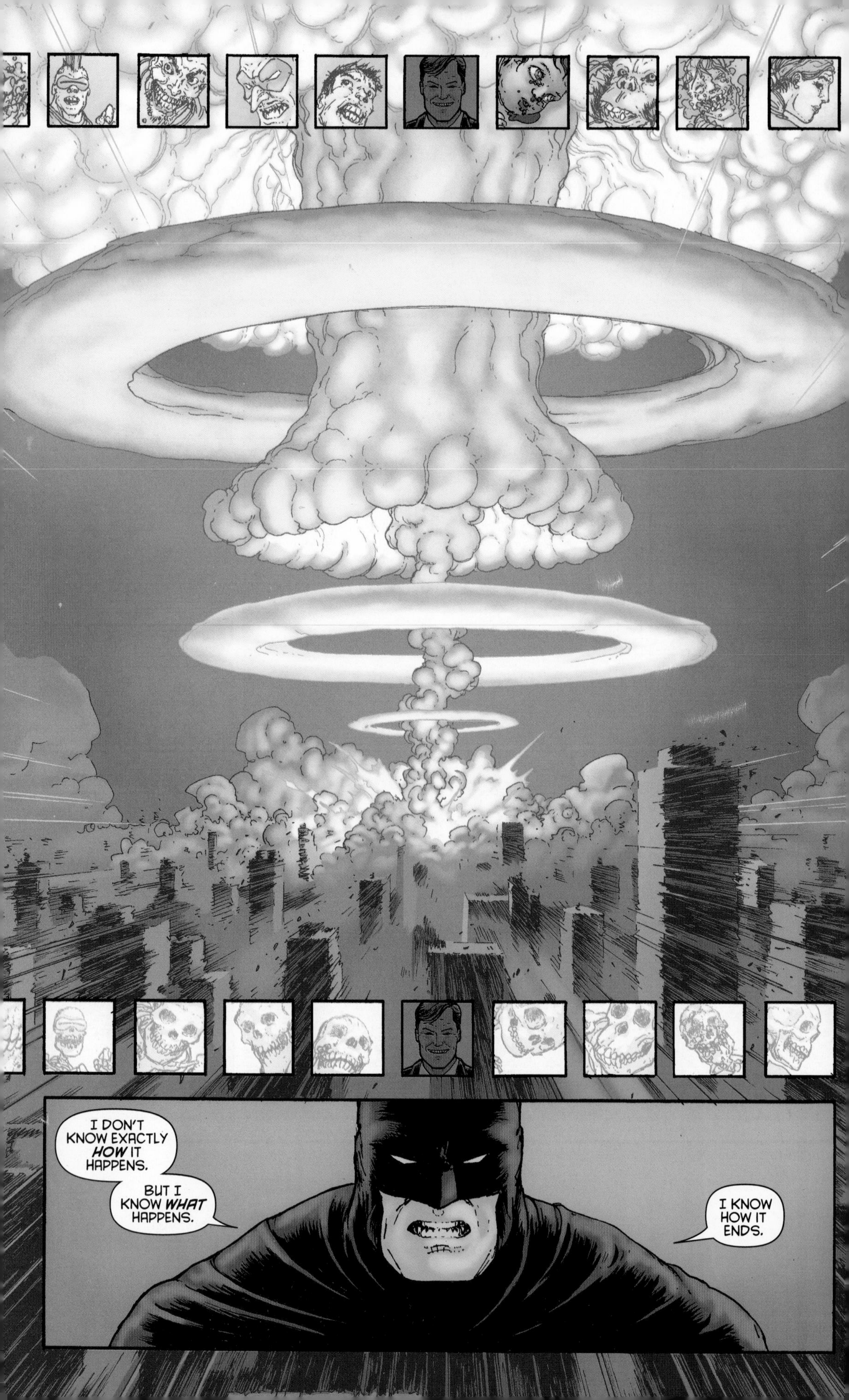
I DON'T KNOW EXACTLY *HOW* IT HAPPENS.
BUT I KNOW *WHAT* HAPPENS.
I KNOW HOW IT ENDS.

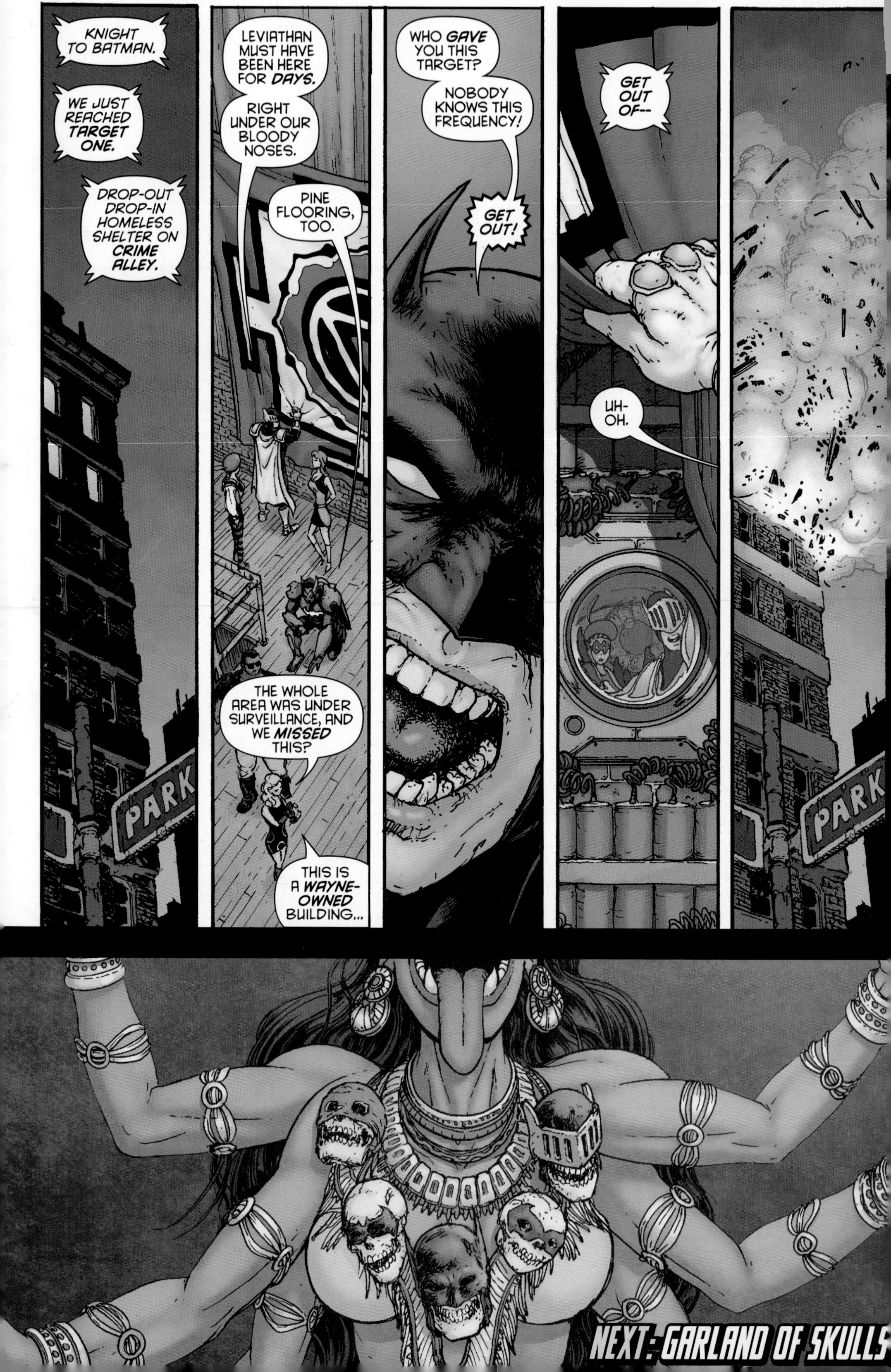

KNIGHT TO BATMAN.
WE JUST REACHED TARGET ONE.
DROP-OUT DROP-IN HOMELESS SHELTER ON CRIME ALLEY.
PARK
LEVIATHAN MUST HAVE BEEN HERE FOR DAYS.
RIGHT UNDER OUR BLOODY NOSES.
PINE FLOORING, TOO.
THE WHOLE AREA WAS UNDER SURVEILLANCE, AND WE MISSED THIS?
THIS IS A WAYNE-OWNED BUILDING...
WHO GAVE YOU THIS TARGET?
NOBODY KNOWS THIS FREQUENCY!
GET OUT!
GET OUT OF--
UH-OH.
PARK
NEXT: GARLAND OF SKULLS

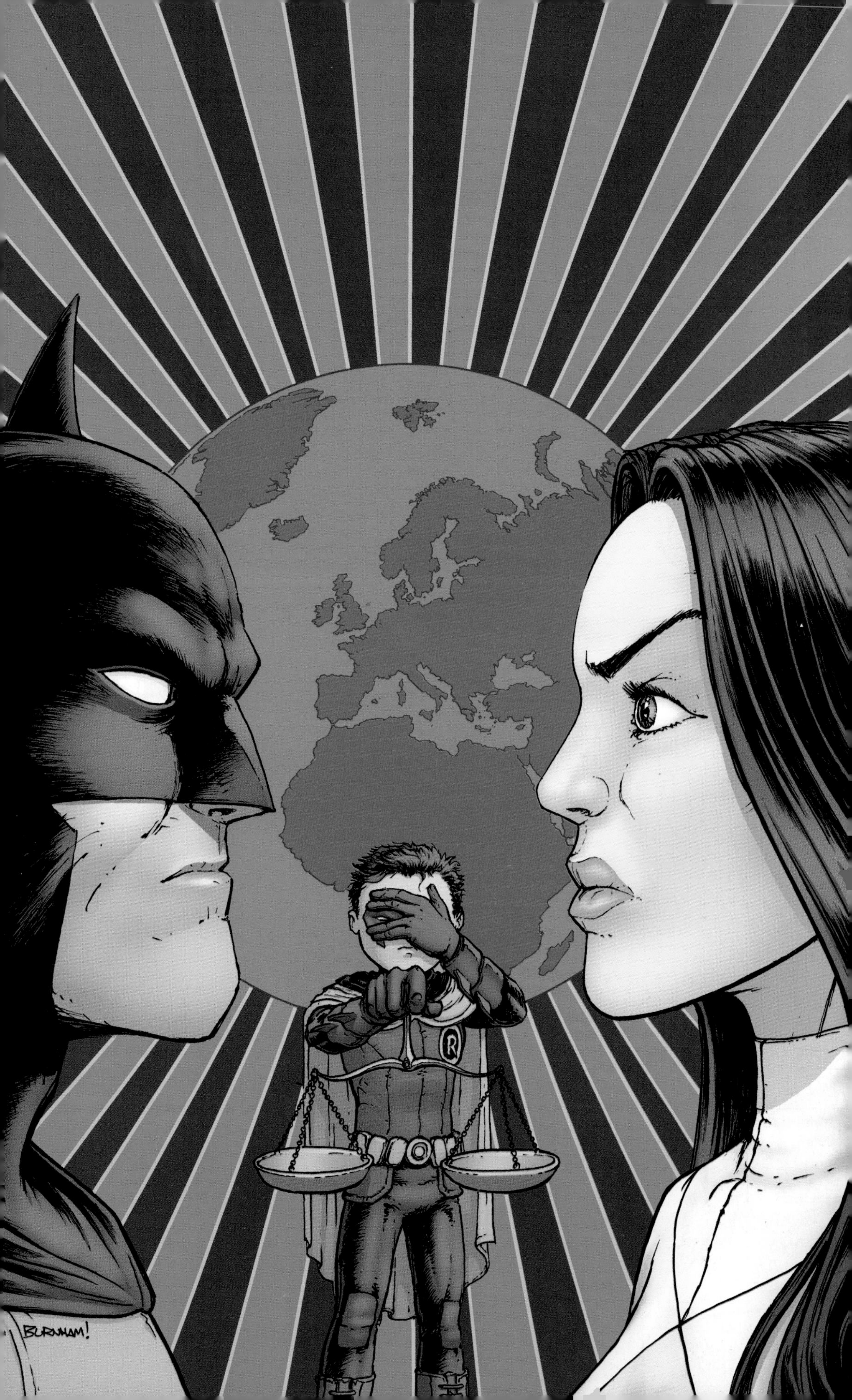
BURNHAM!

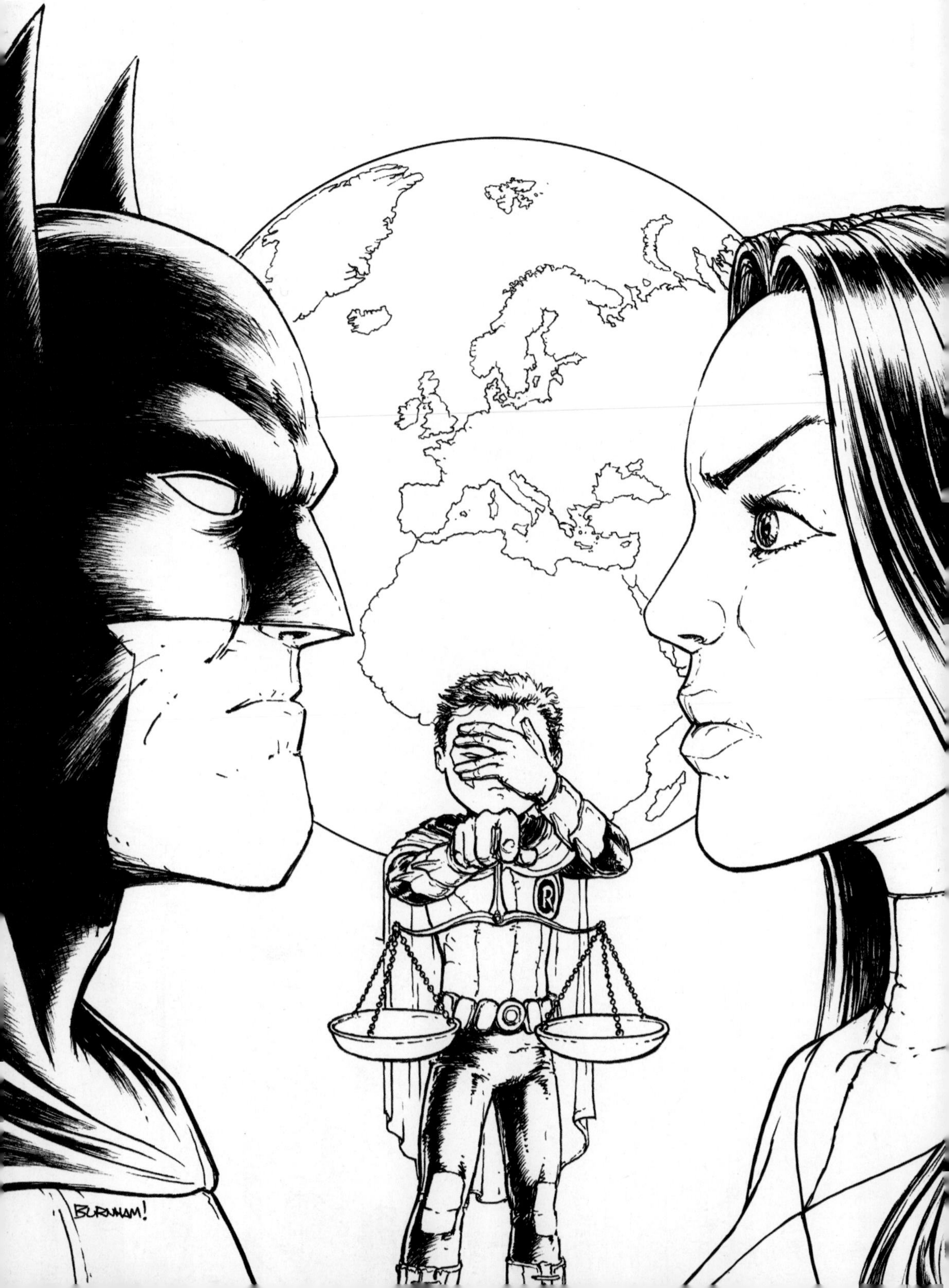
BURNHAM!

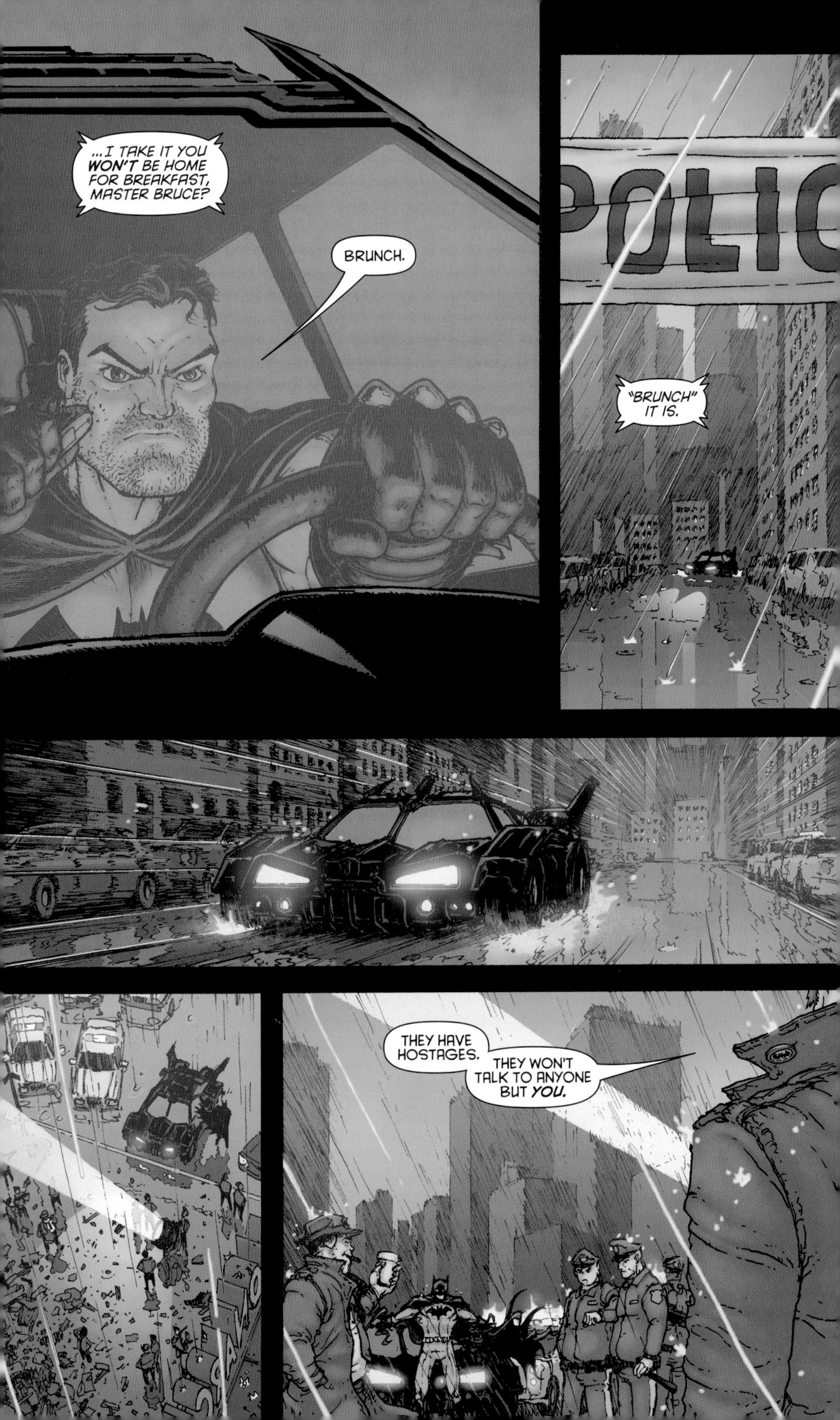
...I TAKE IT YOU WON'T BE HOME FOR BREAKFAST, MASTER BRUCE?
BRUNCH.
POLIC
"BRUNCH" IT IS.
THEY HAVE HOSTAGES.
THEY WON'T TALK TO ANYONE BUT YOU.

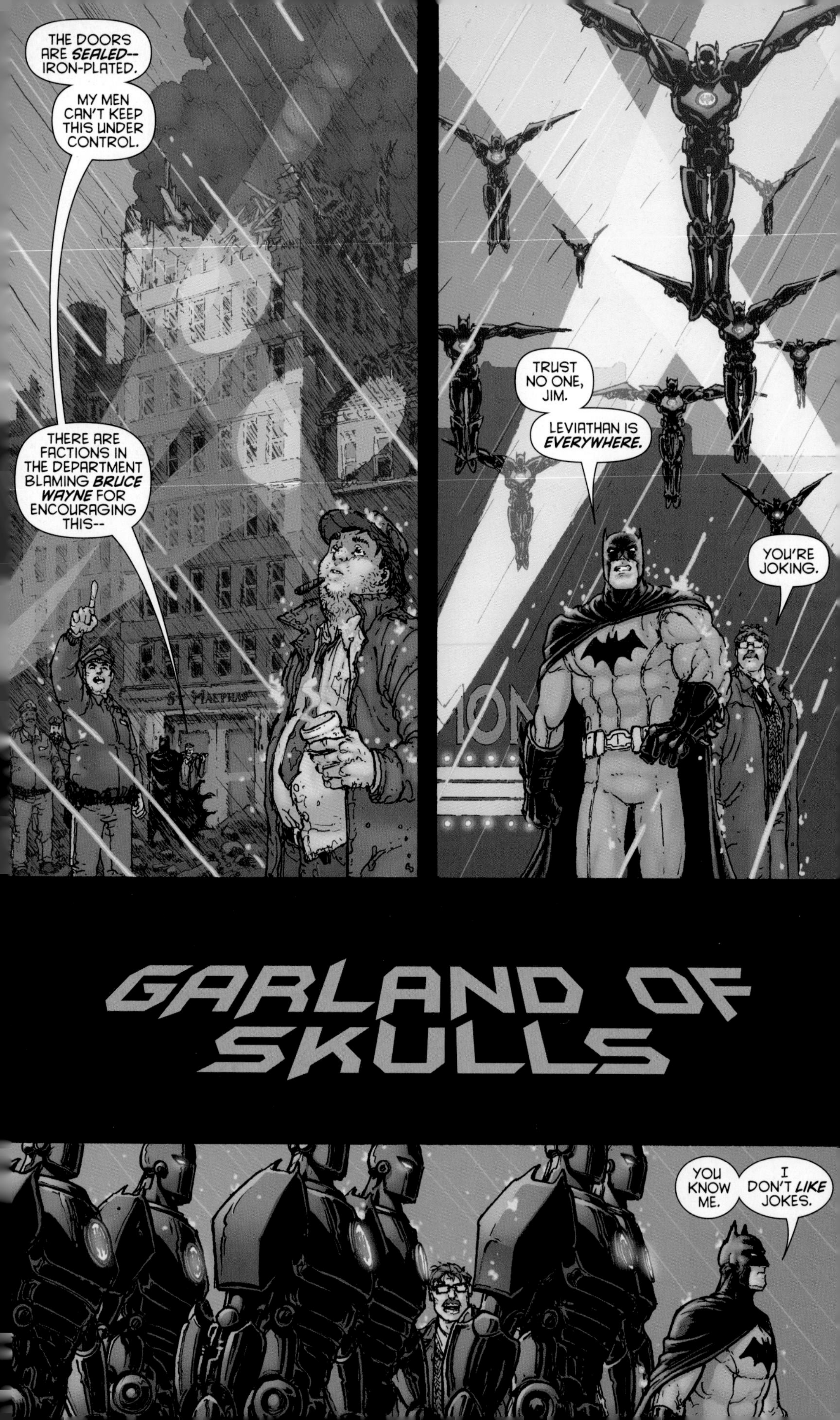
THE DOORS ARE *SEALED*-- IRON-PLATED.
MY MEN CAN'T KEEP THIS UNDER CONTROL.
THERE ARE FACTIONS IN THE DEPARTMENT BLAMING *BRUCE WAYNE* FOR ENCOURAGING THIS--
TRUST NO ONE, JIM.
LEVIATHAN IS *EVERYWHERE.*
YOU'RE JOKING.
GARLAND OF SKULLS
YOU KNOW ME.
I DON'T *LIKE* JOKES.

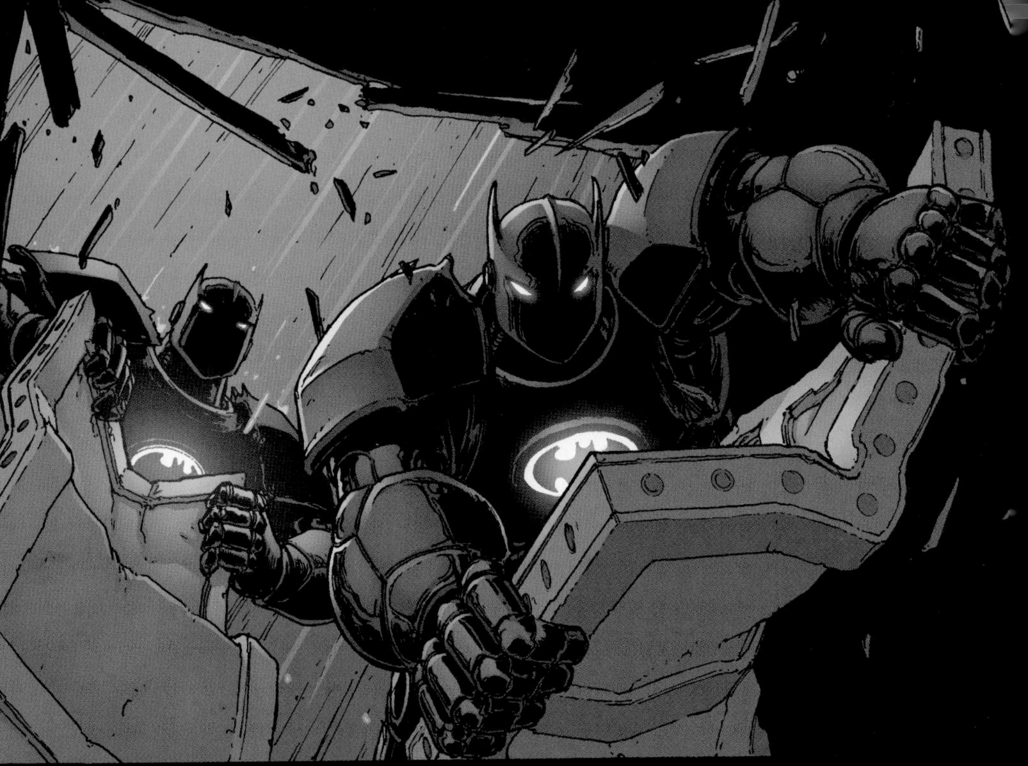

GRANT MORRISON WRITER   CHRIS BURNHAM ARTIST

ANDRES GUINALDO AND BIT ADDITIONAL ART PGS 13-16

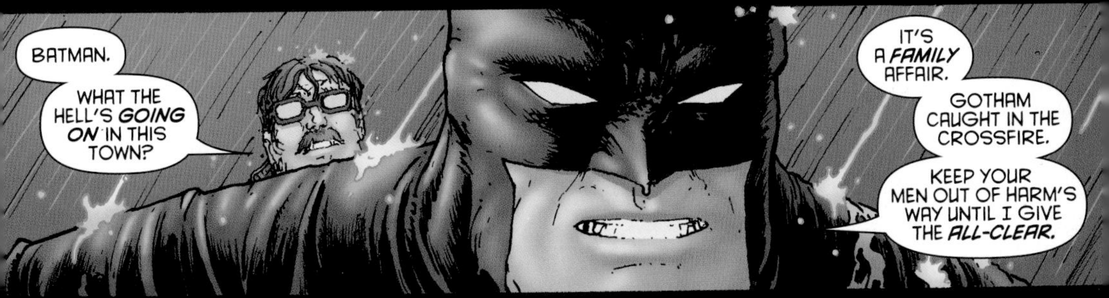

BATMAN.
WHAT THE HELL'S GOING ON IN THIS TOWN?
IT'S A FAMILY AFFAIR.
GOTHAM CAUGHT IN THE CROSSFIRE.
KEEP YOUR MEN OUT OF HARM'S WAY UNTIL I GIVE THE ALL-CLEAR.

NATHAN FAIRBAIRN COLORS   DAVE SHARPE LETTERS

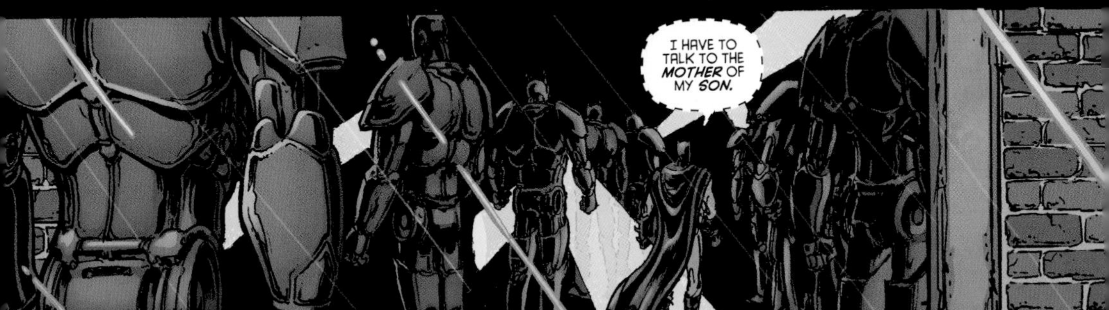

I HAVE TO TALK TO THE MOTHER OF MY SON.

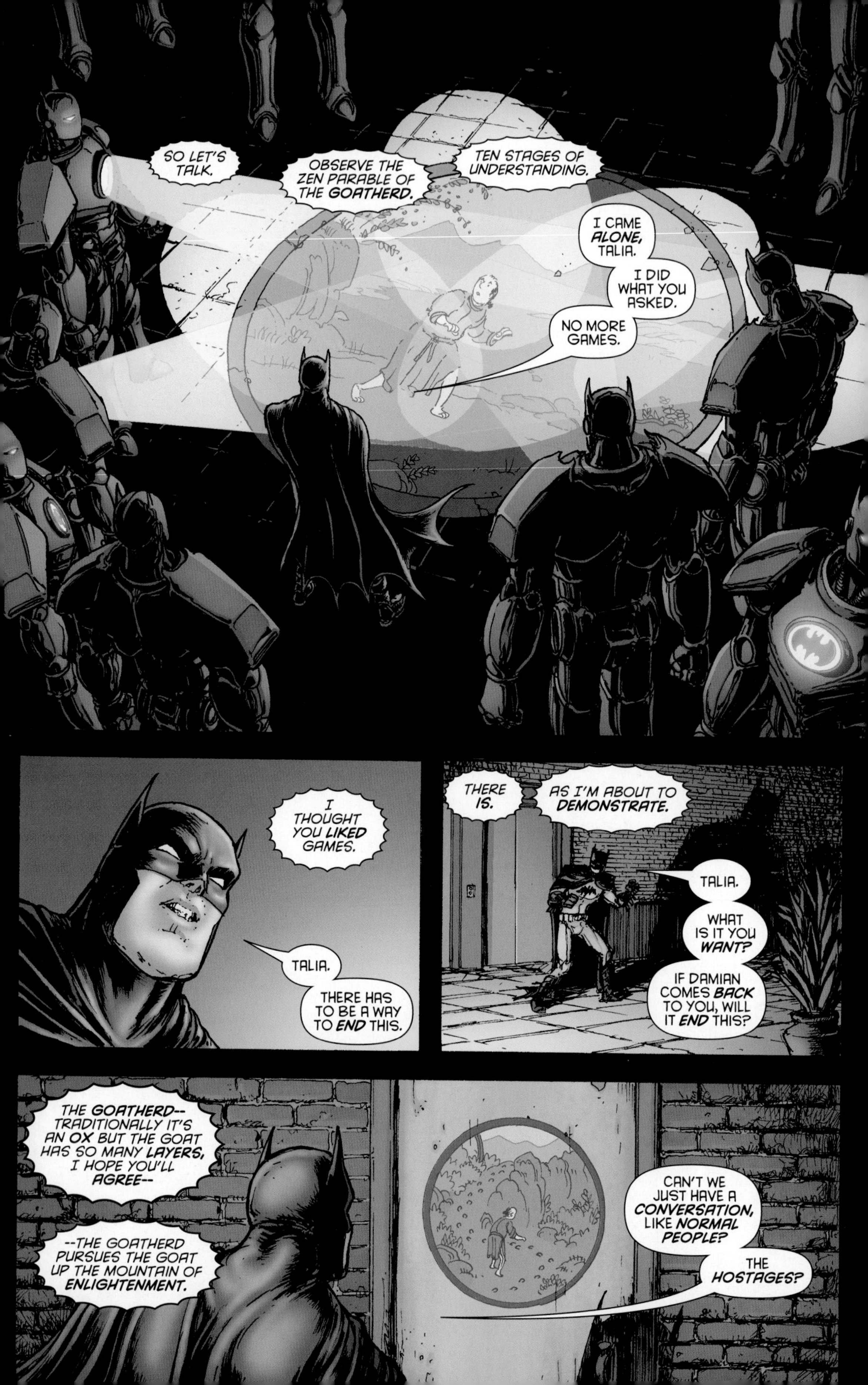
SO LET'S TALK.
OBSERVE THE ZEN PARABLE OF THE GOATHERD.
TEN STAGES OF UNDERSTANDING.
I CAME ALONE, TALIA.
I DID WHAT YOU ASKED.
NO MORE GAMES.
I THOUGHT YOU LIKED GAMES.
TALIA.
THERE HAS TO BE A WAY TO END THIS.
THERE IS.
AS I'M ABOUT TO DEMONSTRATE.
TALIA.
WHAT IS IT YOU WANT?
IF DAMIAN COMES BACK TO YOU, WILL IT END THIS?
THE GOATHERD-- TRADITIONALLY IT'S AN OX BUT THE GOAT HAS SO MANY LAYERS, I HOPE YOU'LL AGREE--
--THE GOATHERD PURSUES THE GOAT UP THE MOUNTAIN OF ENLIGHTENMENT.
CAN'T WE JUST HAVE A CONVERSATION, LIKE NORMAL PEOPLE?
THE HOSTAGES?

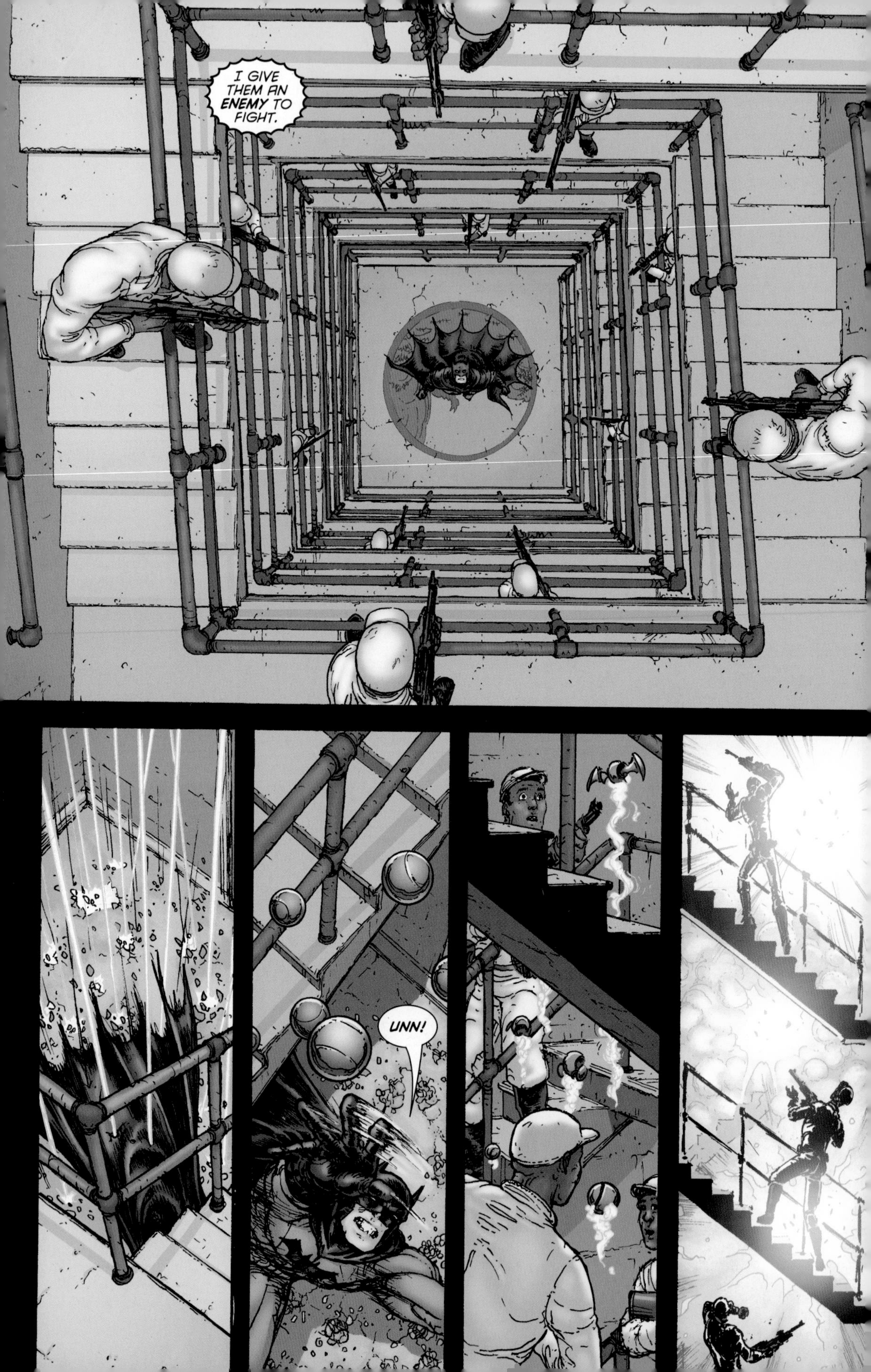
I GIVE THEM AN ENEMY TO FIGHT.
UNN!

-KKT-

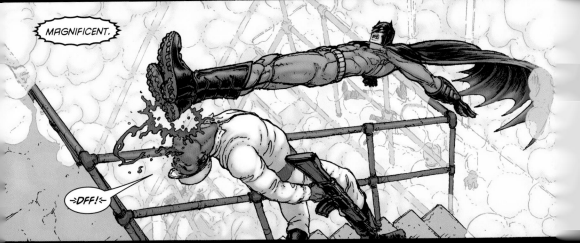

MAGNIFICENT.

-DFF!-

RESPIRATION,
HEARTRATE--
OLYMPIAN.

NONE OF
YOUR RECENT *ORDEALS*
SEEM TO HAVE AFFECTED
YOUR STRENGTH AND
STAMINA...

...OR YOUR
CUNNING.

"*CATCHING THE
GOAT*"--PICTURE
FOUR OF
THE GOATHERD
SEQUENCE.

A TEST
OF *TOUCH.*

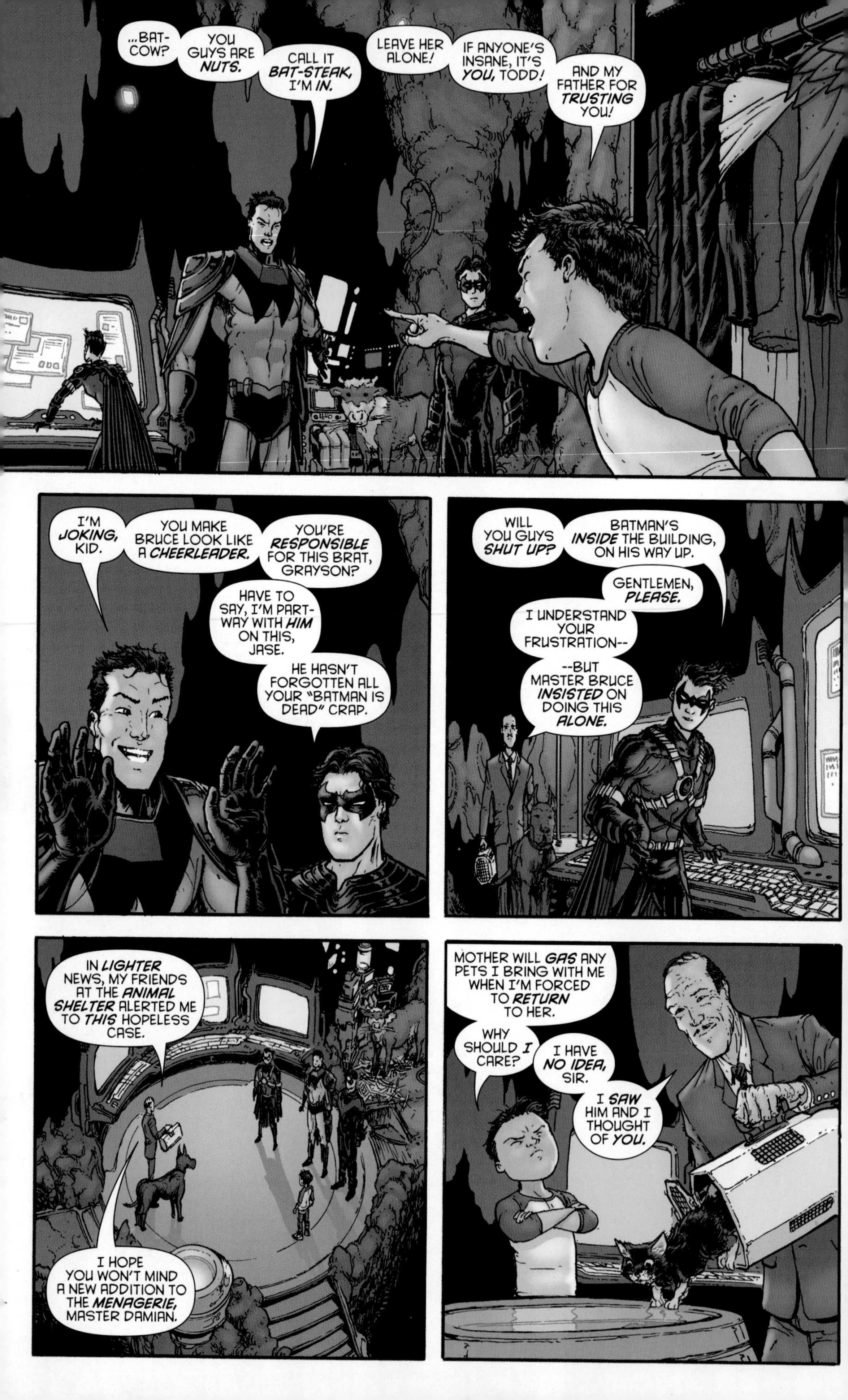
...BAT-COW?
YOU GUYS ARE NUTS.
CALL IT BAT-STEAK, I'M IN.
LEAVE HER ALONE!
IF ANYONE'S INSANE, IT'S YOU, TODD!
AND MY FATHER FOR TRUSTING YOU!
I'M JOKING, KID.
YOU MAKE BRUCE LOOK LIKE A CHEERLEADER.
YOU'RE RESPONSIBLE FOR THIS BRAT, GRAYSON?
HAVE TO SAY, I'M PART-WAY WITH HIM ON THIS, JASE.
HE HASN'T FORGOTTEN ALL YOUR "BATMAN IS DEAD" CRAP.
WILL YOU GUYS SHUT UP?
BATMAN'S INSIDE THE BUILDING, ON HIS WAY UP.
GENTLEMEN, PLEASE.
I UNDERSTAND YOUR FRUSTRATION--
--BUT MASTER BRUCE INSISTED ON DOING THIS ALONE.
IN LIGHTER NEWS, MY FRIENDS AT THE ANIMAL SHELTER ALERTED ME TO THIS HOPELESS CASE.
I HOPE YOU WON'T MIND A NEW ADDITION TO THE MENAGERIE, MASTER DAMIAN.
MOTHER WILL GAS ANY PETS I BRING WITH ME WHEN I'M FORCED TO RETURN TO HER.
WHY SHOULD I CARE?
I HAVE NO IDEA, SIR.
I SAW HIM AND I THOUGHT OF YOU.

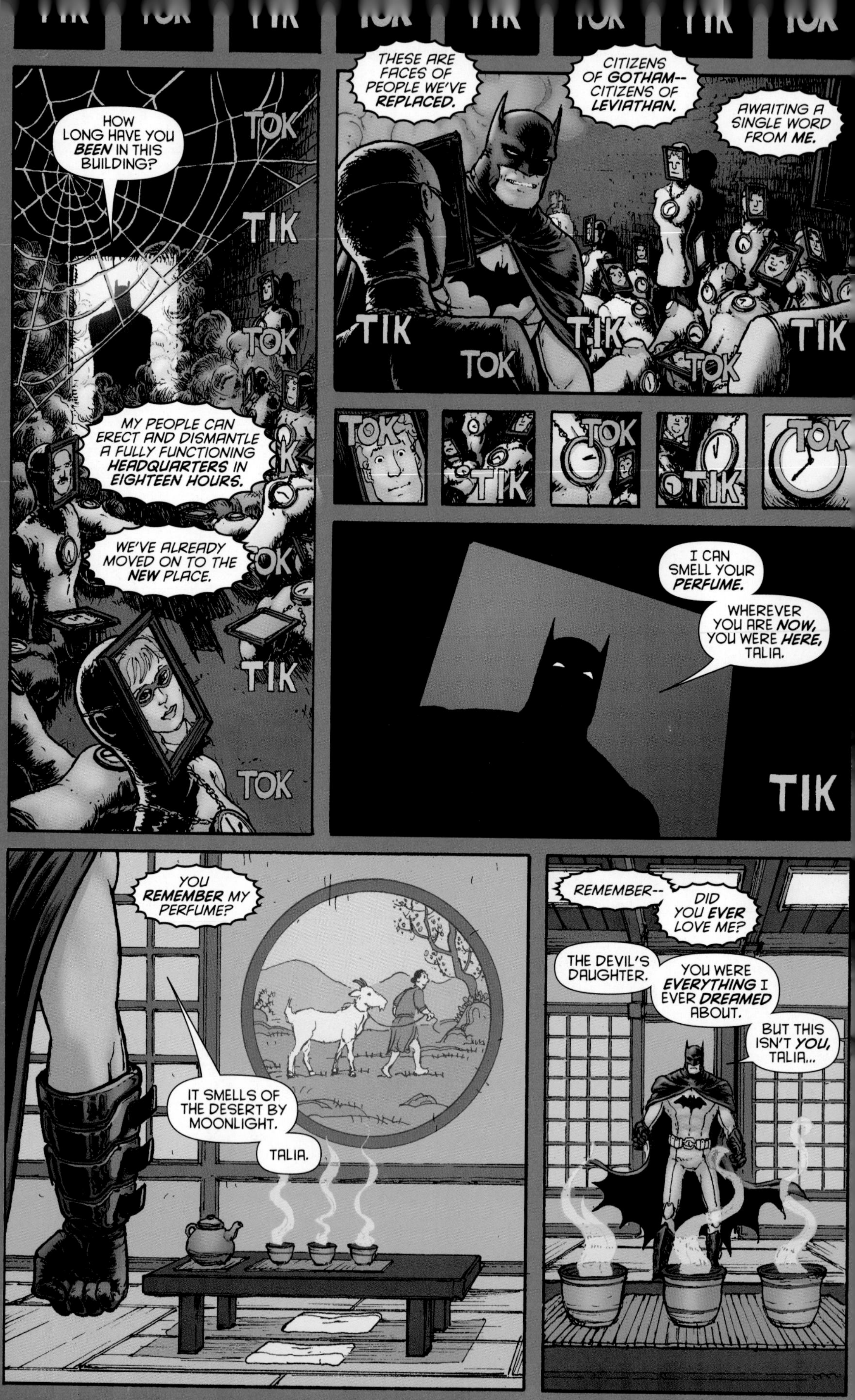
TIK TOK TIK TOK TIK TOK TIK TOK
HOW LONG HAVE YOU BEEN IN THIS BUILDING?
TOK
TIK
TOK
MY PEOPLE CAN ERECT AND DISMANTLE A FULLY FUNCTIONING HEADQUARTERS IN EIGHTEEN HOURS.
WE'VE ALREADY MOVED ON TO THE NEW PLACE.
TIK
TOK
THESE ARE FACES OF PEOPLE WE'VE REPLACED.
CITIZENS OF GOTHAM-- CITIZENS OF LEVIATHAN.
AWAITING A SINGLE WORD FROM ME.
TIK
TOK
TIK
TOK
TIK
TOK
TIK
TOK
TIK
TOK
TIK
TOK
I CAN SMELL YOUR PERFUME.
WHEREVER YOU ARE NOW, YOU WERE HERE, TALIA.
TIK
YOU REMEMBER MY PERFUME?
IT SMELLS OF THE DESERT BY MOONLIGHT.
TALIA.
REMEMBER--
DID YOU EVER LOVE ME?
THE DEVIL'S DAUGHTER.
YOU WERE EVERYTHING I EVER DREAMED ABOUT.
BUT THIS ISN'T YOU, TALIA...

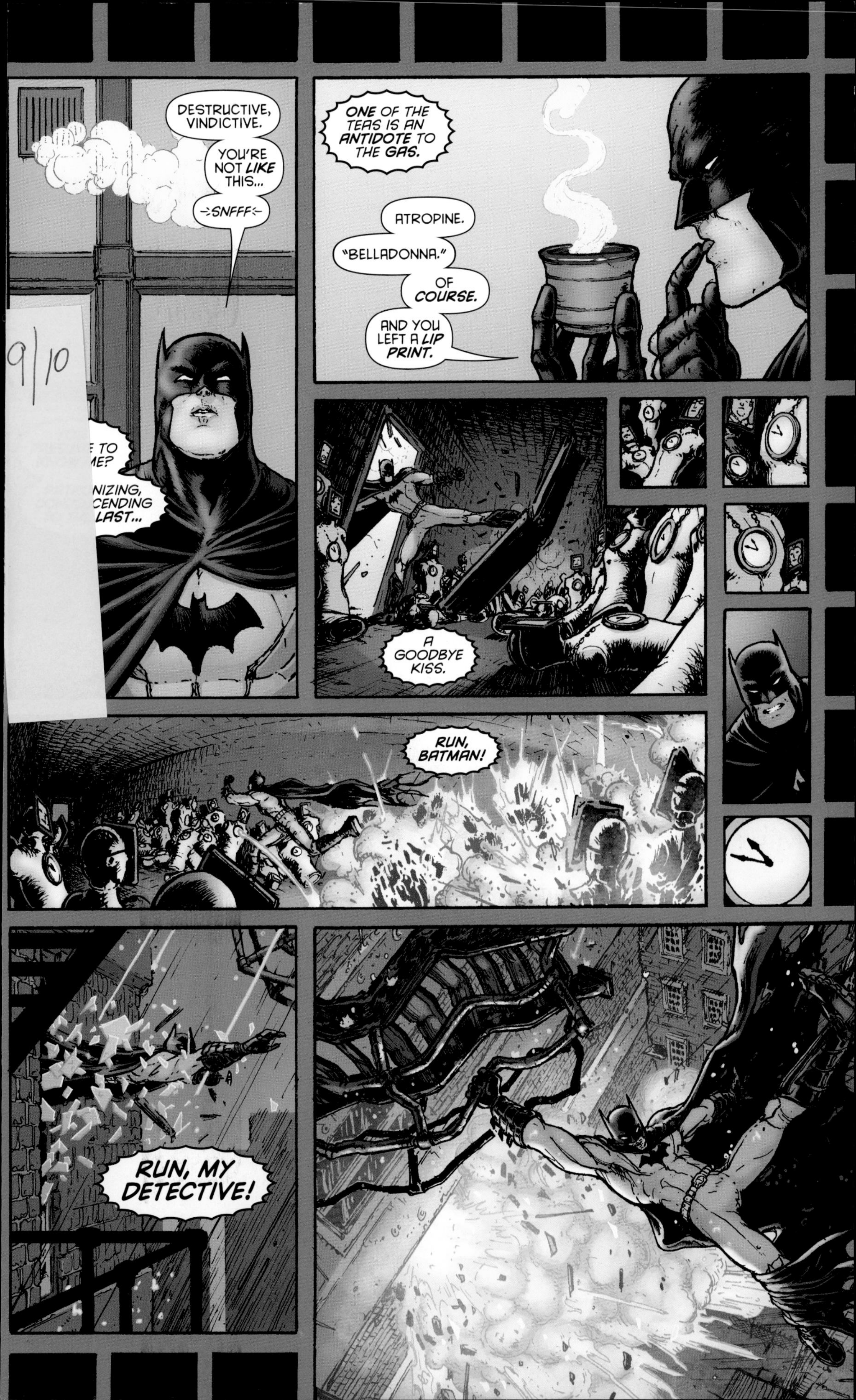
DESTRUCTIVE, VINDICTIVE.
YOU'RE NOT LIKE THIS...
-SNFFF-
ONE OF THE TEAS IS AN ANTIDOTE TO THE GAS.
ATROPINE.
"BELLADONNA."
OF COURSE.
AND YOU LEFT A LIP PRINT.
A GOODBYE KISS.
RUN, BATMAN!
RUN, MY DETECTIVE!

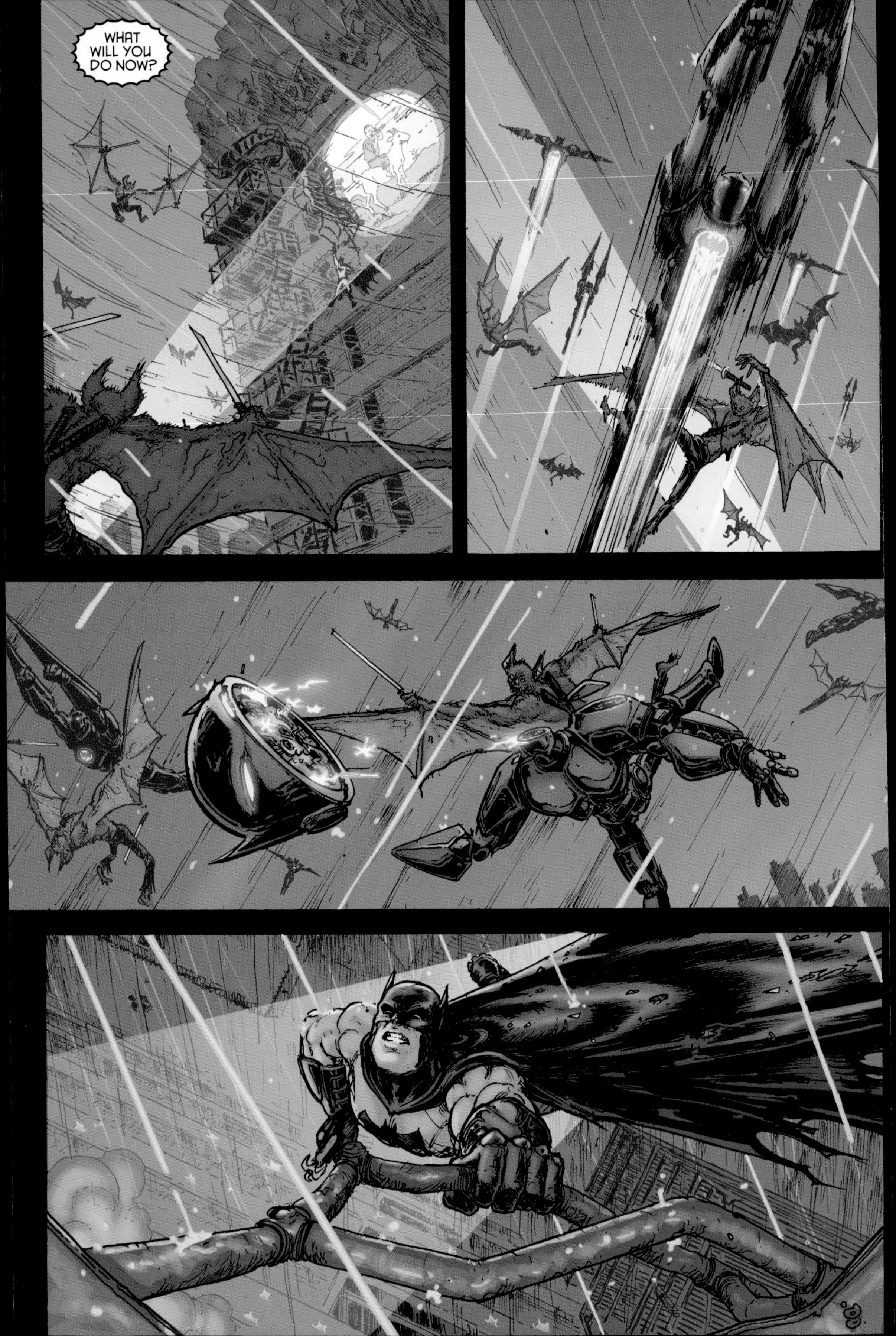
WHAT WILL YOU DO NOW?

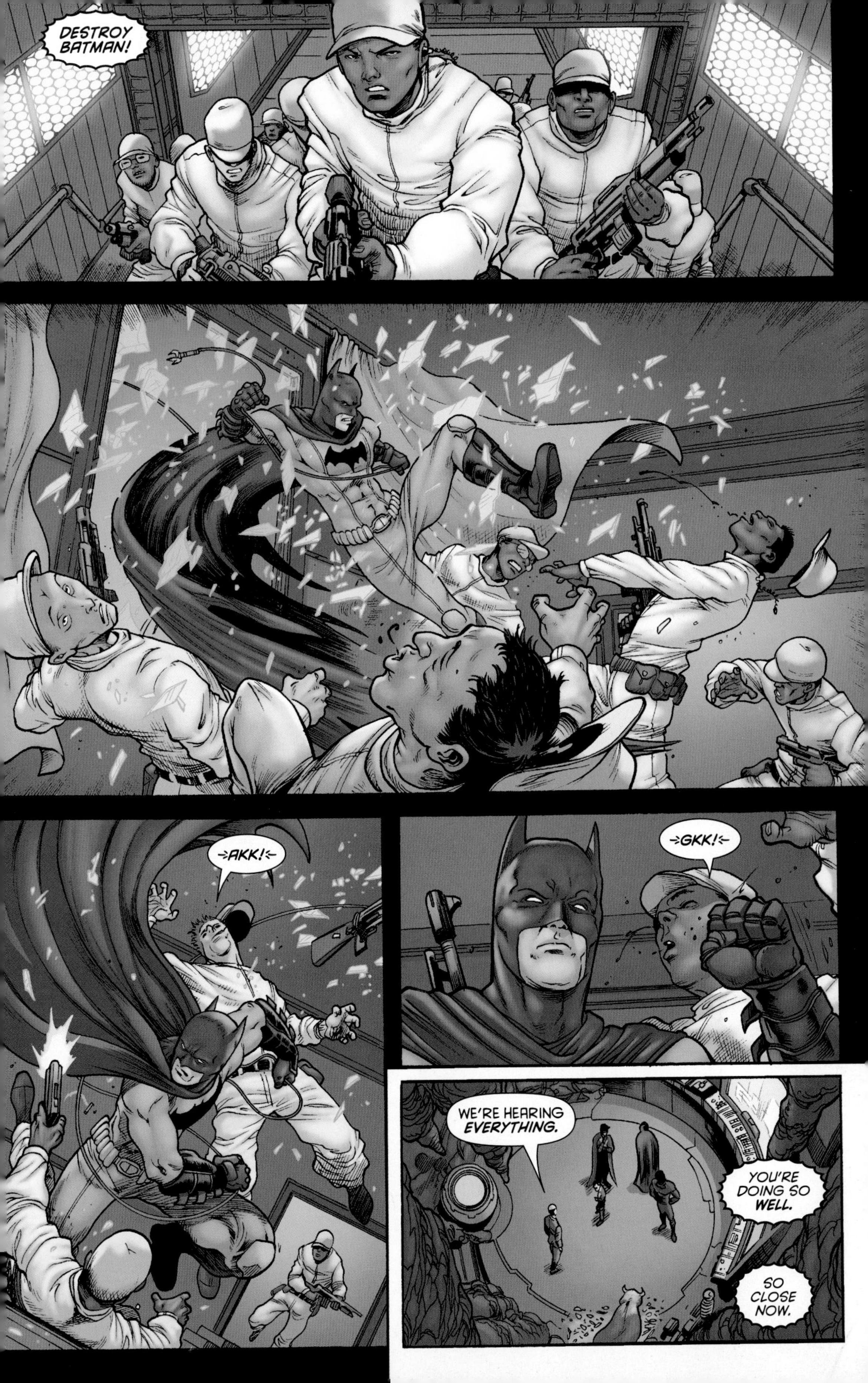
DESTROY BATMAN!
AKK!
GKK!
WE'RE HEARING EVERYTHING.
YOU'RE DOING SO WELL.
SO CLOSE NOW.

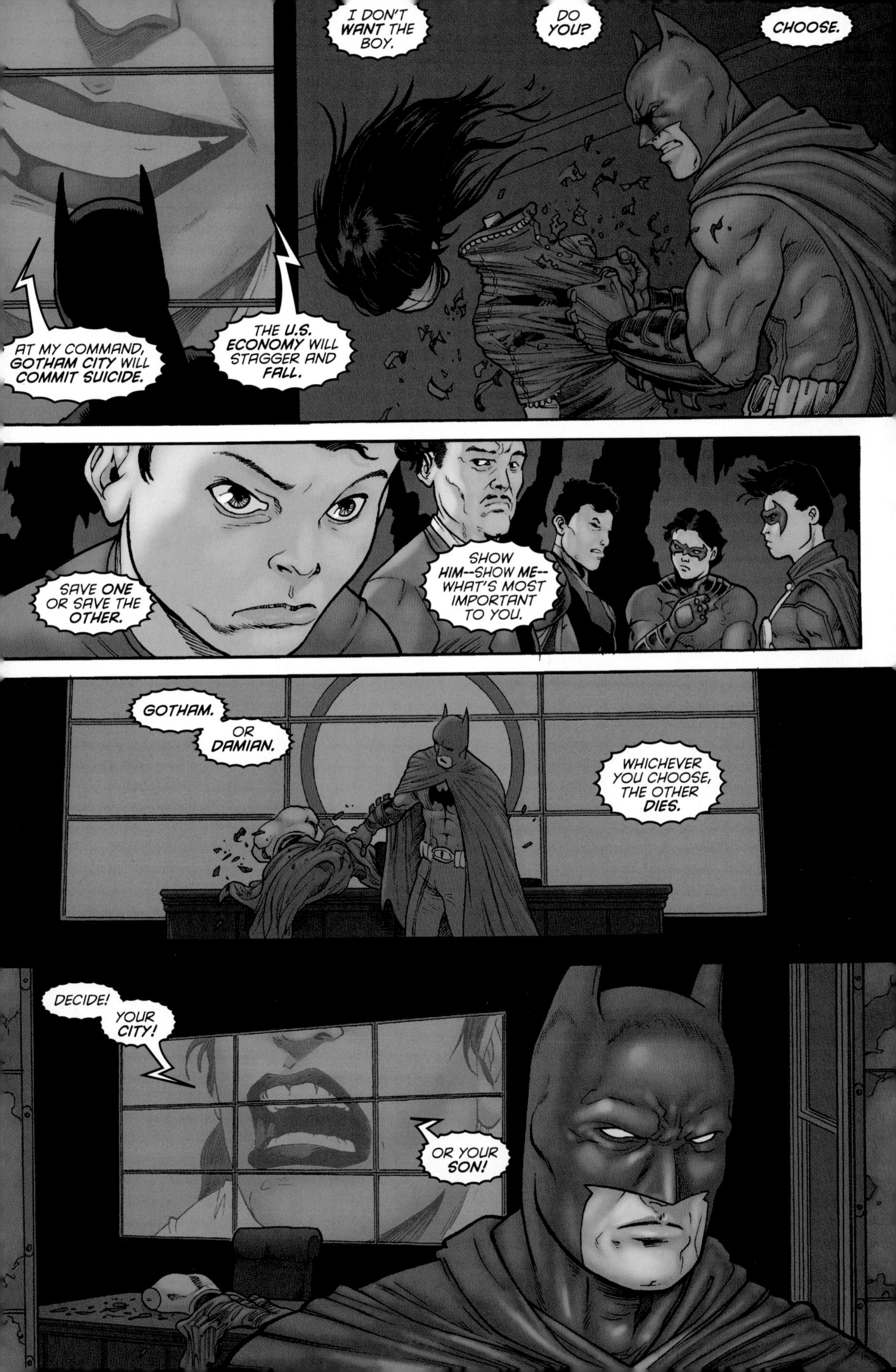
AT MY COMMAND, GOTHAM CITY WILL COMMIT SUICIDE.
THE U.S. ECONOMY WILL STAGGER AND FALL.
I DON'T WANT THE BOY.
DO YOU?
CHOOSE.
SAVE ONE OR SAVE THE OTHER.
SHOW HIM--SHOW ME--WHAT'S MOST IMPORTANT TO YOU.
GOTHAM.
OR DAMIAN.
WHICHEVER YOU CHOOSE, THE OTHER DIES.
DECIDE!
YOUR CITY!
OR YOUR SON!

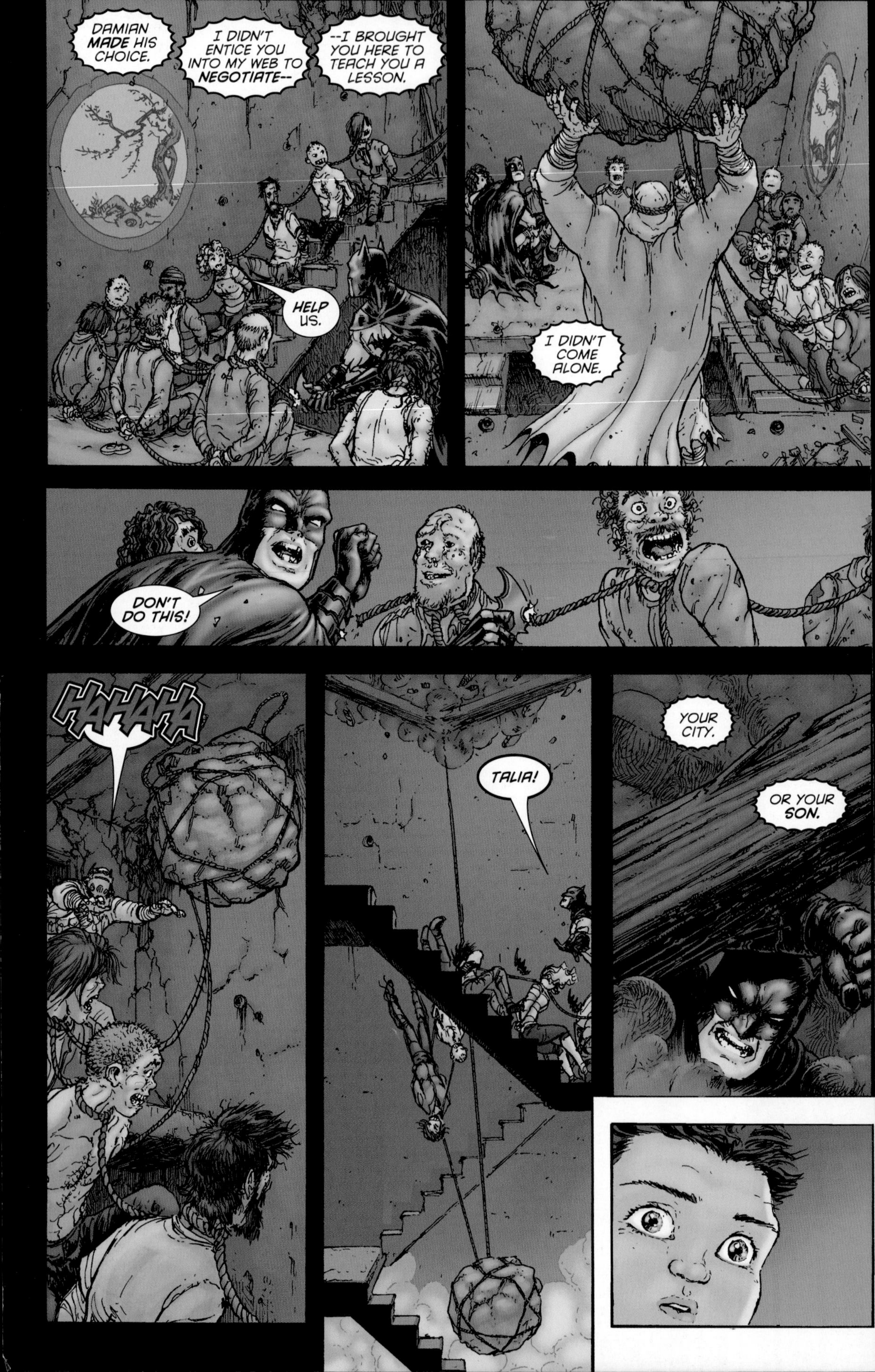
DAMIAN MADE HIS CHOICE.
I DIDN'T ENTICE YOU INTO MY WEB TO NEGOTIATE--
--I BROUGHT YOU HERE TO TEACH YOU A LESSON.
HELP US.
I DIDN'T COME ALONE.
DON'T DO THIS!
HAHAHA
TALIA!
YOUR CITY.
OR YOUR SON.

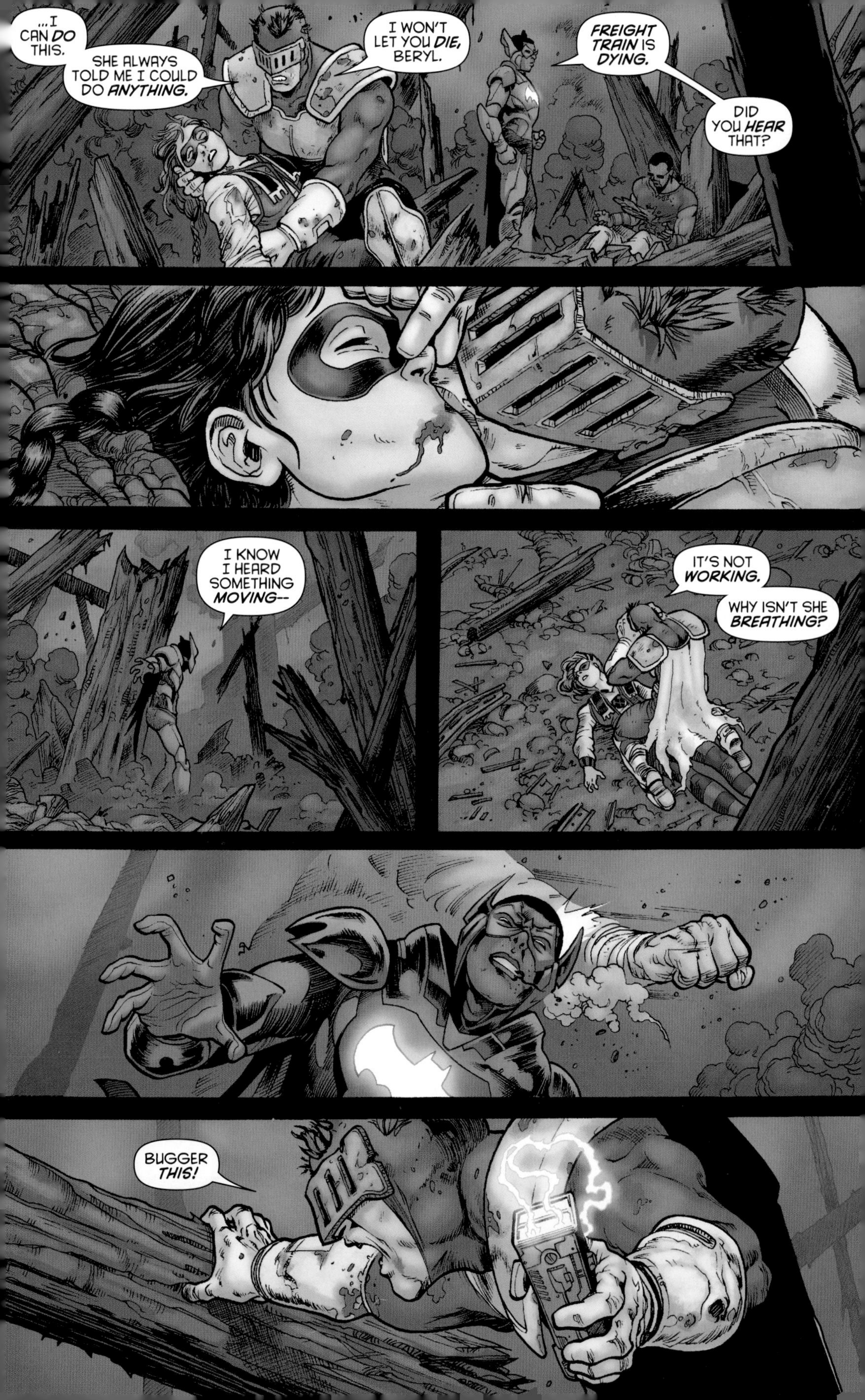
...I CAN DO THIS.
SHE ALWAYS TOLD ME I COULD DO ANYTHING.
I WON'T LET YOU DIE, BERYL.
FREIGHT TRAIN IS DYING.
DID YOU HEAR THAT?
I KNOW I HEARD SOMETHING MOVING--
IT'S NOT WORKING.
WHY ISN'T SHE BREATHING?
BUGGER THIS!

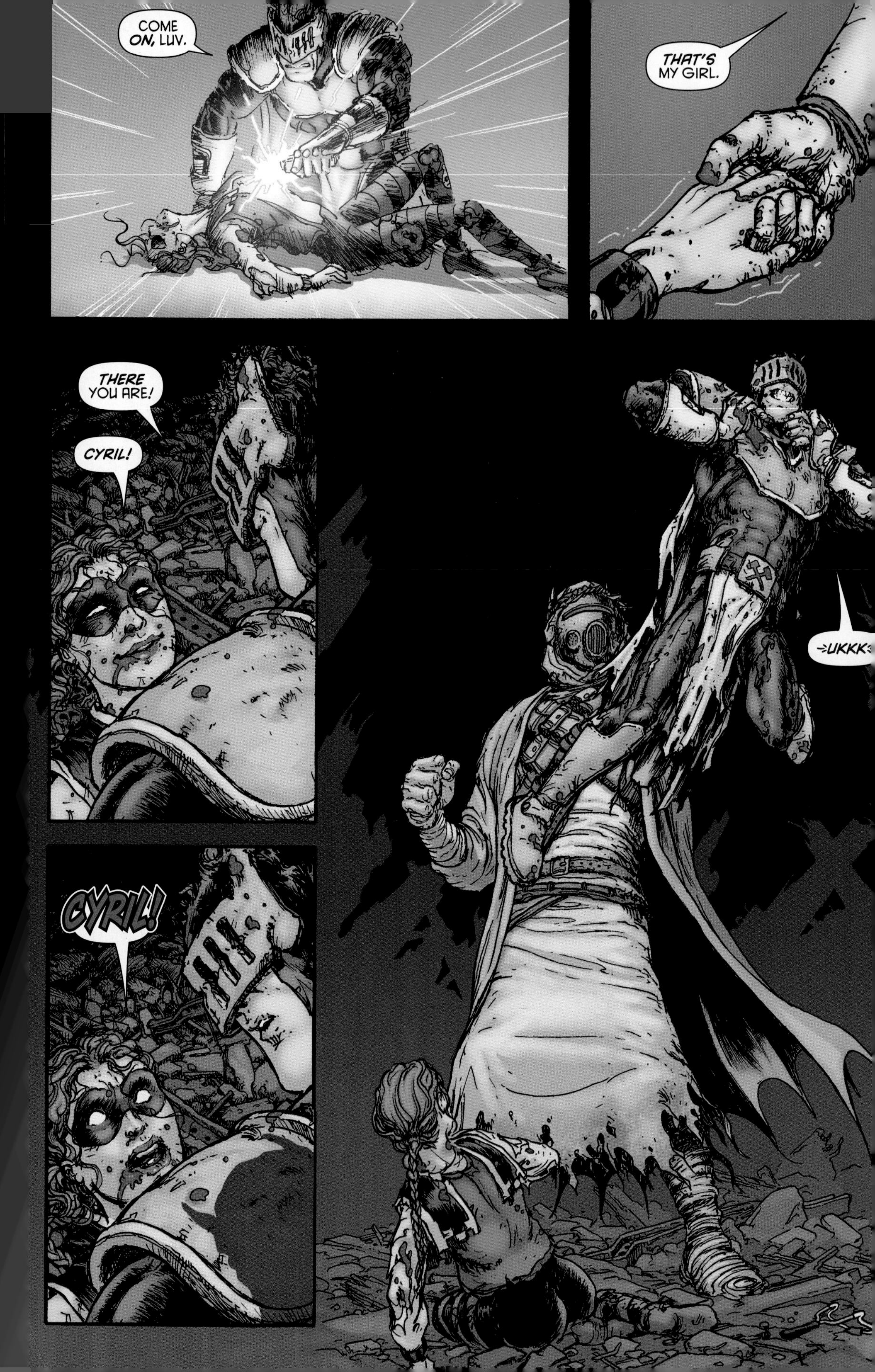
COME ON, LUV.
THAT'S MY GIRL.
THERE YOU ARE!
CYRIL!
CYRIL!
UKKK

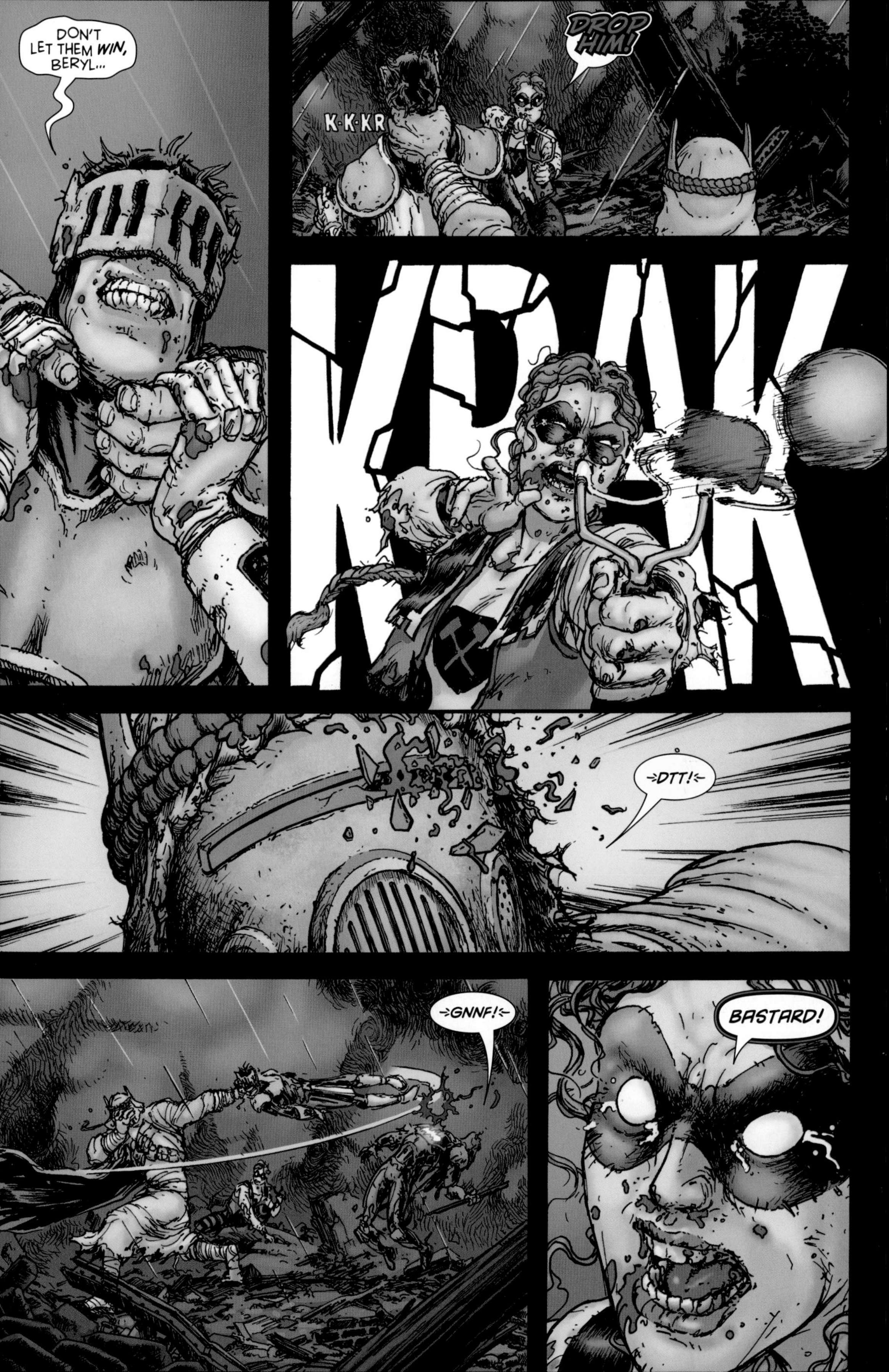
DON'T LET THEM WIN, BERYL...
DROP HIM!
K·K·KR
KRAK
DTT!
GNNF!
BASTARD!

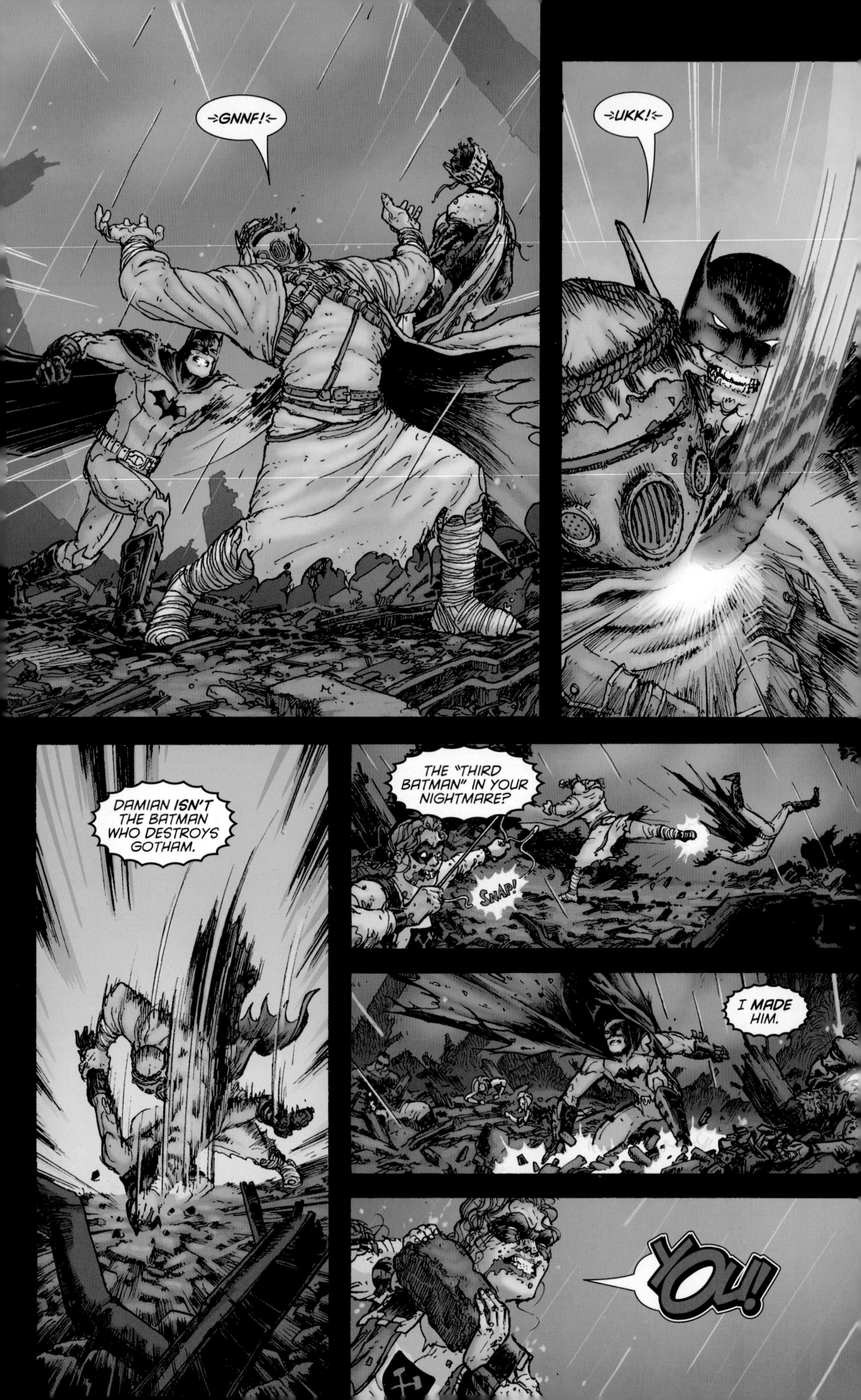
GNNF!
UKK!
DAMIAN ISN'T THE BATMAN WHO DESTROYS GOTHAM.
THE "THIRD BATMAN" IN YOUR NIGHTMARE?
SNAP!
I MADE HIM.
YOU!

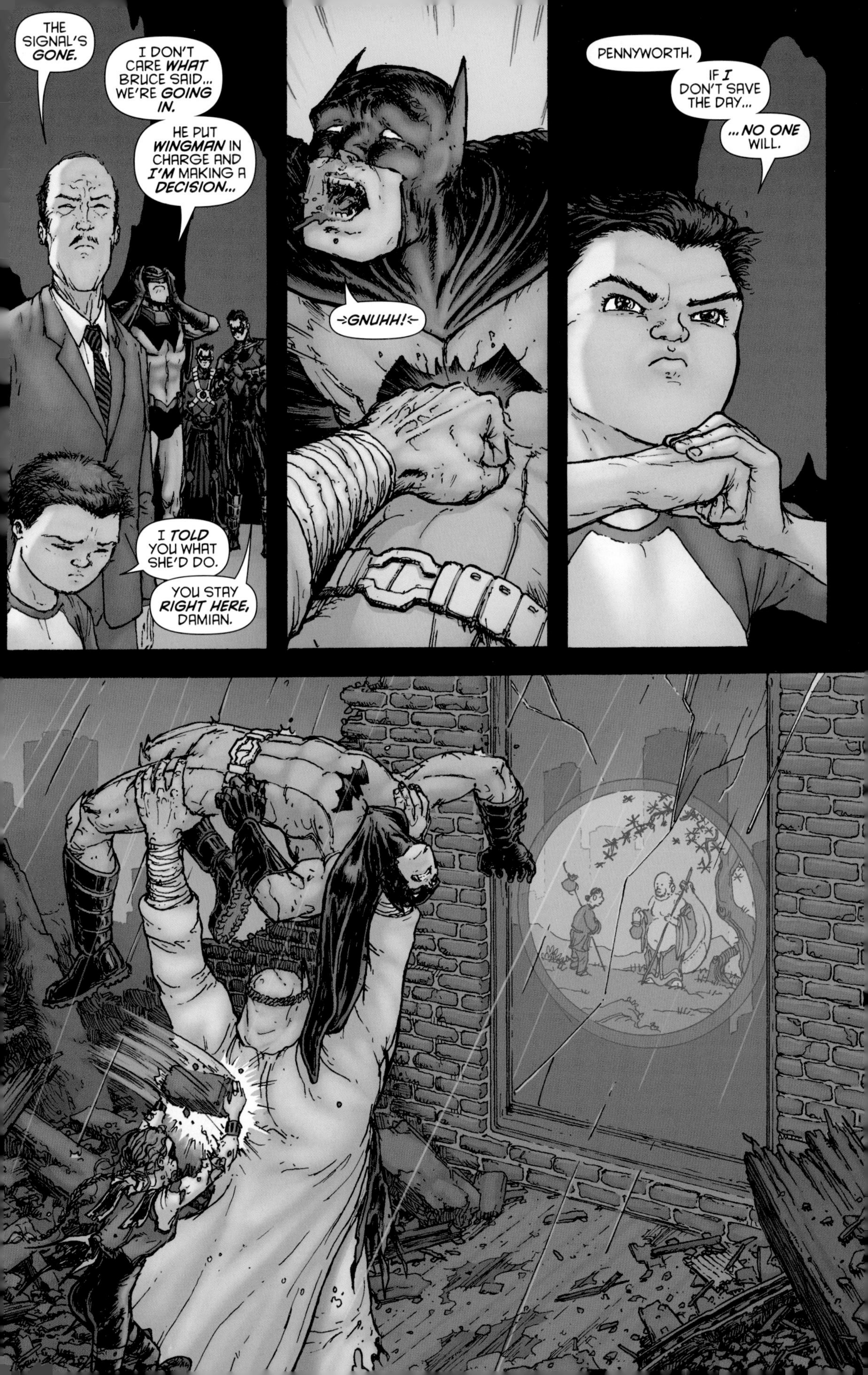
THE SIGNAL'S *GONE.*
I DON'T CARE *WHAT* BRUCE SAID... WE'RE *GOING IN.*
HE PUT ***WINGMAN*** IN CHARGE AND ***I'M*** MAKING A ***DECISION...***
I *TOLD* YOU WHAT SHE'D DO.
YOU STAY ***RIGHT HERE,*** DAMIAN.
-GNUHH!-
PENNYWORTH.
IF *I* DON'T SAVE THE DAY...
...***NO ONE*** WILL.

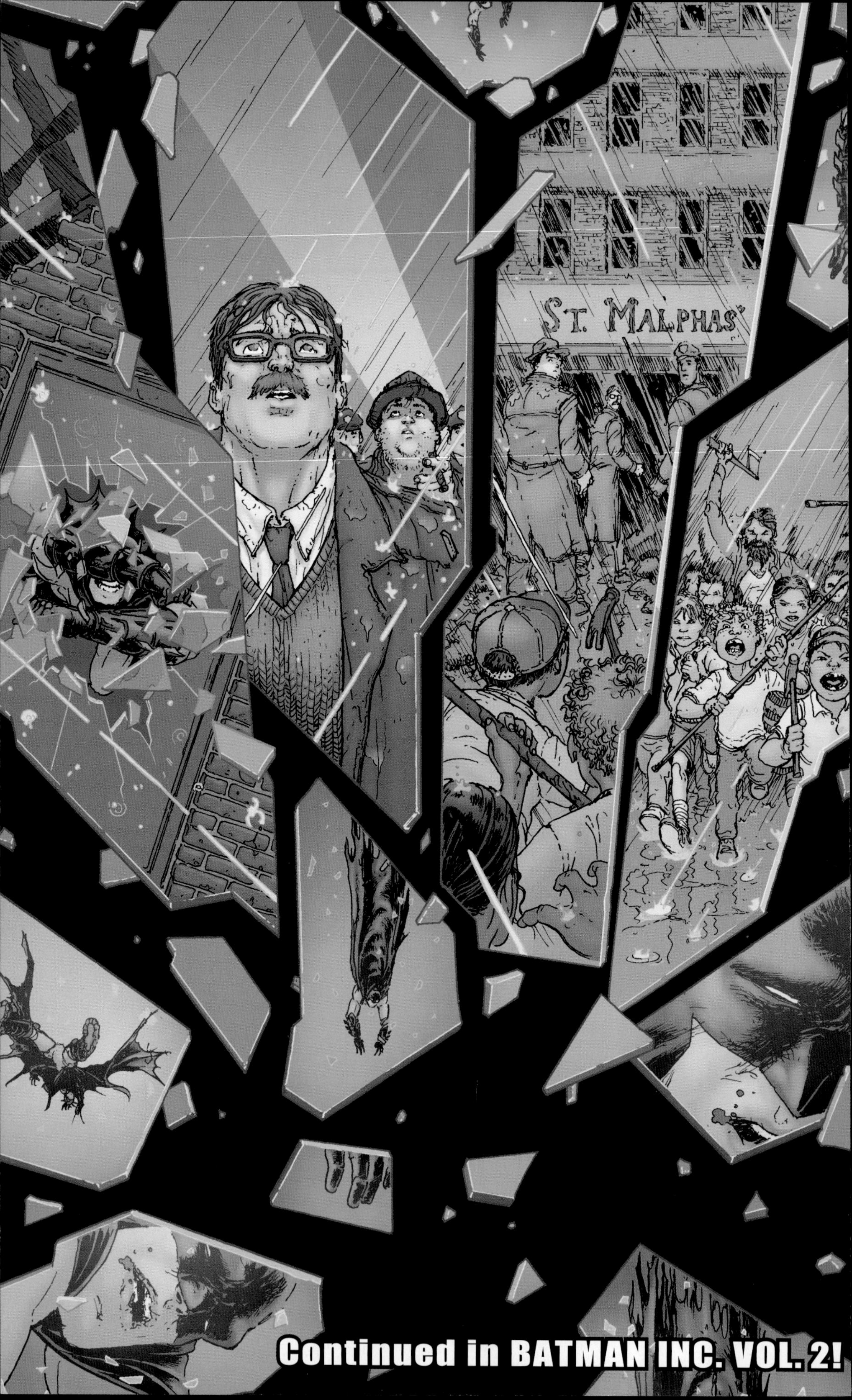
ST. MALPHAS'

Continued in BATMAN INC. VOL. 2!

VARIANT COVER GALLERY

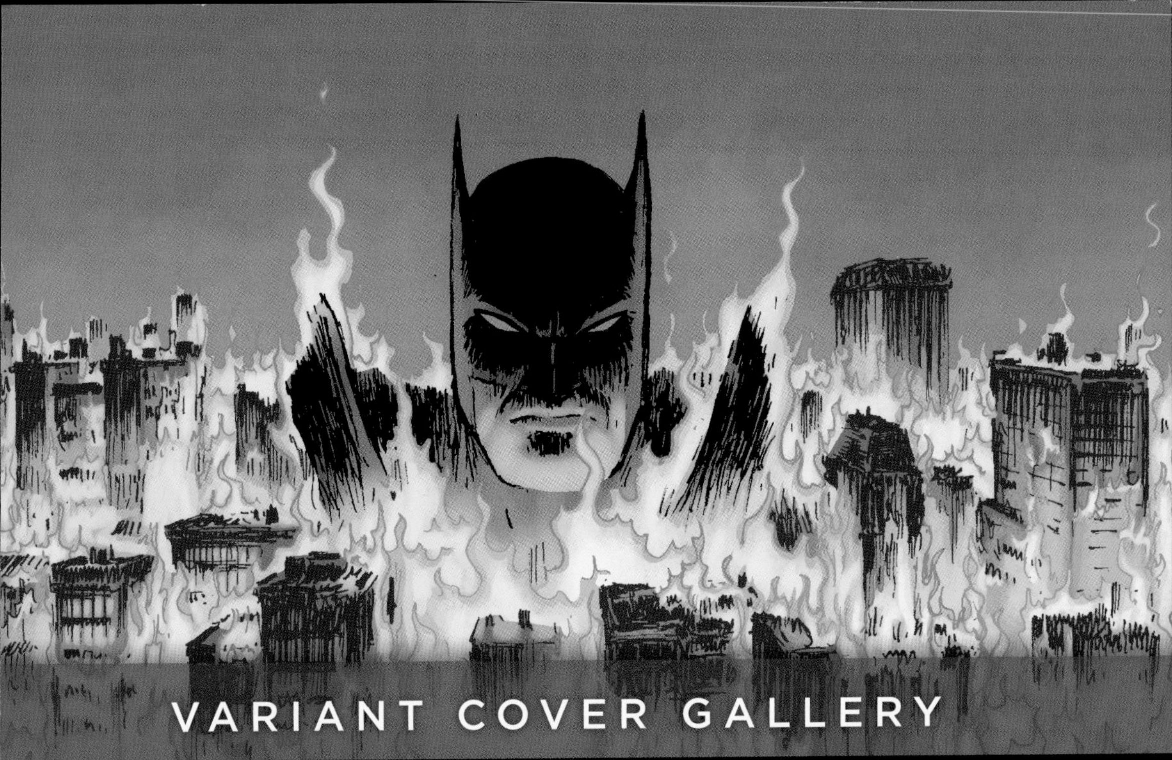

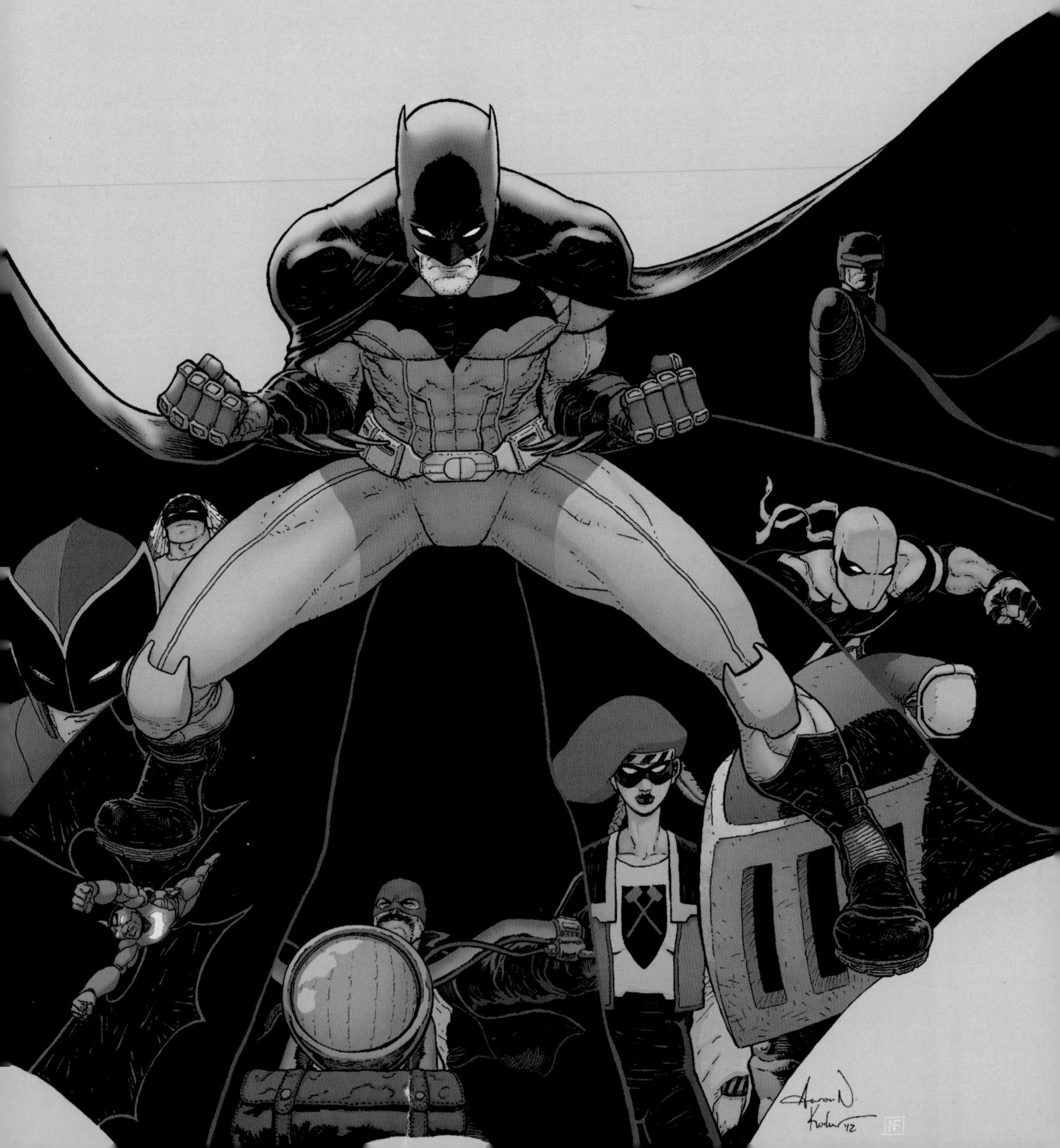

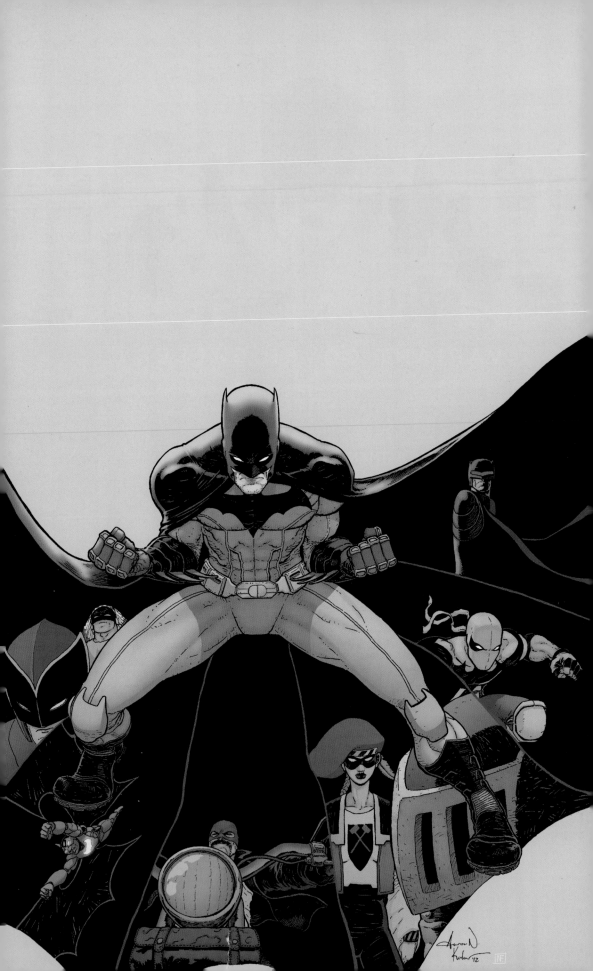

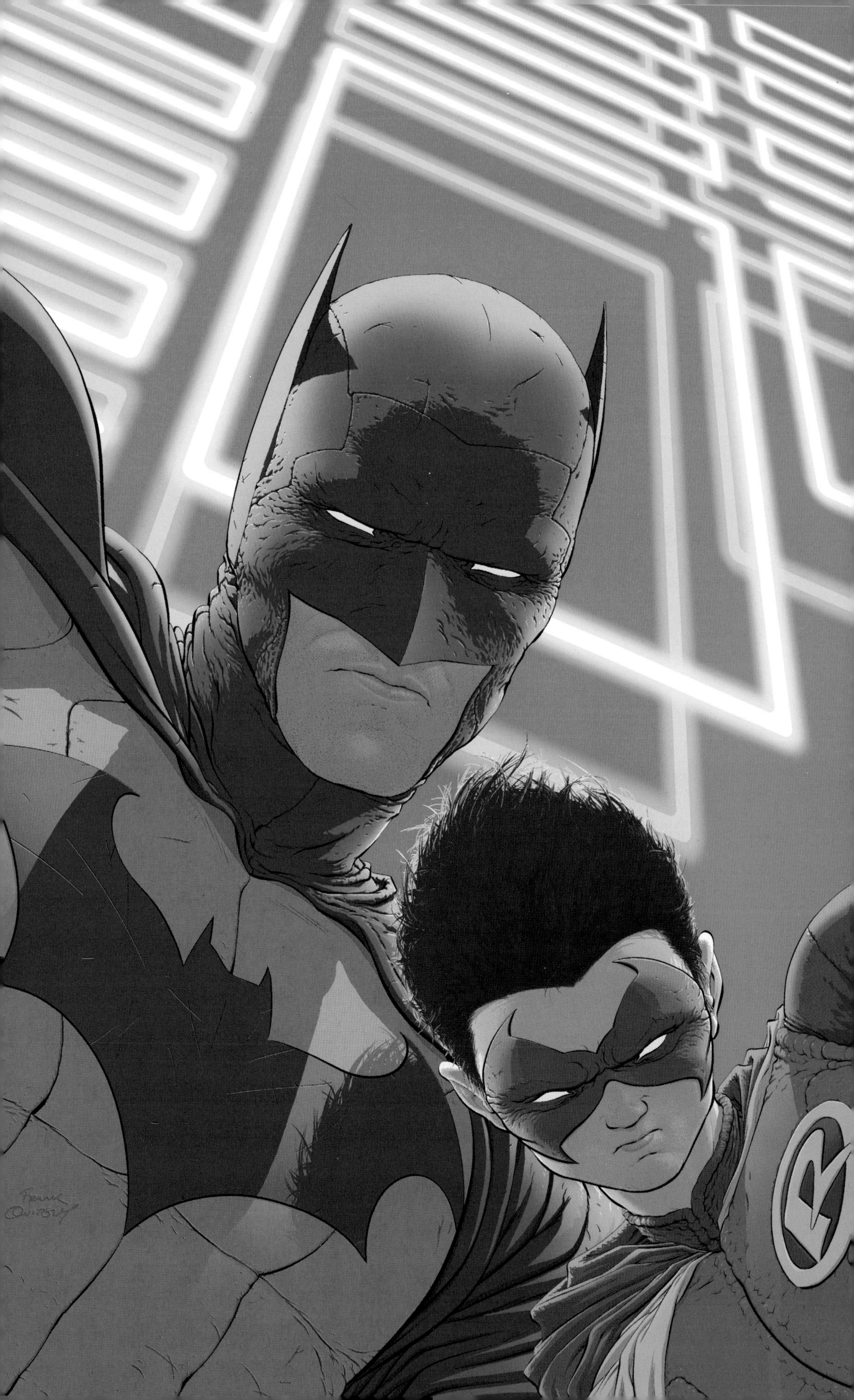

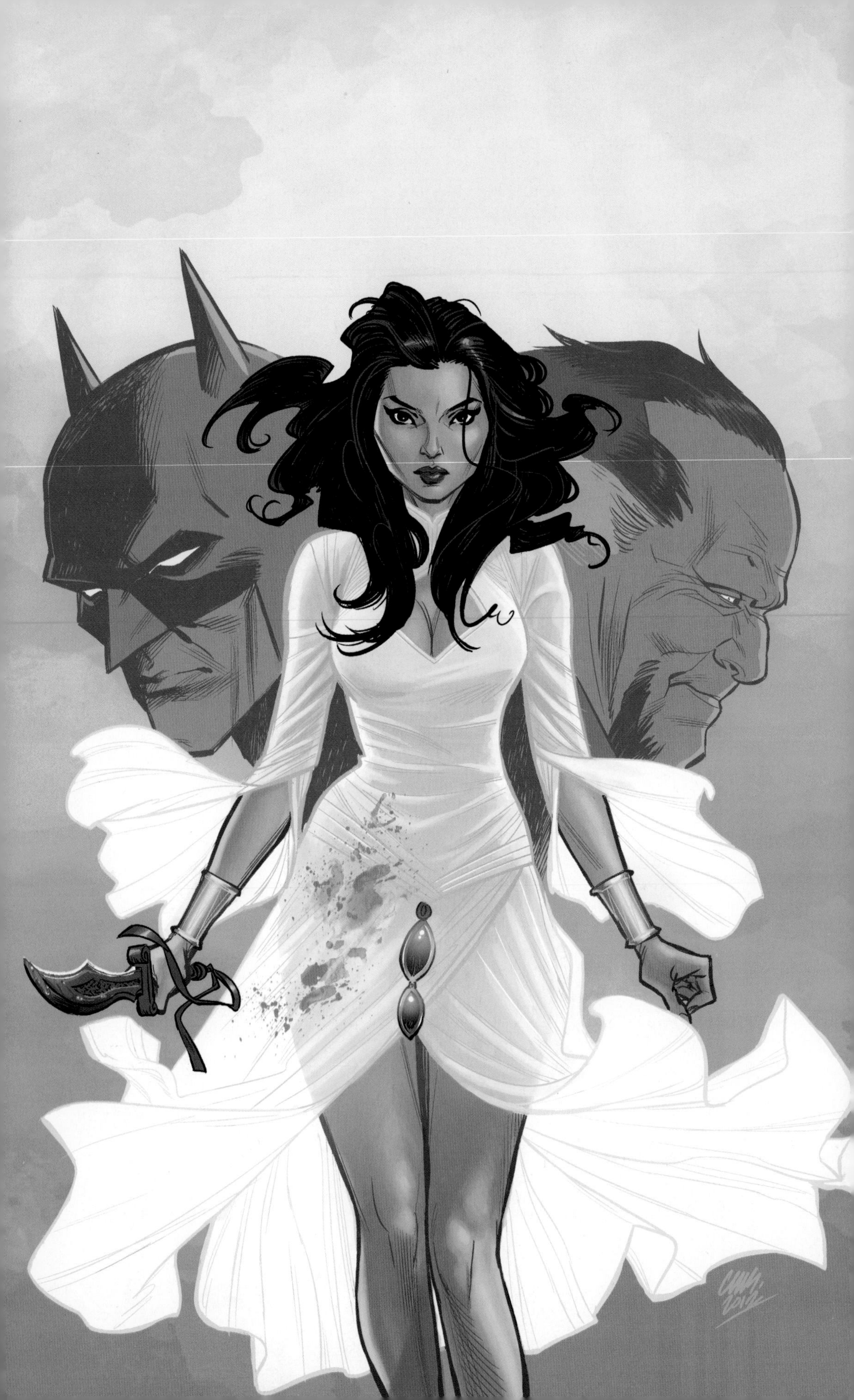

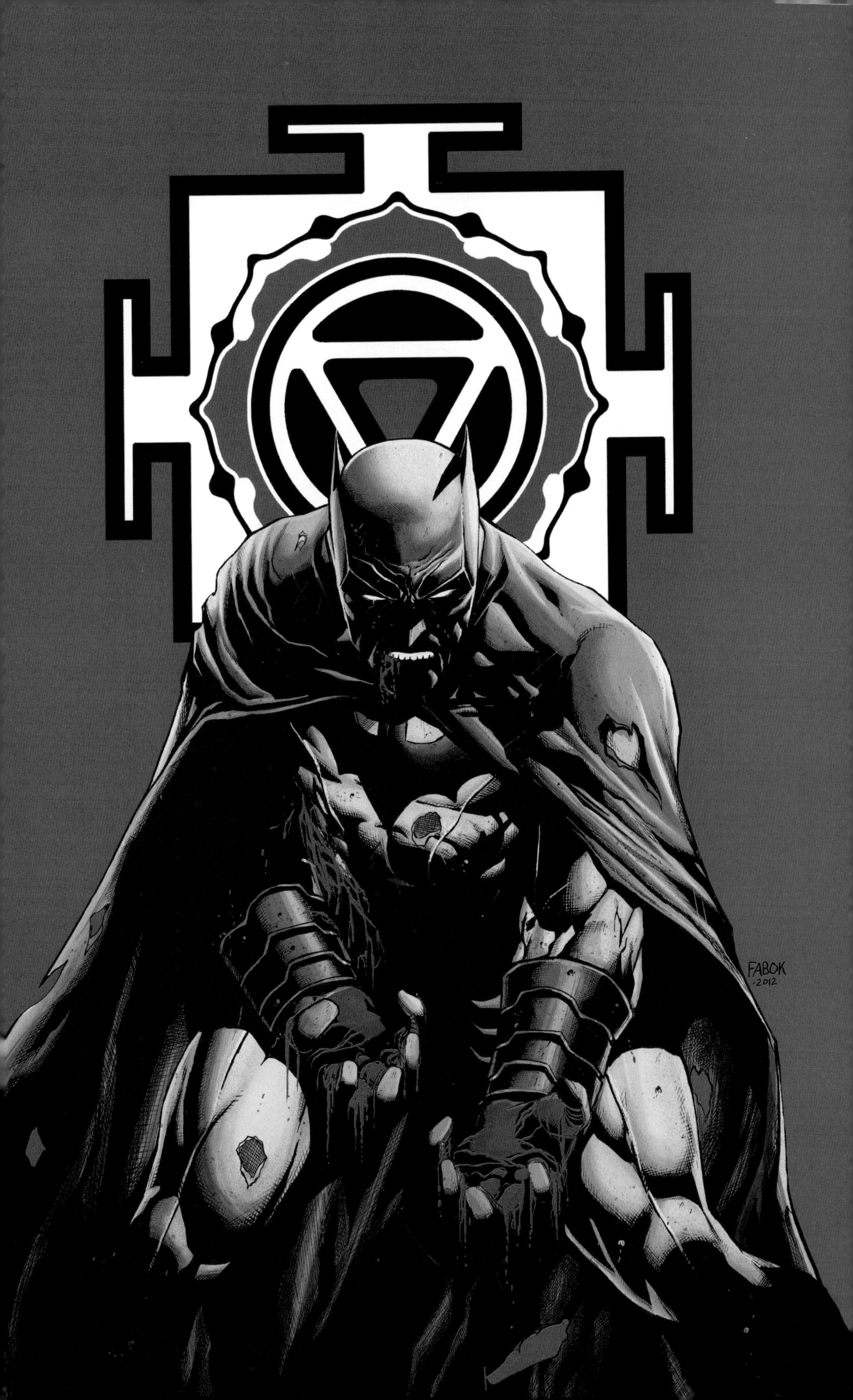
FABOK
·2012·

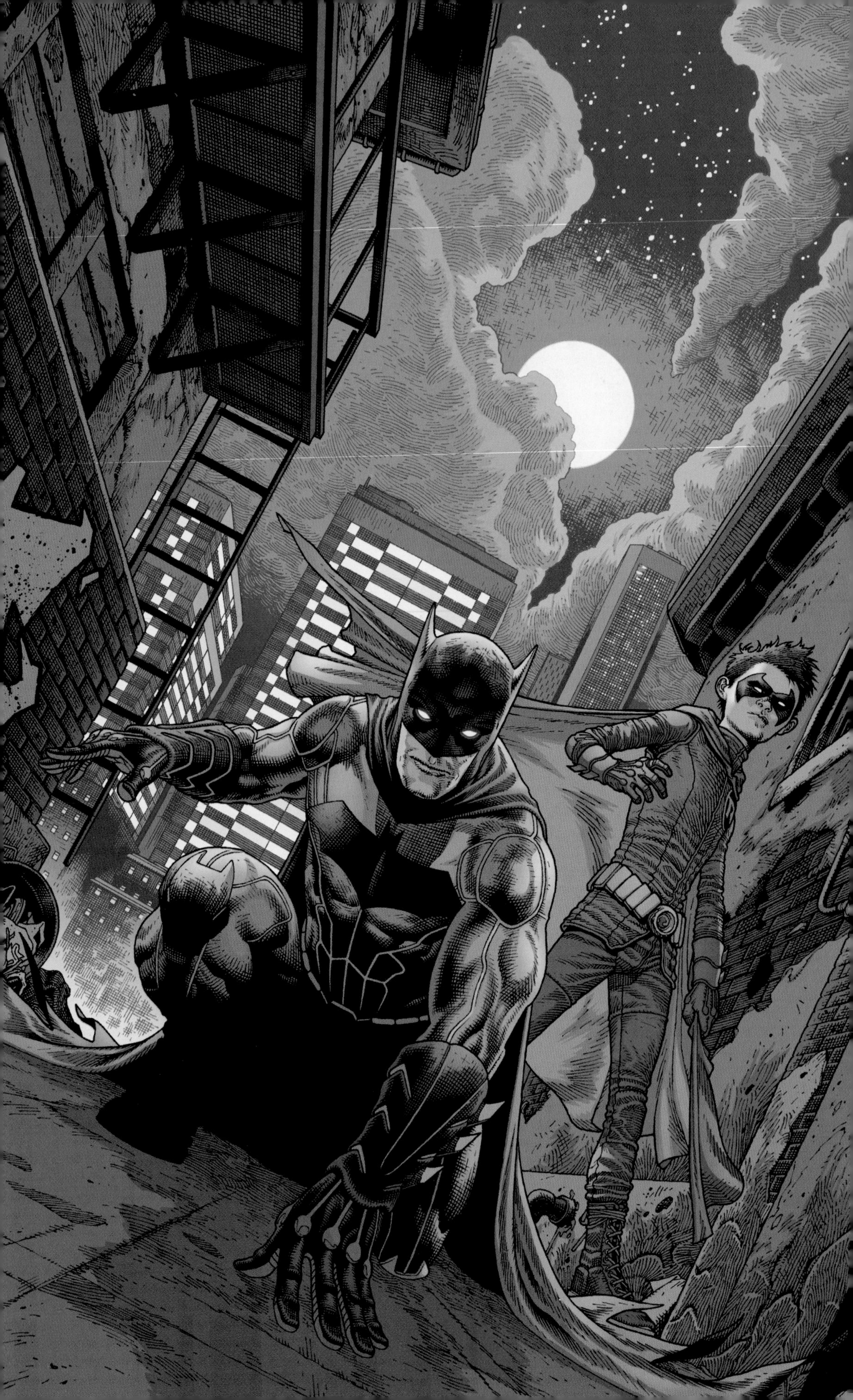

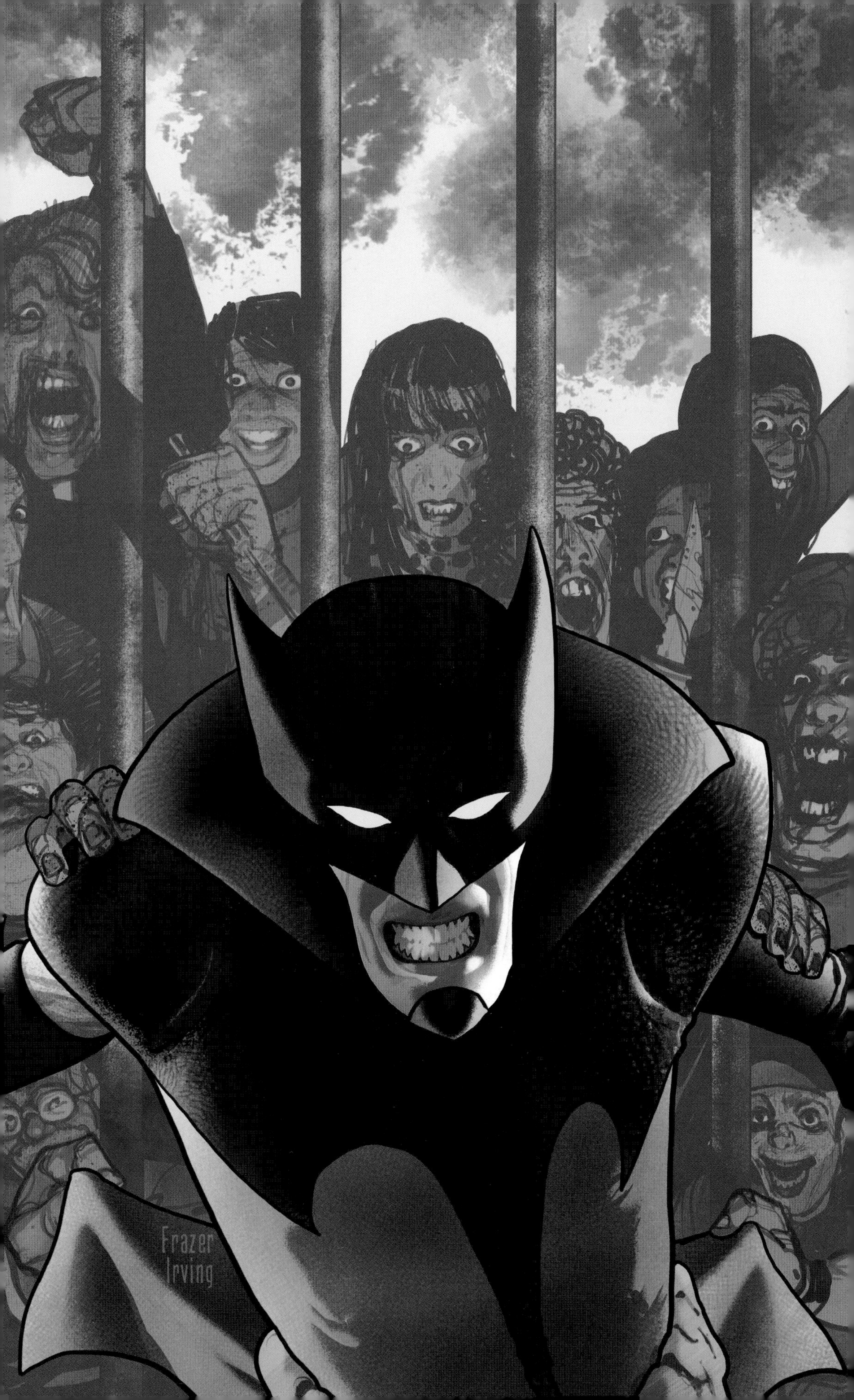
Frazer
Irving

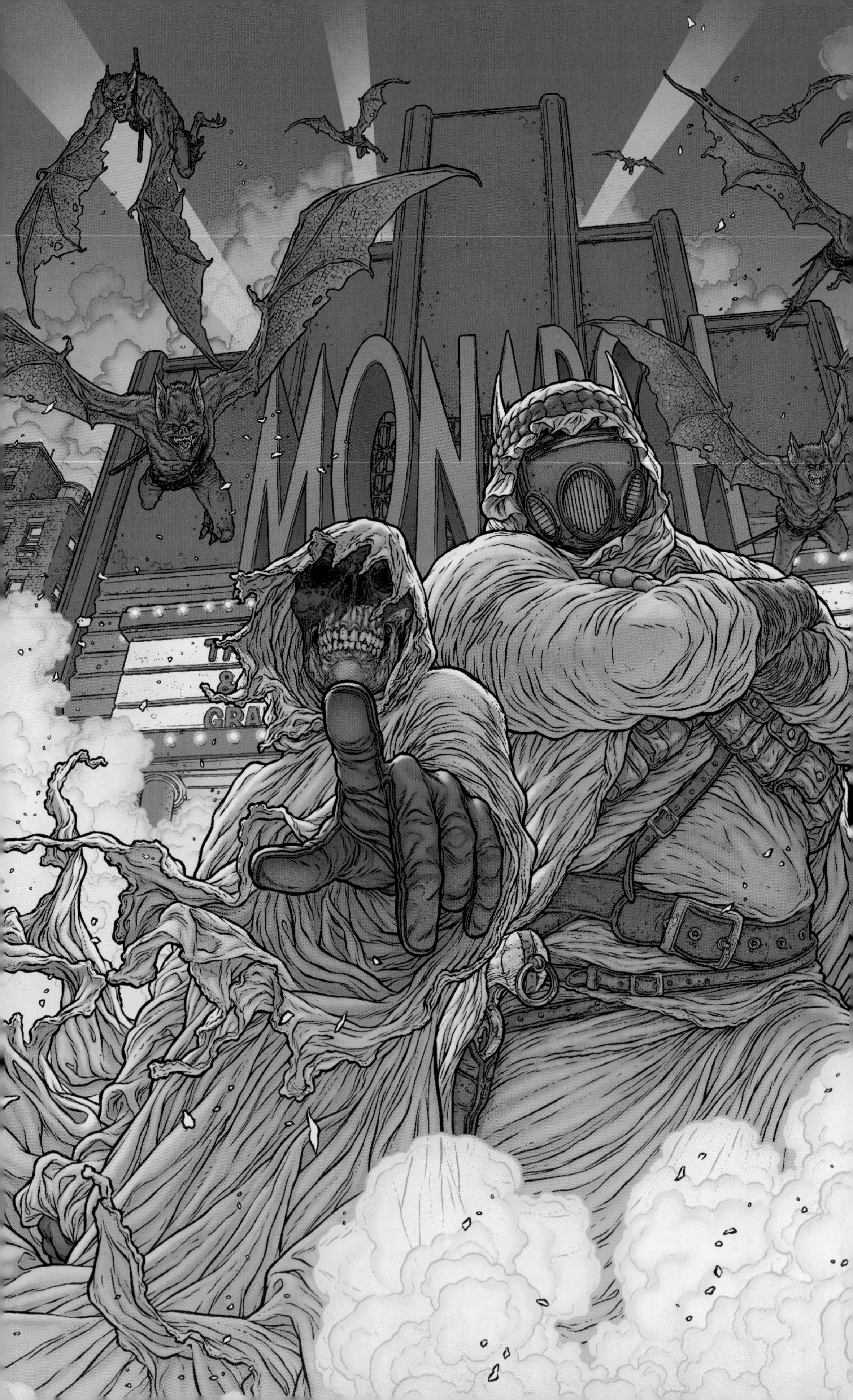

"A stunning debut. This is definitely in the top rank of the revamp."
—THE ONION / AV CLUB

"Snyder and Capullo reach new heights of collaboration here, with Capullo making inspired storytelling choices that add additional layers to Snyder's narration and dialog."
—VANITY FAIR

START AT THE BEGINNING!

BATMAN VOLUME 1: THE COURT OF OWLS

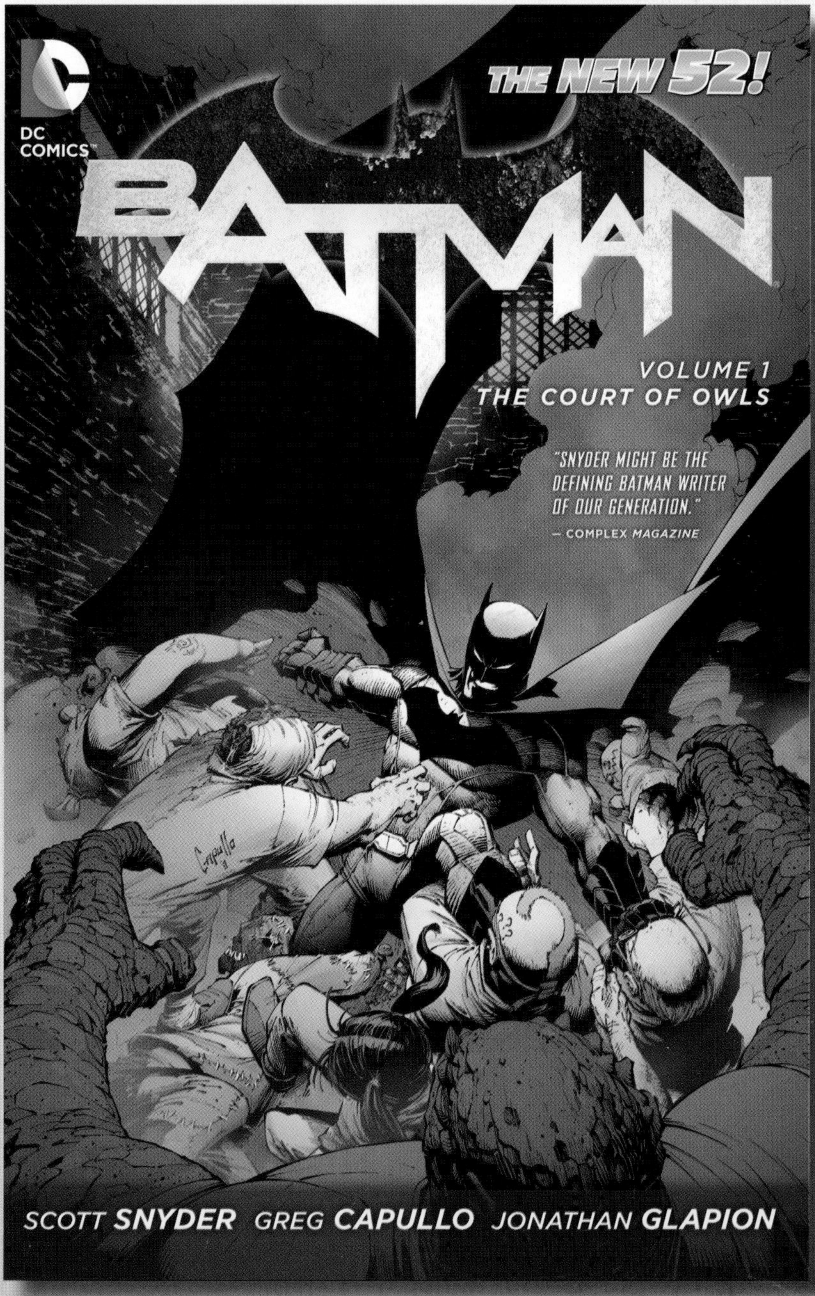

DC COMICS
THE NEW 52!
BATMAN
VOLUME 1
THE COURT OF OWLS
"SNYDER MIGHT BE THE DEFINING BATMAN WRITER OF OUR GENERATION."
— COMPLEX MAGAZINE
SCOTT SNYDER GREG CAPULLO JONATHAN GLAPION

BATMAN & ROBIN VOLUME 1: BORN TO KILL

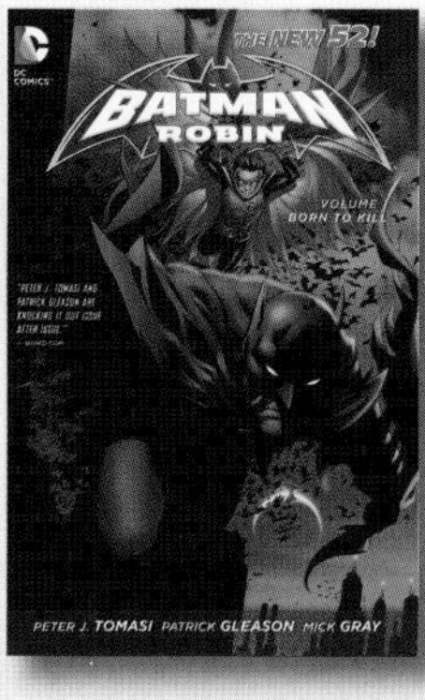

THE NEW 52!
BATMAN
ROBIN
PETER J. TOMASI PATRICK GLEASON MICK GRAY

BATMAN: DETECTIVE COMICS VOLUME 1: FACES OF DEATH

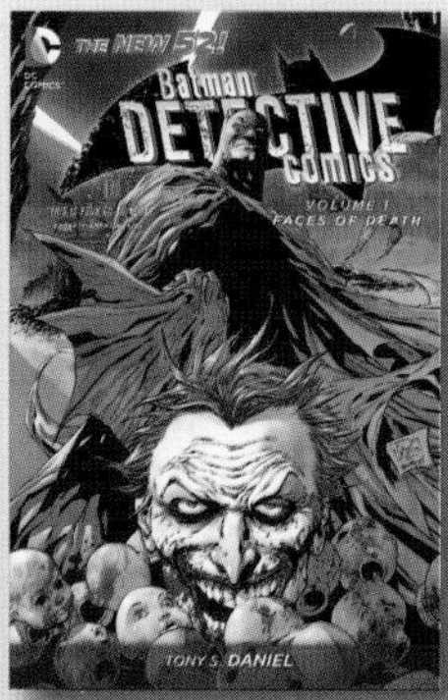

THE NEW 52!
Batman
DETECTIVE
Comics
TONY S. DANIEL

BATMAN: THE DARK KNIGHT VOLUME 1: KNIGHT TERRORS

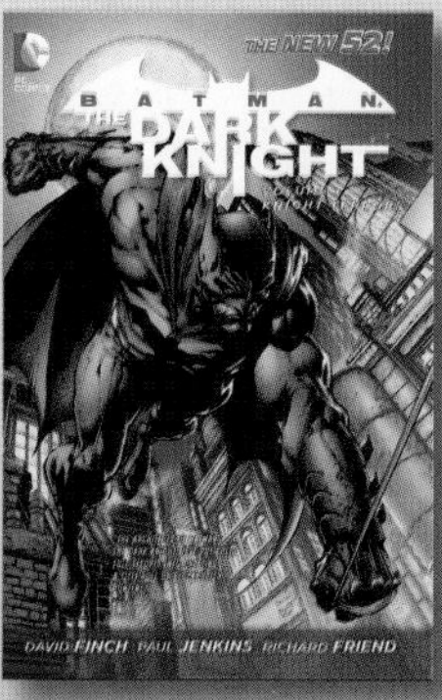

THE NEW 52!
BATMAN
THE DARK KNIGHT
DAVID FINCH PAUL JENKINS RICHARD FRIEND

"Game-changing redefining of the Caped Crusader."
—ENTERTAINMENT WEEKLY SHELF LIFE

"A wildly entertaining ride that's been at all times challenging, unsettling, amusing, inventive, iconic and epic... one of the most exciting eras in Batman history."
—IGN

FROM *NEW YORK TIMES* #1 BEST-SELLING WRITER

GRANT MORRISON
with ANDY KUBERT

BATMAN: THE BLACK GLOVE

with J.H. WILLIAMS III and TONY S. DANIEL

BATMAN: R.I.P.

with TONY S. DANIEL

BATMAN: THE RETURN OF BRUCE WAYNE

with FRAZER IRVING, RYAN SOOK and other top talent

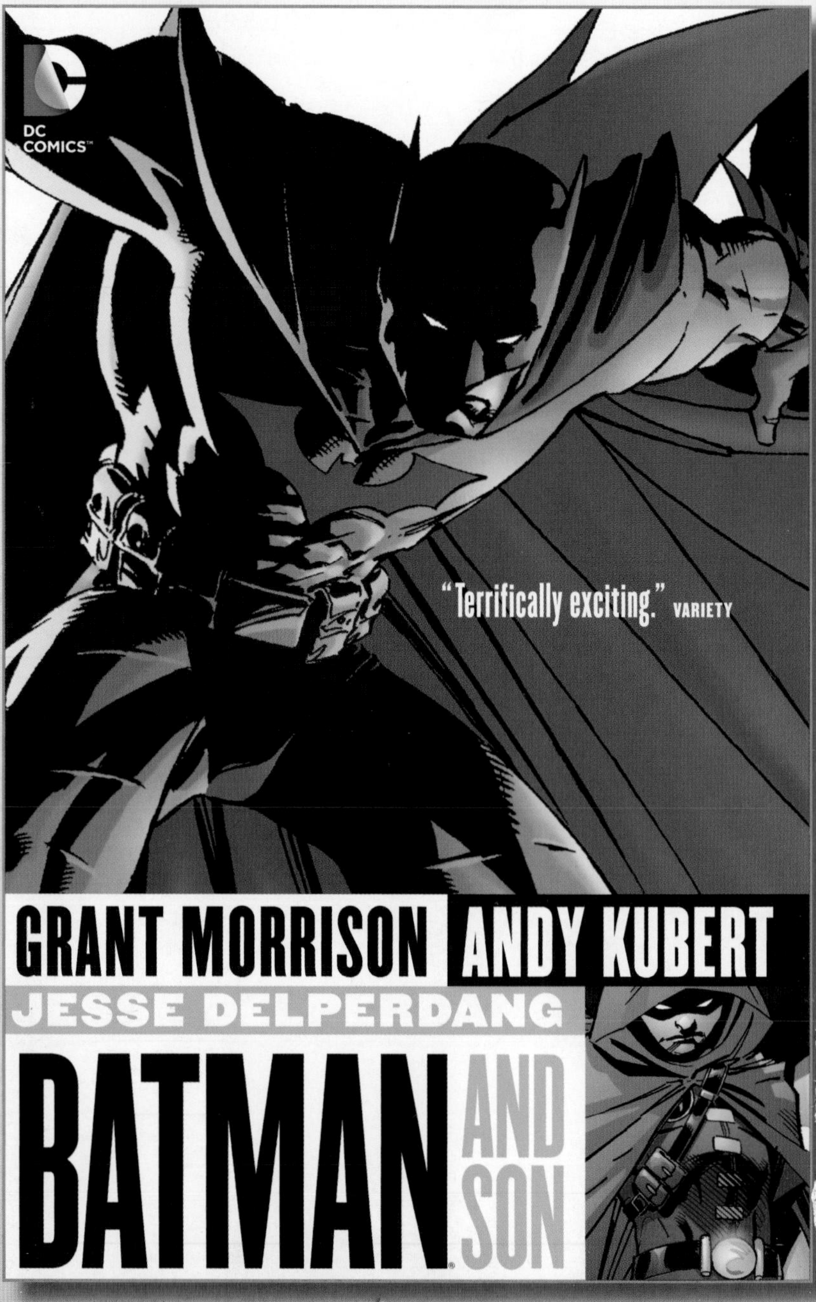

"Terrifically exciting." VARIETY

GRANT MORRISON   ANDY KUBERT
JESSE DELPERDANG

BATMAN AND SON